ENCOUNTER WITH THE TEXT

THE SOCIETY OF BIBLICAL LITERATURE
SEMEIA SUPPLEMENTS
William A. Beardslee, Editor
Dan O. Via, Jr., Associate Editor
J. William Whedbee, Associate Editor

THE SWORD OF HIS MOUTH: FORCEFUL AND
IMAGINATIVE LANGUAGE IN SYNOPTIC SAYINGS
by Robert C. Tannehill

JESUS AS PRECURSOR
by Robert W. Funk

STUDIES IN THE STRUCTURE OF HEBREW NARRATIVE
by Robert C. Culley

STRUCTURAL ANALYSIS OF NARRATIVE
by Jean Calloud, translated by Daniel Patte

BIBLICAL STRUCTURALISM: METHOD AND
SUBJECTIVITY IN THE STUDY OF ANCIENT TEXTS
by Robert M. Polzin

STORY, SIGN, AND SELF: PHENOMENOLOGY AND
STRUCTURALISM AS LITERARY CRITICAL METHODS
by Robert Detweiler

CHRISTOLOGY BEYOND DOGMA: MATTHEW'S CHRIST
IN PROCESS HERMENEUTIC
by Russell Pregeant

Encounter with the Text
Form and History
in the Hebrew Bible

edited by

Martin J. Buss

FORTRESS PRESS
Philadelphia, Pennsylvania

SCHOLARS PRESS
Missoula, Montana

Library of Congress Cataloging in Publication Data

Main entry under title:

Encounter with the text.

(Semeia supplements ; 8 ISSN 0145-3254)
Consists of essays by members of a task force formed under the aegis of the Society
of Biblical Literature.
Bibliography: p.
1. Bible—Hermeneutics—Addresses, essays, lectures. 2. Bible. O. T. Genesis
XXV-XXXV—Criticism, interpretation, etc.—Addresses, essays, lectures. I. Buss,
Martin J. II. Society of Biblical Literature. III. Series.

BS476.E48   1979   220.6   78-31182
ISBN 0-8006-1508-5

7694D79   Printed in the United States of America   1-1508

TABLE OF CONTENTS

Preface

The theory of interpretation is undergoing intensive reconsideration, as is witnessed by the fact that a considerable number of studies have been devoted to method in recent years. A continuing issue is the relation of the past to the present; associated with this problem is the question whether the form-critical tradition has appropriately connected the general with the particular. To examine such fundamental problems, a task group on "Methodology and its History" was formed under the aegis of the Form Criticism Seminar of the Society of Biblical Literature. This task group had an official life span of five years, from 1971 to 1975; its joint endeavor continued, however, until 1978.

The task group decided to cooperate in outlining and demonstrating central principles of hermeneutics. Recognizing that many forms of interpretation are possible, each member concentrated on a certain approach in a presentation designed to contribute to the larger picture. These contributions were shared with other participants for their comments, in the light of which revisions could be made. The present volume, which eventuated from that cooperation, is thus neither a collective product nor a miscellany of independent articles. To show how approaches relate to each other in dealing with a common body of material, the narratives of Genesis 25–35 serve as a source of illustration, whenever possible.

Diversity of point of view was encouraged in the group. Yet the proposals contained in the various essays are largely complementary. Some emerging differences of opinion are noted at appropriate points; whether these might have been reduced through further discussion is difficult to say.

Special appreciation needs to be expressed here for persons who contributed to the discussion of the task group: George Coats, Walter Eisenbeis, David Greenwood, Mary Wakeman, Paul Larose, Michael Platt, and John Van Seters. There are many others who deserve thanks for aiding the completion of the task. Since their list is extremely long, gratitude must be expressed to them privately by each author. It is deeply felt.

Part I

The Word as Embracing History and Structure

Introduction

Martin J. Buss

The relation between particular history and general structure is an old question which has reached a new degree of urgency. At the end of the eighteenth century, a strongly historical approach triumphed, after an extended period of preparation, in close conjunction with a position viewing particulars as primary. This approach rejected an earlier outlook which stressed tradition and stability and was oriented toward a harmony of universal essences. A hundred years later, the limitations of historical criticism became apparent in a perspective connected with social movements seeking to transcend individualism. Since that time, attempts have been made in virtually all disciplines to integrate general considerations.

Within biblical studies, H. Gunkel developed an intensive concern for genres, understood as standardized forms within a culture. His orientation remained fundamentally historical, but he made a major historical error in projecting into the past an image of "pure" types. In critical endeavors by others, on the other hand (for instance in the field of literature), structural analyses sometimes neglected historical perspectives. The crucial question of the present time is whether a genuine synthesis of form and history can be effected.

In the essay below, I argue that it is possible to develop a position which will incorporate the particular and the general in such a way that they are not merely combined but are seen as aspects of a more fundamental reality. This reality cannot be fully understood precisely because it is ultimate; yet it can be apprehended through images. Communication, which involves both individuality and sharing, furnishes an image of love and justice relevant to the current social situation.

Specific themes set forth in the essay include the following: (1) communication as an opportunity and task of the present; (2) the variety and multidimensionality of structures, with probability relations; (3) the paradoxical interplay between uncertainty and information in history; (4) meaning as pointing to the possible and as moving toward a goal; and (5) the significance of insight into connections for orienting and enhancing life. The aim is to clarify the process of interpretation as an integral part of existence.

One of the ways in which form and history can be related is to apply structural analysis to narratives. The studies by Lévi-Strauss, Greimas, Barthes, and others surveyed in Hugh White's essay exhibit this path. Narratives are "historical," like all literature, in that they exist as unique objects in time. Furthermore, their pattern approximates that of history.

The strength of structuralism lies in its attention to general features of literature in terms of logical relationships. White's survey leads the reader through the thought of major critics in this tradition in such a way that one can think with them. Each takes account of history in a special way. For Lévi-Strauss, and others influenced by him, the mediation of oppositions (which are never finally resolved) introduces a dynamic element. Greimas outlines the role of alienation and reintegration in narratives and presents the structures of "test" and "struggle" as irreducibly diachronic themes. Barthes—not a thoroughgoing structuralist—stresses the general significance of the concrete word; as he sees it, the free act of writing presents the possibility of reconciliation for the subject, who is born in an awareness of difference.

All of the authors discussed by White are concerned with problems of communication in general and with linguistics and semiology (the theory of signs) in particular. For instance, according to Barthes, God appears as "logothete" (language founder) in the story of Jacob's crossing. White suggests that these semantic models be explored further for their potential usefulness in biblical study.

Chapter 1

Understanding Communication

Martin J. Buss
Emory University

A. Communication: Present Concerns

Communication is a dynamic relation between two entities. It implies both individuality (for the two partners) and sharing, that is, a holding in common. In its general sense, the term "communication" refers to any process of "transmitting, imparting, or giving to" another. What is transmitted is known as "information," since it "imparts form." These broad meanings, which are quite old, are utilized in recent conceptualizations which stress the continuity of interactions at different levels of existence.

An interest in communication is characteristic of the present century. The development and use of telephone, radio, radar, television, computers, and of new means of transportation constitute a second phase of the industrial revolution, with a stress on interdependence. Broad movements of intellectual conception are connected with this social change. The previous emphasis on history, associated—in different forms—with individuality and power during the first phase of industrialization, receded in favor of orientations toward mutual and general relations (cf. the notion of "post-historic man" in Mumford: 165–84, following R. Seidenberg / 1 /). Of course, such a shift in perspective is gradual and does not proceed in uniform fashion; sometimes it over-reacts against the old.

In philosophy major attention has been directed to language. That includes the use of artificially defined signs in symbolic logic, the examination of ordinary speech by "language analysis," and a considerable concern with language in comprehensive views of reality. Language is at once material and mental, reaching from the human to all of known reality (via mathematics); it is observable, active, and social ("intersubjective"), and expresses relationships and potentialities. It thus provides a focus by which to go beyond a one-sided individualism as well as to narrow a contrast between matter and mind, phenomena associated with earlier tendencies. Many of the relevant reconceptualizations are already present in the pragmatism of C. S. Peirce (dating from 1867 to 1910). He opposed nominalism (for which individuals are primary) as well as dualism and assigned a central role to the "sign" /2/. Somewhat later, Karl Jaspers (influenced by Peirce /3/) made communication the cornerstone of his philosophy; he both discussed interpersonal relationships as the origin of the self (1931:338) and argued in favor of unlimited communication between groups (1948). Such, and similar, reflections are now being used in integrative views by many thinkers /4/.

The development of new modes of transmission and observation has led to a formal, mathematical framework for "communication theory." This framework includes several major foci. One—often called "information theory"—measures the complexity and variation of messages, channels, and codes, and discusses ways of protecting messages against interference (Hartley and especially Shannon, 1948); it involves the mathematics of probability, with "entropy" (unpredictability) as the standard for the potential amount of information. Another, called "cybernetics" by Norbert Wiener (in 1948), examines the relation between signals and goals in mechanical or organic systems; its central concept is positive or negative "feedback," which can be represented mathematically by "directed graphs" or "digraphs" (networks of movement). A third deals with the usefulness of messages for a recipient within the context of "decision theory," which examines probabilities in relation to preferences (Savage [with a "personalistic" theory of statistics], R. Ackoff [Buckley: 209–18], MacKay, Nauta, Menges). Other aspects of the theoretical complex deal with questions regarding the nature of human and nonhuman interactions. The different elements will contribute to discussions below in regard to structure, history, and meaning.

Communication theory has great unifying power which extends

across both political and disciplinary boundaries. Its basic categories have now been axiomatized, so that the presuppositions and operations are open to inspection and to appropriate modification for particular purposes. Applicability of the theory extends to all known levels of existence, although these levels are by no means identical to each other in their patterns. For instance, potentiality or need for "information" is formally equivalent to "entropy" (unpredictability of details) in thermodynamics (Fisher: 47 and others) and to "uncertainty" in quantum theory (Gabor). Communication theory now furnishes key concepts in the fields of biology, psychology, linguistics, sociology, anthropology, and aesthetics /5/. Particularly significant is the development in psychology. Models of "information processing" connect body with mind; therapy can be understood as dealing with both interpersonal and intrapersonal communication (Ruesch and Bateson, Mucchielli, Peterfreund, Mandler). Such conceptualizations are especially important in relation to religious experience, for they provide for it an understanding which is both rigorous and appropriate to the subject matter, thus contributing to the integration of science and theology.

It is likely that both divergence and convergence are needed for cognitive advance. A long-term trend toward specialization has aided the accumulation of knowledge. In recent centuries this trend has accelerated to the point of threatening the unity of knowledge. A contrary move toward interaction and integration, however, recognizes and establishes connections between the various disciplines (e.g., Wendland: 243; Mathews *et al.*; Bonhoeffer: 200; Polanyi: 72; McLuhan: 254). Thus G. Ebeling notes that "systems theory, information theory, cybernetics, or structural analysis," together with their mathematical form, reach toward the humanities, although he is skeptical of their relevance (1975:94, as was Betti: 135–36). More enthusiastically, H. Rapp and C. Welsh argue on the basis of communication theory for a theology which interprets reality as a whole. For the study of the Bible, K. Meyer zu Utrup and N. Wagner have applied cybernetic and related concepts as an interdisciplinary step. In a general manner, G. von Rad expressed hope for "the greatest gift which can be given to us: once more a common language" for faith and science (1974:140 [from 1967]).

In the age of individualism, so-called "secularization" and an emphasis on Christian uniqueness (cf.TeSelle: 168) represented an increased splitting apart of lived reality. The split aided human freedom and power, but undermined ethical concerns and spiritual wholeness (similarly, Moltmann: 269–87). For instance, the viciousness of North-American slavery and the Nazi extermination of Jews were due in part to a widespread attitude that judicial affairs are not the church's business /6/. Ethical involvement requires understanding and interaction among various groups; at the present time, that includes relations with Marxists. In the words of L. Russell, the reality of a common humanity allows one to "move beyond identity toward mutuality" with all people (165). Within the Bible, several Genesis stories emphasize the ethical sensitivity of non-Israelites /7/. Such an appreciation for members of other groups does not mean an acceptance of any activity that may occur; on the contrary, a considered involvement leads to significant criticism.

Important theoretical considerations speak in favor of a broad vision for theology. On the one hand, expressions of faith can be studied by the human sciences in such a way that light is shed on the character of faith (Buss, 1965). On the other hand, faith itself—at least in its biblical form—views God as involved in all of reality (Rust; Peacocke: 149–93). Theology, as is widely acknowledged in theory, deals not with an aspect of existence but with its totality in relation to the Infinite. The special sciences, applying intelligent effort, correspond to what Israelites considered to be "wisdom" under God. Just as wisdom plays an important role in biblical literature, both in a relatively pure form and as an aspect of priestly and prophetic speech, so scientific knowledge can and must be supported and appropriated by theological disciplines /8/.

A partially correct, but seriously misleading, contrast which emerged in the division of knowledge and experience is that between history and nature (as still in Bultmann, 1934:3). When the distinction between these two categories became prominent early in the nineteenth century, the idea of a progressive evolution had taken hold in reference to human change, but in the realm of biology the notion of the fixity of species still reigned /9/. The contrast set human freedom over against subhuman regularity and cycles. Further investigation has made clear that long-range development, apparently coupled with a degree of indeterminism, is a feature of the entire known world. At the same time, it is amply clear that human events are not altogether arbitrary but can be understood to a large extent in the light of connections or according to patterns (e.g., Bernheim: 85–145; Dilthey, V:258; Hempel: 241–43). It is quite proper to make a distinction between particular events and general processes—as did W. Windelband and H. Rickert about 1900—but this distinction does not coincide with a difference between the human and the nonhuman (with Pannenberg: 123–24).

Rather, on all known levels the world contains both particularity and generality. Objects and events are general in the sense that they have a describable form; furthermore, the potential effect of an activity has a mathematically continuous side, such as of a field or wave. At the same time, all objects or events act as particular wholes. The combination of continuity and particularity in an event shows itself in statistical phenomena or probability relations /10/. Probability represents the observable aspect of significant action, for the latter requires both a certain freedom for the acting individual and a degree of predictable effectiveness. Without a combination of influence and surprise, there would be no genuine events and no meaningful future. The logic for an open future was outlined by Aristotle in connection with his discussion of tenses (*On Interpretation*, 19a) and received attention in the Middle Ages. It has been developed in considerable detail since the latter part of the nineteenth century in interaction with both science and art (Feuer: 178–80).

Communication is closely related to probability in joining particulars within a relationship. Specifically, measures for information can be stated as equivalent to those of conditional probability (the likelihood of one event, given another), so that either of these can be derived from the other. Indeed, some mathematicians (e.g., Kolmogorov) regard information as conceptually simpler than probability. Insofar as both variability and connection are universal, it is possible to view information as an aspect of all known processes /11/.

The highest and deepest form of communication is surely love. Because of the comprehensive character of love—which includes both freedom and pattern—Peirce suggested *agapism* as an overarching theory of reality. Although *agape* can describe the ground and fulfillment of existence, it seems too ideal for the more negative aspects of experience (Peirce included negativity in *agape*,

Martin J. Buss

6.287, 304) and too tender for subhuman relations. The broader term "communication," however, serves readily as an over-all symbol by which to express interaction in reality. This symbol fits well a tradition of the creative and redemptive word of God.

In formulating what is ultimate, theology must employ a metaphor which reflects a basic experience of the world. In an aristocratic age, God was pictured readily as Monarch. In the post-feudal "bourgeois" or early industrial period, the image developed into a dual notion of Artisan (cf. Barbour: 40–42) and Personal Spirit. Such symbols were not without justification in their respective contexts but they do not adequately express a fundamental orientation at the present time and therefore give an impression of the "death of God." In recent decades, probably the most impressive "root metaphor" (Pepper) is that of communication. Influenced by Peirce, Josiah Royce characterized God as the Interpreter (319), on the grounds that interpretation is a communal process establishing a world. Writing at about the same time, Franz Rosenzweig employed the symbols of mathematics to provide a key to the phases of the All. Close to him stood a number of other "dialogical" thinkers; these included Martin Buber, who defined God in terms of the relational word "Thou." Quite differently, Karl Barth emphasized the "Word of God," which he set in considerable opposition to man and distance from nature (III/4:332–33; nevertheless, Howe: 75–91 has shown parallels between Barth's theology and modern physics). Emil Brunner, influenced in part by Buber, viewed God as "the Self-Communicating One" (199). More recently, "speech event" or "language event" has been identified as divine reality by Ernst Fuchs and Gerhard Ebeling, although they describe it only in terms of an engagement of human beings with the Gospel (Fuchs: 248; Ebeling, 1963:328). According to H. N. Wieman, creative interchange is ultimate /12/. Rejecting separation and reification, Mary Daly (32, 198) holds God to be "The Good Who is self-communicating Be-ing, Who is the Verb from whom and with whom all true movements move."

If interpretation is grounded in communication as fundamental, nothing will be foreign to its path. The logic of relationship, including mathematics, and all the sciences belong to it, as does intuitive sensitivity to the individual and to the whole.

B.   Interrelationships (Structure)

The study of interrelationships involves the recognition of structure. Structure exhibits the relations of smaller units within a larger one (B. Russell: 250). The larger whole may be a verse, a book, or a culture; the parts may be words, themes, or standard forms. Structural analysis is a part of all thoughtful endeavors, but it can receive different kinds and degrees of attention. It can be employed as a means to some other end, such as historical reconstruction or technological application. Or it can be an intrinsic goal, in aesthetic enjoyment or intellectual contemplation.

Variety

The status of structures concerns a long-standing philosophical debate between "realism" (according to which structures are real or ultimate) and "nominalism" (for which structures are only mental or are merely names). Nominalism is logically and historically associated with individualistic modes of existence, while realism expresses a collective and universal sense. Elements of both positions are combined in a communicational perspective, in which source and recipient are viewed in interaction. An object does indeed exhibit a structure in the sense that its parts—however defined—truly stand in certain relationships. Yet there are a very large number of ways in which wholes and parts can be identified, and these parts stand in different kinds of relations. Therefore no single structural analysis can lay claim to exclusive validity. Each analysis is relative to the procedures and interests of the observer (Pool, *passim*; Ashby). In a particular description, one should thus speak not of "the structure," but of "a structure" or of "structures," of an object. A textual study can pay attention to logical relations between content elements / 13/, to the sequential arrangement of items (traditionally known as "composition" / 14/), to spatial and temporal relations between scenes depicted, to the roles of figures in a story, or to a large number of other features (cf. Olsson: 74–248).

The recognition of relativity should not be confused with a relativism according to which no right or wrong description can be made (against Hirsch, who fails to make the needed distinction, with

Crane: 27; similarly, Martinet). Relativity means, rather, that all statements must be made in relation to a frame of reference, or—metaphorically expressed—that assertions are answers to questions. One of the crucial aspects of information, as defined technically, is that it can only be stated in terms relevant to a certain set of concerns and expectations (so, e.g., Nauta: 227); consequently, it is neither purely objective nor purely subjective. Since general considerations are implied by questions in an investigation, it is not possible to "begin with individuals," as a nominalist position encourages one to do /15/. Because of the variety of potential considerations, however, it is also not possible to point to the "essential" form of an object (expressing what it fundamentally *is* or is designed to be) in an Aristotelian sense /16/.

The observation that different configurations can be recognized applies to literary genres (cf. Hernadi, Hempfer, Gülich and Raible). Gunkel made a major contribution in drawing attention to generic patterns but erroneously implied that only one view of genres is correct (e.g., 1933:10). Generic study serves the goal of furnishing as much insight as possible in a brief compass; it does so by relating repeated features (e.g., characteristics of psalms) to a single model. A form-critical analysis therefore needs to select and organize the data in a manner most helpful for its particular purpose. Thus Gunkel's category of "Zion psalms"—odd in its placement among other genres—is useful in that it compresses information about a number of poems. Yet significant classifications can be carried out according to different principles (cf. Rofé, Culley: 70, Sawyer, and, for multiple classification, Lindsay and Norman: 391). This multiplicity is reflected in the varied and flexible character of generic labels within biblical literature.

In a communicational perspective, a genre is best viewed as an open or virtual class which describes a possibility, rather than as a class of actual objects which meet a certain description /17/. The genre of lament, for instance, is not constituted by the collectivity of all psalms of this type, but by the type itself, i.e., by what constitutes a possible psalm of lament. One advantage of such a conceptualization is that it is in line with the way genres function in human life, namely as expectations of the speaker or hearer. Types may represent a pattern of expectation within a culture regarding what can or will be said. They can also be viewed as theoretical entities, independent of the habits of a culture being studied. Such theoretical genres describe what is possible in principle and become an expectation for the theorist.

If genres are understood as open classes, it is not difficult to recognize their interaction. Normally, more than one possibility is realized in a given phenomenon. Thus the book of Job reflects elements of several forms, such as dispute, lament, comedy, and irony, just as the genres of ancient Greek and Mesopotamian literatures were fluid and interacted with one another /18/. The flexibility and multiplicity of structures is an important recognition of modern study. While much of traditional science was oriented in a quasi-Aristotelian manner toward mutually exclusive categories, modern science (although presupposing classification) sees the need to "progress from classification to mathematics" in order to capture "the complex possibilities of multiple relations" within a system (Whitehead, 1925:43; 1933:150, 176). Biblical form criticism can incorporate the richness of patterns reflected in mathematics by recognizing a multidimensional array of overlapping forms.

Multidimensionality serves both simplicity and complexity. Experimental studies have shown that the human organism perceives best by paying attention simultaneously to several axes of discrimination. When focusing attention on a single scale, an unaided ear or eye can discriminate between about seven items on that scale. When additional types of contrast are added, the number of effective distinctions along any one axis is reduced, but the total number of distinguishable forms rises; e.g., three dimensions with four steps each will yield 64 categories. Observation is most effective when attention is paid to a very large number of dimensions, with a binary or triple disjunction in each (Garner: 122–29). These data regarding information processing show the psychological basis for the widespread occurrences of binary contrasts in language and culture. The perceptual system also supports triple contrasts, with three positive steps or with a neuter position between a positive and a negative one; other, such as fourfold, divisions are of course not ruled out.

The simultaneous operation of several twofold or threefold contrasts is well known in systems of phonemes. The same basic principle is apparent in other aspects of language. Hebrew has three "persons," two "genders," two (or three) "numbers," and two aspectual "tenses"; its seven stems of verbal conjugation designate three levels of action, each with two or three "voices"(active, passive-reflexive). On a larger scale, speech acts—as analyzed in part by Aristotle *(Rhetoric)*, Searle (66-67), and others—reveal several major dimensions: emotive tone in respect to oneself or others (positive, negative, or neutral), time orientation (past, present, future), rank relationship (toward one of higher, lower, or equal rank), and assertive character (affirmation, imagination, question). Culturally defined genres tend to agree fairly closely with this general organization, although numerous variations are standard in different traditions. The system of Israelite genres includes the following dimensions, or sets of contrasts: 1) the nature of the speaker and addressee, divine or human (e.g., law is largely divine speech directed to human beings); 2) particularity (especially in history and prophecy) or generality; 3) the temporal orientation; 4) a focus on the individual or on a group; and 5) a positive or negative tone /19/.

It is doubtful that conventions for expression apply independently to each precise genre. Most likely, an individual lament utilizes the forms applicable to its components: a human speaker addressing God, individuality, negativity, etc. Some clerical psalms present divine speech to a general, repeatable audience; they are, then, in this regard both similar to and different from prophecy, which presents divine speech in relation to particular occasions /20/. Within biblical Hebrew, most conventions probably are available to any speech act for which they are appropriate. If this is true, a speaker can generate various constellations of speech. In such a "generative rhetoric," the number of basic elements to be learned is much smaller than the number of possibilities they engender /21/. Of course, a special genre representing an intersection of more basic elements may develop some peculiarities not predictable from the components.

If conventional forms are not, for the most part, assigned to mutually exclusive genres, there is less need to speak of an "imitating" or "borrowing" of forms than is often thought. The appearance in prophecy of hymnic language, of laments, and of invectives (critical descriptions preceded by *hoy*) is quite natural; the fact that descriptions of evil in Hosea are similar to those in psalms does not mean that they were taken over from the other tradition /22/. Again, there is no need to ask whether the prophetic call was derived from the call of a political leader or vice versa; both uses are found also outside of Israel and presumably form within Hebrew two different realizations of a summons to represent authority. Similar observations hold in regard to calls to attention and other expressions appearing in different contexts.

A multidimensional organization, with cross-classification, requires greater intellectual maturity than a hierarchical "tree" system in which comprehensive genres, like psalms, are separately divided into subtypes, such as hymns. It is reasonable to believe, however, that the common Israelite possessed the needed capacity to employ it both consciously and unconsciously /23/.

Uncertainty

The detailed forms which can be expressed in a communication system have been called "logons" (Gabor). The larger the number of such forms, the greater will be the unpredictability of each, if all are equally probable. In other words, entropy (unpredictability in detail, also called "uncertainty") generally increases with variety. Under natural conditions some forms will appear more frequently than others. Shannon's measure of entropy for the surprise value of a message takes account of the relative frequencies, for these affect the average predictability of occurrences /24/. A complex form or one stated in a complex manner is usually less common and thus more surprising than the simpler elements combined within it. For instance, there are fewer critical prophecies than there are prophecies or criticisms in general. A system with complex forms thus will tend to have higher "uncertainty" than one with simple forms.

Entropy constitutes a potential for information (Nauta: 177). Information as a process reduces the recipient's uncertainty in that what was unknown becomes known; the information yielded by a signal which has been received is, therefore, equal to its prior uncertainty or unpredictability. Thus, in order to be able to increase information, one must increase entropy in a system. This is a profound—although very simple—insight of communication theory. If the perceivable variability of a source or channel is high, rich and surprising messages can be conveyed.

For a human being, as for any system, there is an upper limit for the speed at which information can be processed. Apparently the human organism seeks communication at a rate near this limit when awake and during certain phases of sleep. Under conditions of sensory deprivation or lack of external input, it produces its own stimuli in hallucinations or in dreams. Similarly, play and art largely represent activity and communication for their own sake /25/. They constitute a living in the present with enjoyment and serve an important long-range function in the maturation of activity and perception (Fiske and Maddi). Indeed, it is likely that communication, or growth on the basis of internal or external stimuli, is the prime intrinsic good within experience /26/.

As shown by experiments, entropy and information are connected with aesthetic value. Two somewhat different connections appear in the "interestingness" and the "pleasingness" of a work of art (see especially Berlyne). Interestingness, shown in the amount of attention given to a structure, increases with subjectively assessed complexity and with numerically computed uncertainty—two measures which closely correlate with each other. It appears that interest is positively related to information or the promise of information. It is possible (although not demonstrated) that the evoking of interest declines with very high levels of complexity, which may no longer be observable. Pleasingness, as rated by an observer, is highest with levels of intermediate uncertainty. The optimum level is relative to the observer's capacity and experience; it is higher for more mature persons and for those trained in a given medium or tradition than for others. If a relatively simple object is encountered repeatedly it becomes less pleasing, while a more complex one gives increasing pleasure with repetition until a plateau is reached. Apparently entropy contributes to aesthetic pleasure insofar as it leads to information but detracts from enjoyment insofar as it is not resolved within a unified whole (similarly, Moles: 162). Literary works of high quality typically include several levels of complexity and unity, so that they can be enjoyed repeatedly.

Unity has long been recognized as a characteristic of beauty. The value of variety received partial attention in ancient times (e.g., with regard to choice of words and plot) and even more in the modern period, when an interest in novelty became widespread /27/. Unity is needed for the perceiving of variety within a work, for consciousness can attend to only a small number of unrelated items; short-term memory, in fact, has a limit of about seven independent items (G. Miller). A uniting of variety is described thus by Arnheim: "The great works of art are complex, but we also praise them for 'having simplicity,' by which we mean that they organize a wealth of meaning and form in an over-all structure that clearly defines the place and function of every detail in the whole" (59–60). In literature, aesthetic unity and richness lie in part on the level of verbal patterns but even more in what is said—with fullness, tensiveness (including irony), and subtlety of meaning (Walzel: 185, 385; Brooks: 178–79; Wellek and Warren, chap. 18; Beardsley: 125–52, 552 [with references]; Ingarden: 395–99). Beauty is by no means restricted to nonscientific language; proofs or theories are "elegant" if they accomplish or account for much by means of a few steps.

A simple richness appears in the Bible, which H. L. Mencken has called "unquestionably the most beautiful book in the world" (289). Since this literature was largely directed to a popular audience—that is in fact one of its strengths—one should not expect highly intricate productions. Yet, Israelite narratives contain delightfully surprising twists, intriguing characters, and stark confrontations (cf. Good, Sandmel, and illustrations below). Fullness of patterning can be seen in combinations of alternatives within a single dimension. Some psalms and prophecies contain both positive and negative elements, while narratives frequently express emotional ambivalence. Both divine and human speech appear in prophetic expressions. Very often, individual and communal concerns are joined. In the stories of Genesis, the level of family relations is closely interwoven with a national perspective; this phenomenon does not represent a weakness, but rather enhances enjoyment /28/.

The amount of what can be communicated within the capacity of a medium or of a recipient is reduced by competition from other messages ("noise"). "Redundancy" in the form of additional signals (more than are necessary in a noiseless situation) can protect against loss caused by interference. Redundancy has other functions as well. Appropriately organized, it enhances unity and intensifies feeling. Rhythm, parallelism, and word or sound repetitions focus the attention of hearers, in addition to aiding their memory. Such regularity, however, must be broken in order to avoid monotony. As a matter of fact, redundant patterns create new opportunities for surprise, namely through the possibility of deviating from them (Erlich: 184; Garner: 339). Redundancy thus forms the basis for more complex structures. Indeed, both music and literature derive their effect to a large extent from the varying of patterns. Thus, for instance, a very regular chiasm is not highly aesthetic, although a partial chiasm aids in organizing a passage (cf. Gammie's essay, below).

Patterns, as they appear in existence, are marked not by complete regularity but by conditional probabilities or implicative tendencies (Meyer, 1956:31, 57; 1973:29, 130; Moles: 57, 74). When a rhythm is set up, its continuation may be expected, yet not with certainty. Similarly, during a festival an Israelite prophet may well, but need not, pronounce an oracle. The strength of implications between phenomena ranges from the somewhat likely to the virtually certain. It is important to note that most culturally defined genres are constituted not by rigid norms but by probability relations (with Todorov: 18). Whatever is rigidly required furnishes no information; it may, however, provide security and reinforce a cultural system (important functions of repeated ritual). It is quite appropriate that psalms are highly predictable, since their aim is not to describe a condition in detail but to issue an unambiguous call for help or to express joy, etc. (Even they vary, so that a large number of them are preserved; see Ridderbos: 100). Other genres serve as vehicles for widely varying content and need to be flexible.

A structural apprehension reduces the manifold character of existence to a manageable form. Although this is an advantage for the mastery of life, it does not yield full contact with it. Some religious experiences seek to meet reality without such reduction. For instance, Zen aims at a perception which is continually fresh; if predictability is erased from consciousness, even a repeated stimulus constantly carries new information (Tart: 485). A highly unstructured state (as described, for instance, by V. Turner) does not provide a good basis for practical achievement, but permits intimate relations with others. According to the Book of Job, the divine is manifested in the structures of natural order, yet God's way in its completeness is beyond human knowledge. Not the lack of information, but an inexhaustible fullness constitutes mystery /29/.

C. History

While forms express what is possible, history represents actuality. The actual is particular—not identical (at least in spatiotemporal location) with any other. This particularity contains the seeds of alienation and conflict, but it is necessary for love. A major aspect of actuality is realistic possibility, or potentiality /30/. Such possibility develops in steps; for instance, the invention of the wheel must in principle precede the building of carts. New options emerge as the result of previously actualized opportunities. Particularity and evolution thus constitute the two basic ingredients of history.

Biblical scholarship has fully incorporated the element of particularity into its framework of operation. In fact, as other disciplines did during the nineteenth century, it has emphasized that element one-sidedly. Form criticism, since Gunkel, countered an individualistic perspective through paying attention to repeated styles and content, in relation to typical situations. Yet, in this tradition, genres have largely been conceived as norms within a single culture /31/ and for many scholars genre criticism has served primarily as a tool for examining particular phenomena.

The methods of particularistic historiography are well known. (They are summarized by Bernheim.) A few fundamental issues, however, require special attention. All historical judgment is probabilistic, so that every historical statement must give an indication of the degree of certainty ascribed to a proposal. If one inference is based on another, rather than directly on primary evidence, reliability quickly evaporates. Constant reliance on hard data and lack of dogmatism constitute the foundation of critical historiography. During the period of intensive historical criticism (from about 1770 to 1880), the goal of obtaining a more correct view of historical development, on the basis of free critical inquiry, was on the whole achieved. For once a question is formulated and a procedure is developed for it, a conclusion warranted by the data is ordinarily reachable within a reasonable period of time. The effective limit of knowledge in regard to the history of biblical literature was probably approached at the turn of the century. This limit must be respected and is not likely to change without new evidence, such as through archaeology /32/.

Searching for so-called "origins"—common in twentieth-century biblical scholarship—is on the whole unhistorical. Origin is basically a religious and perhaps a philosophical category; the appropriate words for historical study are "earlier" and "later." A confusion of languages and procedures becomes apparent in attempts to determine an "original" *Sitz im Leben* of a genre. The notion of a life-situation is very useful if it refers to a human role in a "form of life" (Wittgenstein, 1953, I: § 23). The idea, however, that a genre arises from a typical spatiotemporal setting is largely mistaken. A genre may have a preferred, or even a prescribed, setting; but often the genre is older, and as a rule a setting serves a genre rather than vice versa /33/. Furthermore, in most cases pure forms do not represent an earlier stage but arise from differentiation (with Mowinckel: 96, against Gunkel); for instance, hymnic language probably belonged to the human process of praise in connection with other elements— including lament, wisdom, and prophecy—before it became the exclusive content of certain psalms. Instead of searching for hypothetical origins, historical investigation properly focuses on three issues: the meaning level of interaction (the human process or role), the organizational factors at a given time (which form a setting), and long-range development (evolution).

Macrohistorical perspectives have been far less adequately developed by biblical scholars than particularistic historiography. One reason for this lack lies in a justified skepticism toward the idea of progress. Evolution, however, does not necessarily imply progress. Another reason lies in a reluctance—widespread in the first half of the present century—to engage in interdisciplinary cooperation. Indeed, a broad vision, made difficult by modern specialization, was explicitly rejected by the so-called "biblical theology" movement (sketched by Childs). In the biblical field, W. F. Albright is almost the only one who concerned himself with macrohistory. He constructed an "organismic" theory and, furthermore, regarded as probable that evolution can be stated in mathematical form; he was confident that "God controls evolution" (3, 179, 184).

The best formulation of development is probably still that of Herbert Spencer, who proposed that the general trend of evolution is toward an increase in differentiation and integration, as aspects of a single process /34/. Spencer's view was highly optimistic. Not long after his writing, however, a more pessimistic outlook arose, propelled in part by the discovery of the Second Law of Thermodynamics, which recognizes a growth of entropy or "disorder" in the physical universe. Since then, it has been a puzzle to many thinkers how increases in complexity, observable in biology and sociology, relate to this increase of entropy. According to a widely followed theory propounded by E. Schrödinger in 1945 (cf.

Buckley: 143–46), "order" is transferred from the inorganic world to the organic. While this theory may be correct in part, it does not distinguish between degree of order, or predictable orderliness (the opposite of entropy) and grade of order, or complexity. These relate, on the whole, negatively to each other /35/. Thus the development of complexity is not contrary to a growth of entropy. The main question of evolution, then, is how richer wholes are formed, that is, how communication makes use of "uncertainty."

A whole may be defined as an entity within which there is a continuing process of interaction, so that an event in one part tends to affect the rest more than would be the case if the parts were relatively isolated. There are many levels of organization and many degrees of integration. In higher animals, a central nervous system serves to guide the whole. Among human beings, some families are closely knit, while others barely hang together. What is it that joins elements together? A number of processes do so: attraction, exchange of particles, resonances, and—especially important—various systems of mutual contribution or "synergy" /36/. Atoms "share" electrons in molecules; in an organism the various parts contribute to each other directly or indirectly. As a unit increases in size, internal communication becomes more difficult, so that there is a limit to growth by agglomeration. When such a limit is approached, further complexity arises when such a whole enters into relations with other similar-sized units within a more inclusive one (T. Parsons: 113; Parsegian). With each level, unpredictability in detail tends to increase, and with this the potential information in an interaction rises. The individualistic divergence which provides the basis of entropy can thus be both overcome and furthered by mutuality.

The contribution which a part renders to a whole is often called its "function" (it is always necessary to make clear the whole in relation to which the function is considered). Such a function is a special form of causality and no more teleological than causality in general. It can be stated in terms of a mathematical function, which determines one object in a given domain on the basis of another (cf. Nagel: 520–35). In both mathematical and realistic functions, a given value can be reached from more than one base; in other words, the same result can be achieved by functional alternatives.

Functions contributing to a whole participate in feedback loops. Negative feedback stills an operation when it reaches a certain "goal"

and therefore plays a crucial role in stabilizing a system. Positive
feedback is openended and increases an operation, until checked by
other processes. Uncontrolled positive feedback involving only part
of a system leads to the destruction of the larger whole (see M.
Maruyama in Buckley: 304–13). But in conjunction with negative
processes protecting structure already attained, positive feedback
leads to the growth of a system in quantity or richness. Such
enhancing processes include pleasure in organisms and the formation
of meaning in cultural life. For instance, biblical narratives informed
the self-definition of hearers; this in turn contributed to the
preservation of the stories, whose impact is now world-wide.

Growth in amount or complexity does not constitute moral
advance but yields an increase in real possibilities, including
destructive ones (so also Wiener: 37). Variety and unpredictability
are paradoxical in that they provide both the need and the
opportunity for information. Uncoordinated and clashing activities
form a problem to which communication responds. Indeed, Jewish
and Christian traditions see in history a growth of both good and evil
(comparable to the interplay between form and uncertainty)—the
good giving opportunity to evil and evil providing occasion for good
(see Buss, 1967:144–47; 1969:132, 140).

An interweaving of good and evil is clearly discernible in the story
of Jacob, who is pictured as a rascal and yet the chosen of God.
Although deception is not condemned very sharply in biblical stories
(especially if done by the weak), Jacob is in no sense a moral hero; in
some ways he is outshone by Esau, especially in the latter's generosity
in reconciliation. The Israelite willingness to be self-critical in this
way can be assessed as spiritually profound. Such self-irony is
continued in later "Jewish humor," which exhibits the generic
character of the Jacob accounts and furnishes a significant literary
form for a conception of history /37/.

The complex character of Israelite narration becomes apparent in
a comparison with V. Propp's analysis of imaginary tales involving
magic. Propp isolates over thirty "functions," i.e., processes which
advance the drama of a narrative, and argues that an individual story
selects from these in sequence. Of these, the first two-thirds appear in
Genesis 25–35. Functions 1–8 deal with trickery for which the victim
may share some blame through violating an interdiction or by failing
to resist the villain. Jacob's acquisition of Esau's birthright, in part

because of the latter's lightheartedness, and his deception of Isaac, who acts rather stupidly (cf., below, pp. 128, 168), fit this pattern. Functions 8a–19 involve the solution of the problem created by the villainy: the hero is dispatched from home, finds a donor who willingly or unwillingly provides magical aid, and defeats the villain in a struggle in which the hero is branded or marked. Jacob's departure, blessing by God, involvement with Laban (are both of them donors?), and struggle with deity (Genesis 28–32) provide a fairly close parallel. It is startling that Jacob plays the role of both villain and hero and that God acts as opponent as well as guide. Roland Barthes, who recognized the connection between Jacob's struggle and the branding "function" (see below, pp. 57, 64), compared the paradoxical role of God with extortion (an act in which support and injury go together). Such a comparison, however, unduly rationalizes the situation. At a similar period in Moses' travel, God meets him with threatening force and is held off by a branding of some sort (Exod 4:24–26). The mystery of a union of positive and negative sides in humanity and deity lies at the heart of these stories /38/.

A careful survey of other traditions is needed for an assessment of the extent to which moral ambiguity is characteristic of different sorts of stories. Complex evaluation is especially appropriate for sagas or historical narratives (as distinguished from fairy tales), since they seek to represent actuality /39/. Yet many imaginative narratives also contain ambiguity, especially in the image of a trickster. The trickster is selfish, lawless, and in need of correction, but dupes primarily the foolish, avaricious, or proud (cf. Radin; R. Armstrong in Pool: 168–69; Lévi-Strauss, 1963:226; J. Ackerman in Gros Louis et al.: 349; and below, p. 155). One can raise the question whether the Israelite interpretation of the name Jacob as "deceiver" reflects the tradition of this figure.

It seems that every significant element of the Bible can be found elsewhere. Still, the total constellation is unique, as is true for highly complex phenomena. Whether Hebrew faith possesses fewer or more peculiarities than do other religions is difficult to determine. Uniqueness may enhance individuality, but it is not inherently related to theological truth or to moral validity (with Barth, I/2:70–71). Thus it is not possible to support the validity of biblical views by claiming for them a special character. On the contrary, an emphasis on peculiarity and on "distance" between individuals, nations, and times—including the notion of different religions (cf. Troeltsch, 1924:32, 80; Westermann, 1960:18–21)—is a feature of historical criticism rather consciously designed to undercut the noncompetitive economy of the Bible (see, e.g., Buss, 1974:26–27). True individuality, as Bosanquet has rightly argued, lies positively in wholeness rather than negatively in idiosyncracy. Uncertainty introduced by variety, however, provides opportunity for communication /40/.

Comparisons within history are not easy, but they are important for interpretation. It is necessary to pay close attention to the functions of items compared, in their respective contexts. Sometimes a surface similarity reflects two very different social roles. More frequently, surface differences mask pronounced parallels in dynamic relations. For this reason functional analysis is crucial for biblical theology. A recipient cannot comprehend a message without recognizing the problem to which it proposes a solution /41/. If one understands the relation of item A to context B, however, one can construct or comprehend an item C which stands in a corresponding relation to context D. This is the pattern of analogy, which combines difference and similarity. Analogy can be used for the comprehension of historical events (e.g., Heinrici: 726) and is crucial for the application of a text to another context (e.g., Lowry: 417–38; Sanders: 406; and Patrick, below); the possibility of comparative study and the continuing applicability of a text imply each other.

The variety of traditions aids the development, preservation, and recognition of messages, through protective and clarifying redundancy together with the new growing from interactions. Within Israel, the duality of North and South provided in part analogous and in part complementary versions of faith, subsequently fused in the biblical canon. Western culture is paralleled and complemented by that of the East (India, China, and contiguous areas). Dual streams like these provide for a wider exploration of possibilities and illuminate each other /42/. For instance, Jesus' words against anxiety and judgment—which seem very strange—are comparable to Taoist theses in such a way that they cannot be brushed off easily as hyperboles. Similarly, Israel's emphasis on economic equality even in a relatively advanced society is supported by the Confucian ideal of the "well-field" system (with equal family plots). In aspects in which East and West differ,mutual enrichment is possible and has already taken place; e.g., Buber's "I and Thou" merges elements of Jewish and Taoist experience. While most persons are likely to value continuity with their background, love and intellectual interest call for an opening to the other. So-called secular movements similarly furnish both clarification and fresh stimuli.

History is to a large extent cumulative (although one must allow for the possibility of sharp discontinuities /43/). Genuine advance does not mean the abolition of the old but its inclusion in a wider perspective. In the intellectual realm that means that progress proceeds not so much through a furnishing of new answers to old questions as through the raising of new issues which may presuppose the older ones. Israelite faith emerged within the spearhead of ancient civilization, near the center of the land mass of Asia, Africa, and Europe. There communications from all directions could and did converge to stimulate cultural development, with its positive and negative sides. In turn, insights presented in the Bible, like those of Greek philosophy in another sphere of life, are still valuable, although they need to be reformulated. Fortunately, modern reformulation can draw on significant contributions by Jews, which continue the biblical tradition in an important way /44/.

It is probably not necessary to produce a Bible again or to establish a new set of dates for biblical material. A more promising task and opportunity for the present is the study of dynamic relationships. Pure (nonfunctional) structuralism would mean a return to the tradition dominant before the rise of historical criticism; nevertheless, recent structuralists point to valuable insights to be retained and developed. Future work must include both structural and historical perspectives, not merely adding them to each other, but merging and transcending them /45/.

The present situation, like any other, contains dangers as well as opportunities. Increasing sophistication in technology, which enhances world-wide connections, undoubtedly poses a severe threat to the quality—and even to the survival—of human life. Responsible action opposes such a threat and involves itself in the positive potentialities of the same process.

D. Meaning

When a relationship is perceived or conceived by someone, it

constitutes a "meaning" for that person. (A sheer relation in itself is
only a "function.") Meaning is largely, although not entirely, a
human phenomenon. In animals instinctive reactions respond to a
stimulus automatically, without a direct reference to consequences;
with increasing complexity, meaning gradually develops in terms of
learned associations between events. Human life becomes
characterized by an extensive and complex network of meanings.

The meaning of signs—which point to the actuality or possibility of
another object or event—has been discussed continuously since
ancient times. Recent discussions are heavily indebted to the
conceptualization of Peirce. He distinguished between three kinds of
signs: (1) the "icon" directly represents a quality or characteristic of a
possible referent (a map exhibits the shape of a real or hypothetical
country); (2) the "index" reflects the influence of an object (swaying
trees show wind motion); (3) the "symbol" or "legisign" is
conventional and usually associated with general ideas (2.247–49,
304). The structure of a sign—as he showed—is triadic. It is not only
related as a signifier to a signified, but it "addresses somebody"
(2.228). It is a sign in its function of leading to a related sign in the
mind of an actual or future person (2.92, 228, 274, etc.). A sign is not
just a thought or a connection resting in itself; rather, it is "informing
thought, or cognition," establishing new connections (1.537, 2.231).
The sign is creative, like sympathy and evolution in general (1.337–
39, 6.32, 8.328–32). Its meaning is "something virtual" (5.289), a
potentiality.

Possibility

Possibility is central to the process of communication, in which it
plays several different roles. One role is the opportunity for
expression given in a code or convention (with Ullmann: 19–21). A
set of conventions, such as Hebrew, is known as a language (*langue*,
in Saussure's terminology); when acquired by individuals, it becomes
their "competence" (Chomsky: 4). The possibility given in such a
system is actualized in the "performance" of a particular utterance or
text (*parole* /46/).

The meaning of a text is a potential or, more precisely, a set of
potentials. A potential becomes realized as the expression is
interpreted by someone in relation to a code and in connection with
relevant circumstances /47/. The author envisions a certain code and

knowledge in the audience. The recipient, in turn, applies to the text a language frame believed to have been used by the speaker. For the interpreting of biblical literature, few data are available concerning the concrete circumstances of individual authors and recipients or their variations in linguistic convention. Moreover, the material has been modified in oral or written tradition so that idiosyncracies are toned down. It is therefore difficult to reconstruct an author's meaning, if that is different from what would be normal in that culture (against Ernesti: §§ 3, 188). On the whole, the interpretation of a biblical text must rest with the determination of its normal potential in the language system /48/. The fact that a text can be connected only somewhat loosely with a specific occasion does not limit its relation to human existence. On the contrary, that fact may indicate an extensive potential for involvement. For "literature," i.e., material suited for repeated use, speaks to a human situation which is more than purely individual /49/. In psalms, for example, "enemies" represent hostile forces in general, which can be particularized differently by those who use a given lament.

Words and sentences indicate possibilities. One of the key strengths of human speech is that it deals not only with objects or events in the immediate vicinity of the speaker, but also with such as are distant in time or space or even nonexistent altogether. Descriptive words designate members of virtual classes, e.g., possible or conceivable trees, not only those actually existing. Sentences similarly designate possible events or states. It has long been known that speech does not refer directly to reality but expresses the content of thought. At the end of the nineteenth century, F. Brentano renewed medieval notions and terminology in characterizing the direction of thought as "intention" (1874, II:124, etc.). In the tradition of phenomenology emanating from him, thought is viewed as oriented outward toward the world, yet the intended world need not be actual. The idea of possibility, stimulated in part by earlier discussions of divine power, has now become prominent in formal semantic theory /50/. A "name," it is true, specifies a particular person or group, but even this entity may exist only in the imagination.

Descriptions forming open classes can be analyzed in terms of components, i.e., as combinations of more elementary features /51/. For instance, the notion of a tree contains the elements of vegetation and largeness. Contrasts formed by single features—such as living vs. nonliving and small vs. large—represent different dimensions cutting across each other, so that the meaning of words exists in a multidimensional space. One advantage of the componential character of word meanings is that images can be formed creatively through the combination of known features, e.g., a cherub (winged bull) or, in technology, the idea of an improved tool.

Possible realities play a central role in literature /52/. Worlds depicted in art can be related to actual existence in different ways. According to an ancient theory, literature "imitates," or represents, human life (Plato, Aristotle). With the development of individualism, emphasis was placed on the poetic personality which expresses itself. Thus Carlyle wrote concerning Shakespeare: "His works are so many windows, through which we see a glimpse of the world that was in him" (110). Interest in progressive movement led readers and theorists to expect imaginative creations of a different world (so, among more recent ones, Dewey: 348, E. Bloch, Frye: 184). These ways of relating to actuality are not mutually exclusive, for a writer may depict both established and alternative states of affairs.

Every actuality exhibits a realized possibility. A biblical story can thus be viewed as factual (for instance, by an ancient audience) without losing its character as embodying a potential. According to Heidegger, the point of historical narration is to indicate a "possibility of existence" (although it may need to be rejected for one's own life, 385). To combine historical actuality with transhistorical meaning was the aim of the traditional belief in the multiple senses of Scripture. In Karl Barth's view, the Bible witnesses to a reality lying behind or in history as its foundation or central movement, so that Christ constitutes "the concrete possibility of the existence of all men" (IV/2:48; cf. I/2:25, etc.). G. von Rad has called such a witness the "kerygmatic intention" of a document (1962:106); the human meaning of texts, however, is inadequately developed in his scholarly writings.

Direction

Alongside the question of possibility arises the issue of value, which governs one's aims. To envision a state as possible does not imply that it is desirable. On the other hand, to say that a condition is desirable does not imply that it is possible in conjunction with other realities and leaves open the question of how it may be brought about. One of the differences between Judaism and Christianity is that the former places value on activities largely within the power of the human being, while the latter takes a special interest in states over which one has no control, so that their possibility is left in God's hands /53/. The presence of the "Old Testament" within the Christian canon means, for some interpreters a least, that the dimension of effective action and social morality is included in Christianity. Jews, on the other hand, recognize the fundamental role of divine activity. Religions, in general, are concerned in a major way with ideal or desirable states and with steps toward reaching these.

Statements about value are part of an "inside" view of reality, one which states the frame of reference within which one exists and acts. A descriptive approach, in contrast, is an outside view. The internal perspective includes an external one, since the understanding of one's situation involves reference to other beings. At the same time, an external (descriptive) view cannot be isolated from, but is a part of, an active orientation /54/. An inside view is necessarily more comprehensive than an external one, for it refers to the whole which includes both oneself and others; it intertwines self-commitment with observation. In so-called "practical reasoning," desired ends and factual data together form the basis for specific decisions (Rotter: 152, Anscombe: 56).

An "inside" view can be shared; on the basis of observable actions and expressions it is possible to enter imaginatively into another's world. In such empathetic participation one can recognize a system of beliefs and desires (cf. E. Stein). The sharing of another orientation is a profoundly enjoyable experience, truly "ecstatic" (beyond oneself). It embodies respect and allows the other to enrich one's orientation in belief and aim. An explicit inside view exists only for beings which can form an image of wholeness and, with it, an image of themselves. With a few possible exceptions, that occurs only in human beings. It is for this reason that a sharing of inner vision is largely limited to human interaction. Nevertheless, it is possible to attribute aims to nonhuman processes on the basis of an "as-if" teleology; such aims express the direction of a being. Empathy can then be extended to these processes, so that one participates sensitively in them.

A human world into which one enters through verbal or nonverbal communication need not be one of full awareness. Indeed, subconscious and unconscious factors play a major role in human life. Such factors must be inferred, since they are not directly given; but that is true also for the recognition of another's consciousness. In fact, it is often difficult to determine whether a given belief or desire is conscious or not, for implicit knowledge hardly differs from conscious thought in its effect on expression. Thoughts repressed because of their threatening character appear in normal speech only intermittently and as oddities ("Freudian slips"). It appears that they emerge more clearly in imaginative literature, where they enjoy a certain safety in a presentation with which both author and recipient identify only in part (Lesser). In biblical literature, confrontation with the dark side of existence appears quite frequently; whether this confrontation was conscious for the writer is less important than whether it is likely to elicit in the reader a similar engagement.

Since literature embodies conscious and unconscious movements of human existence, the psychology of literary works is a most important aspect of criticism /55/. Such a psychological interpretation does not need to deal specifically with an individual author's experience and thought (as for Schleiermacher: 81) but can lay bare the "emotional dynamics" expressed in a text (Voss and Harsch: 148). Furthermore, it need not wait for application to particular recipients (although, with Wink, that is an important step eventually). Rather, a psychological, together with a sociological, examination can aid in clarifying for a public audience forms of existence exhibited in, or readily elicited by, a text.

In its dynamic structure, human life reflects a small number of basic dimensions of experience, especially the following three: nature of evaluation (positive, negative, or mixed), degree of arousal (major or minor), and effective role (dominance, receptivity, or relative equality) /56/. Gratitude, for instance, involves a sense that one has received some good. The psychologist Osgood has found that ordinary descriptive words ("father," "stone," etc.) can be placed into a semantic space with the primary dimensions of evaluation (good or bad), activity (motion vs. rest), and potency (strength of effect). Even more clearly, "expressive" symbols represent basic emotional and pragmatic structures. Thus an actual tree or the word "tree" can express flourishing vitality. Individuals (Leary: 154–91) and groups communicate to themselves and to others their roles and hopes through such symbols. An analysis of relational patterns, then, is crucial for understanding the meaning of symbols.

Ricoeur—examining active life—argues that symbols precede thought (1967). One needs to distinguish, however, between emblems (such as a sacred stone or a name) and metaphors (such as the word "lion" for hostile power). Emblems are objects or expressions directing life with only limited intellectual content. Metaphors, on the other hand, include an awareness of a more literal meaning, which is employed for the sake of the action or experience it embodies. Metaphors presuppose formal thought, although emblems need not. Symbols referring to what is ultimate hint at the fundamental organization and movement of existence (cf., e.g., Sewell); they imply a fairly high degree of awareness.

Like all activity viewed internally, speech is oriented toward a goal (cf. Parsons and Shils, C. Morris, Austin, Searle, Hutchison, Leont'ev). The goal sought by a speech act is a reaction in the audience; to recognize this purpose is crucial to understanding an expression /57/. The aim of many prophetic words, for instance, is to bring about a change of activity in the hearer. Other prophecies, including many of those known as apocalyptic, encourage perseverance in the face of external pressure. Ordinarily it is not difficult to discern the purpose of a word, for there is a logical connection between the pragmatic thrust of a text (e.g., criticism or promise) and the desired response (such as change or trust) /58/. Thus Genesis texts revealing a divine origin and an ambiguous human past naturally evoke—if they are accepted—such affects as gratitude and at least partial self-criticism.

For the recipient who accepts a message, its meaning has an "organizing function" (MacKay: 35). A word about or from the ultimate has a high potential in this regard. One can say that it carries a large amount of "semantic information," if this is defined as the number of items implied by a given message /59/. Ordinarily, a notice which attracts attention is one which has a carry-over to other parts of the recipient's cognitive system. Religious and similar holistic declarations are intrinsically rich in such information. They shape not only a small portion of existence but give form to (inform) its pattern as a whole, so that every aspect is affected in principle. In Genesis 25–35 God's speech appears at critical points /60/ to give direction to life.

E.   Understanding

To obtain insight into an action or expression means to reduce its uncertainty. Maximum information is obtained when a very large uncertainty is reduced to a very small amount. For a system involving more than one element, understanding takes place when the elements are seen as appropriate in the sense that one element implies another, which in the realm of practical reasoning may mean that a certain step is likely to lead to a given goal. For instance, Jacob's flight makes sense in view of danger and a normal human desire for safety, although other ways of meeting the issue can be imagined. In mathematics and logic, relationships are necessary and inevitable, given certain assumptions. In the actual world, connections are looser, ranging from very low to very high probability, requiring or yielding different amounts of information. How tight a connection needs to be in order to be viewed as "appropriate" is a matter for individual judgment /61/.

An important step in the process of gaining understanding involves a recognition of actual correlations within the system to be understood. For instance, D. Verner has shown that Jacob is described more frequently as the son of Rebekah than as the son of Isaac, while the reverse holds true for Esau. Such correlational "content analysis" has been employed with considerable success for sociological and psychological purposes as well as for literary study; with or without formal statistical calculations, it is useful for biblical investigation /62/. One of the advantages of such an approach is its focus on the data themselves in relation to statable hypotheses. There is no limit to the kinds of phenomena that can be investigated in this manner: sounds (for assonance), words (for semantic, syntactic, or poetic issues), verbal "components" (to determine the dynamic pattern of a text, for instance in terms of emotional quality), or ideas extracted from sentences or passages.

Correlations carry no meaning unless they are interpreted in the light of an ideal structure or model /63/. A back-and-forth relation obtains between the correlational data and a model chosen or constructed to account for them. In scientific procedure with access to more than one sample, the test of a model is applied to a sample different from the one which initially suggested the model. For the study of unique phenomena, it is not possible to pass on to other data, although a certain amount of comparison with other complexes is possible /64/. The examination of an individual text necessarily oscillates between a constructive view and specific observations. The normal result of such an operation is that the text increasingly makes sense as one's view is refined. For instance, the fact that Jacob is often called Rebekah's son coheres with a thesis (developed by Allen, below) that Rebekah plays a major role in the history of salvation.

The possibility for understanding a phenomenon increases with an expansion of the horizon. For instance, Rebekah's prominence in Genesis 27 (where she guides Jacob) remains a relatively meaningless phenomenon until it is placed within a larger context. A more comprehensive framework deals with the role of women in existence, with the nature of Israelite faith, and with other relevant issues. A broader view can take account of further texts (biblical or otherwise) and of what may be known about social and psychological processes. Since the ultimate horizon is infinite and since one must allow for indeterminacy, complete understanding is impossible.

When little uncertainty is left in a text, most of the available information will have been extracted. What happens to the information? It may be forgotten, for there is no law guaranteeing its preservation. Ideally, however, it will be incorporated into the mental structure of recipients, who are enabled by it to act more intelligently and sensitively /65/. The models by which reality is understood can serve as suggestive models for life (Geertz: 8, 34). What fits one situation can fit another, insofar as the two are comparable. Although decisions require a degree of openness in order to be meaningful, they gain in wisdom and power from insight into connections within reality.

An informed "regard" enhances life; such a view—connecting intellect with concern—is expressed in the Hebrew Bible with the aid of a number of words for understanding, knowing, attending, and teaching. The broader implication even of words addressed to a quite particular situation was seen by Israelites. For instance, the conclusion of the Book of Hosea indicates a general application of the words of that prophecy: "Who will be wise and understand these things, discerning and recognize them? For straight are the ways of Yahweh—the righteous walk in them, but the transgressors are brought to stumble in them." Certainly, interpretation cannot be separated from a transformation of existence; whether a message has been understood can be determined only from the recipient's response (even the devils react, in a "shudder," Jas 2:19).

Not all texts speak to all issues. On the contrary, one of the essential insights of genre analysis is that different problems in life call for different responses. A psalm of lament deals with a condition of trouble. A certain kind of law is designed to solve ordinary conflicts between members of a group (Buss, 1977). Narratives provide orientation in life. The problem situation addressed by a text is ordinarily stated or implied within it /66/. The *topoi*, or standard elements of content, represent typical questions and answers, reflecting experience. The most crucial task of the examination of forms ("form criticism") is not a discovery of arbitrary conventions but a recognition of what solutions represent a fit response to a given concern.

To a considerable extent, historical study relativized the past in such a way as to weaken its significance for the present (so also Gunneweg: 107). This negative function played a significant role in liberating human society and culture from external authority and unquestioned tradition. When this freedom has been obtained, however, it is necessary to seek guidance unless ethical action is left simply to impulse. To offer guidance has been an aim of modern anthropology, which attempts to examine particular phenomena not so much for their own sake as for the light they can shed on others. Thus Radcliffe-Brown stated in 1929: "If anthropological science is to give any important help in relation to practical problems of government and education it must abandon speculative attempts to conjecture the unknown past and must devote itself to the functional study of culture" (41). Much of biblical scholarship, as has already been pointed out, continues in the older style here described and is not devoted to showing the significance of the Bible in a critical manner.

An understanding of relationships aids a new kind of liberation, which goes beyond a negative freedom from past authority to the positive freedom of meaningful action. The first kind of freedom is associated with the revolutions overthrowing aristocracy. The second kind belongs to the exerting of rights and the enjoyment of opportunities by all. Both are needed and are to a large extent possible /67/. If dynamic relations are grasped through social and psychological investigation, one can effect a "translation" of an ancient word in such a way that a functional equivalent (cf. Nida: 59) is obtained. Furthermore, when directions are seen as appropriate to existence, they act as an intrinsic guide rather than as an external imposition on one's actions.

It is often possible to discern the appropriateness and inner logic of biblical patterns. For instance, in Israelite prophecy ultimate salvation is always announced as a divine act. Indeed, an infinite reality cannot well be produced by finite human activity. The psychological correlate of this insight is that the ultimate is met receptively. More specifically, an analysis of expressions in Israelite prophecy shows that a certain form of eschatology (such as Hosea's) embodies both self-transcendence and fulfillment. Self-transcendence, which appears also in the Jacob stories, is an integral part of faith in God and plays an important role in social existence. Like the God of the Bible, "high gods" in religious traditions are normally not called upon in competitive magic, but are related primarily to ethics and to a view of the world as a whole. Such an outlook recognizes that the ultimate cannot be manipulated and that an orientation toward it implies concern for other beings /68/. Many other, and simpler, examples of appropriate elements can be given for law, wisdom, psalms, and narratives, with the aid of the human sciences. Often a form-critical analysis reaches what appears to be a very obvious conclusion, such as that a psalm of lament complains of evil and calls for help. Yet it is precisely in seeing a close connection between phenomena that insight is reached /69/.

The individualistic tradition, which still strongly dominates biblical study, lays little emphasis on insight. The will and action of a nominalist God is fundamentally inscrutable and must simply be believed or obeyed. Apart from reference to God, nominalism favors descriptions over norms or guidance. Biblical scholarship accordingly often oscillates between critical description and capricious faith, calling the one "historical" and the other "theological." In contrast to this outlook stands a philosophical position oriented toward essences. Its weakness is insufficient attention to freedom and change. A united perspective appears in such notions as probability and relationship. If love and *sedeq* ("rightness") are ultimate, neither individuality nor sharing is more basic than the other.

Three aspects of interpretation can be identified, then, by the terms fact, form, and faith. Fact represents the particular actuality; form, the possible or general; faith, one's apprehension of the whole or ultimate, which includes and transcends the other two. In Israelite faith the name Yahweh symbolizes the more particular side of deity; the designation Elohim, the more general /70/. These two sides are held together in communication. As both are apprehended together, one can recognize what the Bible—or any word—has to "say."

Notes

/1/   On the beginning of the present era in the last decades of the nineteenth century and on its social condition, cf. Buss, 1974:32 (the break is placed similarly by Whitehead, 1941:271) and note especially the movements of labor and feminism.

/2/   Peirce not only anticipated but also to a large extent actually influenced subsequent thought; his early impact was largely indirect, e.g., through William James. Like others, Peirce was aware of the political and economic (libertarian and competitive) correlates of nominalism (1.17, 6.294). That in a practical, social perspective, dualism is transcended was noted by K. Marx (162). R. Palmer now argues for an integrative "post-modern" perspective, with special reference to Nietzsche. Peirce, and then Russell and Whitehead, developed a logic of relations.

/3/   Peirce's influence extended through J. Royce to G. H. Mead, a major source of Jaspers' thought. The recent discussion of communication by J. Habermas is probably indebted to Jaspers; it explicitly refers to Peirce (91–112).

/4/   E.g., influenced by Peirce, G. H. Mead (324, etc.), and J. Habermas, K.-O. Apel and H. Peukert view communicative interaction as the basis of both knowledge and ethics. Logic and linguistics are converging in the work of R. Montague, T. van Dijk (1977), and others (e.g., the many contributors to Keenan). It should be observed, however, that this "new" movement picks up an old and widespread concern for language (see, e.g., Gusdorf: 11–21, 127).

/5/   In biology, one refers to "codes" and "messengers." Linguistic theory now deals with statistical and multidimensional patterns (cf. Herdan for a survey), with the flow of information through a discourse (such as the use of pronouns, relations between "topic" and "comment," and "presuppositions" [cf. now van Dijk, 1977:117, 219–28]), and with the nature of communicative action. Among anthropologists, Lévi-Strauss (1963:83, 296–310; 1966:75, 268; 1976:66, 255), Leach (e.g., 3), and M. Douglas employ communication (and specifically information) theory. For overviews of virtually all phases, see Pierce, Smith, and Silverstein.

/6/   North-American slavery was unusually vicious, apparently in part because Protestant churches played a weak role in protecting slaves; American theology has learned much from that. R. Herrmann (29) rightly complained in 1933 diary entries that the church was publicly silent on the destructive side of the Nazi revolution. /7/ Gen 20:4–11; 21:26; 33:1–11. These passages employ Elohim as a designation for deity. (The view—expressed by Jaroš: 58, 401–2 and others—that E is critical of Canaanite religion is based primarily on passages in which Elohim does not appear, at least not as a name. E.g., " 'elohim" in Exod 32:16 is best translated by "divine"; Num 23:9 stands within a passage largely using the name Yahweh. For a tradition of religious wisdom in the Northern Kingdom, see Buss, 1969:69, 82.)

/8/ On wisdom as an aspect of various types of speech, including narratives and prophecy, see Buss, 1967:149; 1969:63–71, 82, 101, 107, 123–24, 139, etc. (Crenshaw rightly argues against regarding certain literary expressions simply as examples of wisdom; but as an aspect or element that tradition appears widely, just as other "forms" should not be regarded as originally or ideally independent.)

/9/ Schelling, I/III:588–89; I/V:218 (although he transcends the distinction ultimately); Hegel, IX:67; Droysen: 9–12, 357 (from 1858). In modern times, the idea of social evolution anteceded that of biological evolution by about a century.

/10/ One reason for probability is the fact that any given event is subject to more than one influence. Bohm showed that the data of modern physics can be reconciled with determinism if one assumes an infinity of influences; such an infinity can never be known, just as (with von Wright: 136) full determinism can never be proved. Thus the question of ultimate indeterminacy is left to intuitive commitment, but that is true for all visions of the whole. Formally it is possible to state causality either externally as conditional probability or internally as action (see, e.g., Nagel: 406–22 on the equivalence of causality and teleology and, further, below, pp. 27–29).

/11/ So, C. F. von Weizsäcker (1971:351–61) and some Marxists (Kirschenmann: 123, 183–84; Kubát and Zeman: 187–200, 254). The speed of light (pure energy) represents the limit for the propagation of (at least ordinary) information and causation. Communication is a useful image for causality, since determinism is not assumed (Brillouin: 69–72) and since it is likely that causality is not a one-way process but a phenomenon of mutual interaction (with Mach: 205–6; cf. Barbour: 331).

/12/ Schillebeeckx (35) applied the "word of God" to all of God's activities. Perspectives of love as basic in reality appear in Charles Hartshorne (stimulated by Peirce), Nels Ferré (15–16, with a cybernetic analogy), Paul Tillich (I:279; III:422), and Martin Luther King, Jr. (11). According to Casalis, the place of God is now taken by the sign which refers to itself (64); one can speak, differently, of a new metaphor for God. Recently, T. Altizer has located God's presence in speech (43, although—in a nominalist fashion—with primary emphasis on otherness and actuality, rather than on sharing and possibility, so that in his presentation silence is ultimate). Whitehead joins particularity and generality in God; similarly, in his view a "proposition" is a "hybrid" of actuality and potentiality (1929:282; applied to Christ by Beardslee: 150). Whitehead's system, however, lacks coherence as well as mystery through its failure to identify God with the ultimate (1929:11,47,73)—perhaps as a differentiated unity ("dialectic") of communication.

/13/ So, Buss, 1969:116–140. Logical (or thought) relations loom large in structural analysis by A. Weiser (22), W. Eichrodt (31), and Y. Kaufmann. For "generative semantics" (diverging from Chomsky), the semantic content is the deep structure of a sentence (see van Dijk, 1972:17–18).

/14/   Sequential structures, together with various stylistic features, have been described by E. Galbiati, L. Alonso Schökel (1963:chap. 9), W. Richter (79–114), and others. Some scholars seek to combine compositional with logical relations (e.g., Fohrer *et al.*: 86); often, however, different aspectual patterns do not coincide (see Oomen: 212; M. Weiss).

/15/   Against Richter (138, etc.) and others. Richter's distinction between genre and individual "form" cannot be upheld, for it is an essential characteristic of forms that they are general. Richter, although seeking an openness to systematic thinking, remains fundamentally individualistic, viewing genres only as abstractions from individuals. The modern philosophy of science has shown that induction from particulars, favored by the nominalistic tradition during the last few centuries, is theoretically weak. (So, rightly, Polzin: 19–26, 48, with Popper—although Popper's view again is one-sided. Induction plays a legitimate role in conjunction wth other procedures. For a criticism of the opposite extreme, which stresses prior assumptions, see below, n. 63.) A different view is represented by Melugin (below, pp. 93, 96). On the variability of starting points or perspectives, cf. White's and Allen's discussions (below, pp. 52, 160).

/16/   Thomas Aquinas states the issue thus: "Since that by which a thing is constituted in its proper genus or species is what is signified by the definition expressing what the thing is, philosophers have taken to using the word *quiddity* for the word *essence*. The philosopher [Aristotle] frequently calls this the what a thing was to be [in Latin, *quod, quid erat esse*], in other words, that by which a thing is a *what*. It is also called *form*" (1949:28). Biblical form criticism often attempts an uneasy (and illogical) combination of the nominalist and Aristotelian positions; both must be transcended.

/17/   This position opposes both Platonism (according to which forms are more "real" than are concrete objects) and nominalism (which is reserved about an ontological status for possibility and emphasizes particular actuality [see, e.g., the descriptions by Faust: 190; and by Horkheimer and Adorno: x, 23]). The issue is a central one in modern logic; cf. below, nn. 50, 52. Cantor's "set" contained possible or conceivable objects (481); Bernays described "classes" as an "open universe" (57). According to Wittgenstein (1922:2.033), "form is the possibility of structure." Husserl's *eidos* ("form") brackets out the question of actuality and deals with "possibility" (29, 47). Quine's semi-nominalist "virtual class" or class "abstract" is similar to what is here called an open or virtual class, but without an ontological status (64–72). (It should be noted that there are many degrees and varieties of both nominalism and realism; see, e.g., Martin: 269. Not very often is either alternative now held in an extreme form, but perhaps a genuine union cannot be fully brought about within philosophy.)

/18/   See Babbitt: 249; Nietzsche, XVIII:157; Grayson: 5. As R. Williams (180) rightly points out, the theory of fixed genres is a neo-classical construction, more rigid than ancient Greek thought on the subject.

/19/   On such intersecting dimensions in genres, see Mowinckel: 39; Westermann, 1965 (in part); Buss, 1969:*passim*; 1974:54–55; Beauchamp; Pike: 136–39; Jason: 415. Generally for language, Hartmann (v, vi) defines "form" in terms of multidimensional combination and "structure" as a relation between possibilities.

/20/   See Buss, 1963. (Many of the relevant psalms are now attributed to Asaph; whether they originated from a group called Asaphites is a question—discussed by others—not immediately relevant here.) It is not likely that oracles within psalms are adapted from prophecy (as found in the prophetic books); rather, they share a component with prophetic speech, agreeing with it in one dimension (divine speech) and disagreeing in another (general vs. particular); cf. the next two notes.

/21/   A generative *rhetoric* can probably be stated in terms of a finite number of rules. A generative *poetics* (cf. van Dijk, 1971, for a survey) is problematic, unless one attributes to poetry an infinite code (Kristeva: 174–80). Traditionally, it has been held that poetry can be taught only to a limited extent, so that poetics focuses on understanding language and life, while rhetoric trains in the production of speech (Buss, 1974:7); it was possible, however, to relate the two, in that poetry provides models for rhetoric. (Güttgemann's "generative poetics" is probably misnamed; his description of genres, 1971b:229, however, is similar to the one presented here.)

/22/   See Buss, 1969:83–105; 1978:169 (invectives are not derived from mourning, although it is not impossible that in some cases they are affected by the latter because of the similarity in style); cf. also below n. 33. Hardmeier recognizes the wide applicability of specific forms, but does not go quite far enough in reconceptualizing genres. Although following "generative semantics" (see above note 13), he does not carry through with a distinction between genres in semantic "deep" structure (267, which transcend a particular tradition; cf. 113–15) and genres as instruments (286, presumably conventions); what he calls "forms" apparently are conventions that serve as expressions for the components of genres. Amos 5:2 can be analyzed as follows: 1. basic speech act: prophetic threat (componentially: a negative projection for a specific group or person on the basis of revelation); 2. prophetic conventions, including the following: a) threats are usually stated in the form of announcements; b) the future can be described as present or past; c) metaphoric and dramatic style is frequently employed; 3. general conventions, among others: a) a certain style for lamenting the downfall of a person or group (expressing negativity with sympathy); b) a widespread habit of personifying groups. Prophetic lament over a nation, as a complex, became a conventional genre in Israelite culture.

/23/   .   In modern children, cross-classification becomes consciously operative before adolescence (e.g., Anderson: 225–56, following Piaget).

/24/   Average unpredictability is highest when all options occur with equal frequencies. For instance, a person who knows how to make five different responses to a frustrating situation but customarily uses only one of these is more "predictable" than another person who knows only two responses but uses these with roughly equal frequency. Thus entropy normally rises with, but is not simply equal to, variety. If one logon is considerably more common than another, an efficient language normally employs a shorter coding for it. (Natural languages make use of this principle, so that word length is inversely related to a word's frequency; Zipf: 19–55.) Shannon's measure for information is usually stated in "bits" (the logarithm, with the base of two, of the improbability of a signal); it corresponds roughly to the number of digits in a binary code, if the signal is economically represented.

/25/   According to R. Jakobson (in Sebeök: 203), the poetic function of language highlights the message as such. Art has repeatedly been compared with play since Kant and Schiller (cf. Gadamer). A major difference between art and science lies in the fact that the former, more so than the latter, creates uncertainty to be reduced; this distinction corresponds to a difference between play and (other) exploratory behavior, which take place under secure and uncertain conditions, respectively (Lieberman: 109).

/26/ Sources of happiness identified so far include primarily interaction with others and especially variety of experience (e.g., Bradburn: 132–46, 227; Izard: 266). Joy, however, arises not from the stimuli as such, but in their being resolved (it comes not from a state, but from a process); an excessive amount yields anxiety.

/27/ In 1671 and somewhat later, Leibniz characterized harmony as "diversity compensated by identity" and as "unity in plurality"; the harmonious is "the uniformly difform" (138, 426). Leibniz held that such a harmony was divinely pre-established, since he denied influence or "communication" among created substances (457). A view of beauty as "unity in the manifold" (Moses Mendelssohn) became widespread in the eighteenth century; according to François Hemsterhuis "the beautiful is that which gives the greatest number of ideas in the shortest time" (see Gilbert and Kuhn: 241, 261, 275, 296–97). Hemsterhuis' formulation furnished inspiration for informational-theoretical analyses of the arts (see Nake for a survey). Modern analyses of this sort have shown the relative complexity and unpredictability of artistic expressions, including literature (e.g., Lotman: 43, 113–14), and how even familiar realities are presented in a fresh way (Mukařovský: xiv and others).

/28/ In Genesis, as in the story of David, family and national relations are so closely interwoven that it is unlikely that they represent stages in the development of these texts. Hardly any of the stories would make sense without both aspects, although the individual motifs undoubtedly have divergent histories. (These histories ordinarily cannot be reconstructed from the story itself but can be traced to some extent through comparative research; see, e.g., Gaster: 164.) A combination of personal and political elements appears also in ancient and modern drama, in historical novels, and in recent studies of psychological factors in history. The conjunction thus reflects neither an odd juxtaposition of genres nor an outmoded form of narrative. These observations, however, do not rule out the possibility that in some instances unresolved tensions occur within the present form of the story as a result of its prior history.

/29/ Similarly, H. Schilling (with a discussion of relevant views).

/30/ On "real," as distinct from formal, possibility, cf. Peirce (2.664, 5.453, 6.217–20), Whitehead (1929:102), P. Weiss (105–15), E. Bloch (237), and N. Rescher (193). Such possibility (or potentiality) can be assigned a probability greater than zero. (Probability measures a relation between future actuality and formal possibility.)

/31/ In Germany, as well as in some other countries, there was a strong movement against both individualism and universalism in favor of nationalism or group identity (e.g., Rosenberg: 537). A more appropriate balance between these three factors is needed.

/32/ Neither more conservative nor more radical conclusions than those (roughly) of Wellhausen are persuasive. For the Pentateuch, the insight remains that four strata can be distinguished to a considerable extent on the basis of style and content (cf. Bentzen). Sharp divisions cannot be made between the strata, but their tendencies can be handled statistically and the strata can be treated as complexes of correlations. For instance, E is probably best understood as material employing

Elohim, but not exhibiting characteristics of P. Whether a continuous document E existed, as implied by Roth below, can be left open; J probably includes a number of traditions written over a period of several centuries (most likely before the Exile). At each step beyond this analysis, hypotheses become increasingly tenuous.

/33/ According to Mowinckel (28), "situation" determines aim and content; that is true only if a human "life-situation" is distinguished from "setting"; setting is generally secondary in relation to the other factors. Against traditional setting theory, see Long, 1976. On role and situation (distinguishable from setting): Buss, 1969:1; 1970:2; 1978; Ruesch and Bateson: 27, 276; Hasel: 383; Joshua Fishman and others in Pride and Holmes: 19–31, 75, 260–335 (according to a personal communication, Fishman—a leader in sociolinguistics—has been familiar to some extent with biblical form criticism); W. Kummer in Gülich and Raible: 37–39; Schutz and Luckmann: 113, 252; Hempfer: 188 (reporting observations by M. Waltz, learning from and correcting Gunkel's notion of "Sitz im Leben"), 225; J. Fabian in Eister: 255–66; Mehan and Wood: 75; K. Berger: 111–27; and, for religious education, Grosch: 35, 63.

/34/ Increase in complexity must be regarded as probabilistic, not inevitable. (Toulmin: 334, like others, rightly argues against inevitability.) That differentiation is normally associated with increase in size can be seen in Blau's data; it is not given sufficient recognition by Teilhard de Chardin, who places an integrating "Omega point" into the future. The development of complexity and, with it, freedom in sociocultural, including religious, history is well known (e.g., Bellah: 44).

/35/ That complexity is related to entropy is recognized in part in connection with the question of evolution by S. Bok and V. Somenzi in Dockx and Bernays: 219–27, 234; Kirschenmann: 72, 151; K. Denbigh in Kubát and Zeman: 84. As has been known for some time, a high-entropy state is "probable" over-all precisely because it is realizable in a large number of ways and thus unpredictable in detail.

/36/ On "synergy," see Maslow: 199–211, following Ruth Benedict; in physics a form of this appears as "binding energy," with a negative cost to the system (so also Weizsäcker, 1974:211, having, furthermore, learned from Shannon the role of entropy as a potential). Peirce regarded love (conceived quite broadly) as the basis of creativity (6.287–317); similarly, Wood. Freud held that eros builds up unities (57). According to J. and R. Maritain, liberating poetic creativity arises from communication (7, 79).

/37/ On early, medieval, and modern Jewish humor, see, e.g., Waxman: 605; Jónsson: 85; Buss, 1969:74, 126; and the Israeli satirist Ephraim Kishon. In a stimulating manner, Kenneth Burke and Haydon White have applied literary models to views of history. According to Burke (171), the comic frame allows a joining of action with self-observation. That holds true especially for the self-ironic comedy of "Jewish humor," which best expresses the character of the Genesis accounts. (Good: 106 speaks of "comic irony" for the pattern of Jacob stories; but "ironic comedy" is preferable, since compassion is dominant.)

/38/ The parallel in Exod 4:24–26 is noted by Gunkel, 1910:360–65, but as an isolated, and thus unparadoxical, motif. (On general similarities of the Jacob and Moses stories, cf. Hos 12:13–14 and Daube: 62–72.) The idea of a moral complexity of God is sophisticated, not "primitive" (with D. Robertson, against Gunkel; Robertson, however, fails to see adequately God's negative aspect in Exodus and God's positive side in Job). On the duality of the experience of the divine, cf. Otto. A. de Pury correctly sees that the Jacob cycle must be viewed as a whole, not in terms of isolated scenes. He briefly compares the cycle with Propp's functions (496–97); in greater detail, Couffignal presents such a comparison, recognizing the complex role of Jacob and interpreting it in terms of an Oedipal relation. May, 1969: 170 illustrated by means of the Peniel story the role of the "daimonic" in creativity. For other examples of paradox see D. Seybold, J. Ackerman, and H. Barzel in Gros Louis *et al.*: 64, 68, 118, 140. Role reversal is an element of humor (Cooper: 167).

/ 39 /   J. Pitt-Rivers tells how he was startled by Genesis stories, until he realized that it "was not moral truth that was being expounded ... but historical truth" (126). Moral complexity appears also in the Hindu epic *Mahābhārata* (Narasimhan: xx-xxiv).

/ 40 /   Barr, 1973:45–46, argues for the possibility of communication. Brueggemann states (in part on the basis of Gen 11:1–9 and the Abraham tradition) that the "idea of a divided, hostile, noncommunicative world is not willed by God" (44).

/ 41 /   Similarly, Collingwood: 29–43. Collingwood, however, stresses the role of an answer in relation to a problem in such a way as to weaken the significance of a thesis for another context. Dynamic analysis (not sufficiently pursued by Gadamer, who is concerned with application) can be used to recognize the appropriate relevance of a text for another situation.

/ 42 /   Fifty percent redundancy appears to be ideal for most systems of communication; it is approximated in these cultural developments.

/ 43 /   So, e.g., Foucault: 8, 169; the mathematical form of discontinuities is analyzed by "catastrophe theory." It should be recognized, however, that an advance is possible only with continuity.

/ 44 /   Jews must be regarded, on the whole, as the truest heirs of the Hebrew Bible (against H. W. Wolff in Westermann, 1960:161). Jewish leaders of the present century include Freud, Adler, Wertheimer, Lewin, Fromm, Erikson, and Maslow in psychology; Durkheim, Simmel, and Lévi-Strauss in sociology; Bergson, Husserl, Wittgenstein, Popper (Wittgenstein's father and Popper's parents had been born in households with overt Jewish affiliation), Langer, Jonas, Bloch, and other notables in philosophy; Einstein, Minkowski, and Pauli in physics; Wiener and Gödel in mathematics; Harris and Chomsky in linguistics (it may be noted that Harris, who started recent developments in text linguistics, was acquainted with literary analysis or "form criticism" of West Semitic, to which he contributed significantly [e.g., Montgomery and Harris: 10, 31]; Chomsky, son of a professor of Hebrew and a student of Harris, developed the germs of his transformational theory in a thesis on modern Hebrew [Mehta: 48]); in addition to many outstanding literary and musical creators. Their work is spiritual, not merely technical, and shows that the line between theological and "secular" disciplines is not sharp.

/ 45 /   The scholarly situation is illustrated by developments in biology. In this field the descriptive-structural approach reached a certain highpoint in the eighteenth century with Linnaeus' classification, before the historical perspective triumphed in the following century with Darwin; since 1900, the analytical or functional method—including and going beyond both of the older steps—has become dominant in that discipline, now involving concepts drawn from communication theory. Both J. Piaget and L. Goldmann develop a functional, or "genetic," structuralism; for other attempts to go beyond static structure, see the work of R. Barthes, P. Ricoeur, J. Derrida, and others.

/46/   Saussure, 1967:40. (It is necessary to go to the manuscripts for Saussure's precise views. The distinction social-individual does not coincide with the distinction potential-actual, as was perhaps recognized by him; cf. Leont'ev: 20; Coseriu: 117, 223.)

/47/   The relation of circumstances to meaning has been treated by P. Wegener (21–29), B. Malinowski (e.g., in Ogden and Richards: 296–336), K. Bühler, T. Slama-Cazacu, R. Montague (95–147), and P. Grice (especially in Cole and Morgan: 43–58). Relating a text to a code and circumstances is the task of the "grammatico-historical" method, which remains valid in principle.

/48/   The redactor's meaning, for texts transmitted, remains somewhat unclear also. On the other hand, it is inaccurate to say that a text as such has meaning.

/49/   The recognition that "literature" to a considerable extent transcends particular circumstances runs from ancient to modern times (see, e.g., Staiger: 33; Eliot: 113; Gadamer: 356–57; S. Schmidt in Gülich and Raible: 66). Particularity of author and audience is especially relevant to prophetic speech, as it is of the essence of prophecy to address actuality with a revelatory word by means of an inspired agent. Many prophetic words, however, speak to a deeply human and thus continuing process.

/50/   For the notion of possibility in semantics (not always with ontological assumptions), cf. Faust; Frei: 98 (on the view of C. Wolff); Prior: 111–70; Lewis: 171–72, 207 (with reference to R. Carnap, J. Hintikka, S. Kripke, R. Montague, and others); and above, n. 17. The characteristics (or "functions") which define an open class of (possible) objects are often named its "intension," while the actual objects covered by this class are called its "extension." Peirce (2.418 [in 1867]) distinguished between 1) an actual object referred to, 2) the character of an (actual or hypothetical) object which forms the "ground" of the symbol, and 3) associated notions not directly expressed by the symbol; Frege, in 1892, made almost exactly the same distinction with the terms "Bedeutung" (reference), "Sinn" (sense), and "Vorstellung" (conception). E.g., "Messiah" designates an intension or sense (in some cases, "final human leader under God") with which different ideas can be associated; messianic texts in the Hebrew Bible predict not a specific individual (e.g., Jesus, who is the extension or reference of the term in Christian belief), but a certain kind of person.

/51/   Crucial studies by linguists and anthropologists are listed in Lyons: 489; essays by Katz, Bierwisch, Dixon, and Hale are conveniently reprinted in Steinberg and Jakobowitz. (Other significant approaches to semantics stress contrasts and associations. For the componential analysis of genres, see above nn. 19 and 22.)

/52/   The role of the "possible" in literature has long been recognized (cf. now Schmidt: 170–90). The nominalist Goodman, however, views fictive statements as possible descriptions of the actual rather than as possibilities as such (51–57). Langer describes all the arts as "virtual" (cf. Vater's paper, below, p. 177).

/53/   Without an express theological concern, P. Nowell-Smith (248, 271–73) points out that one may be praised or blamed for one's basic value orientation although one cannot will to change it (for to will to do so already implies that one no longer holds it). On the whole problem, cf. Buss, 1961. The logic of value is formalized in "deontic" logic (since Mally in 1926), a division of "modal" logic, which includes also the logic of possibility and tense logic.

/54/   Also for Dilthey experience is a holistic structure which includes reference to others (V:201–7, 247; VII:238), although he contrasted the natural and human sciences. Peirce viewed the meaning of observational sentences as inextricably connected with a "practical maxim expressible as a conditional sentence having its apodosis in the imperative mood" (5.18; cf. 5.2, 9, 402); he thereby laid a foundation for discussions regarding verifiability and use as criteria for meaning, which have included some positions more extreme than his—such as Wittgenstein, 1977:59, which seems to ignore the theoretical aspect. (On Peirce's influence on British thought and thus on Wittgenstein, cf. Thayer: 304–13. Peirce, however, was weak in the area of describing goals.)

/55/   For surveys of approaches both to consciousness and unconsciousness, see Wellek and Warren (chap. 8), Lawall, Strelka, Spiegel, Batson *et al.* (one-sidedly against ontology), and Detweiler. The psychology of the reader is stressed, e.g., by N. Holland and W. Iser. Buss, 1969, attempted a social psychology of the book of Hosea, with special attention to the nature of eschatology; one can regard the study therefore as an application of semiology, defined by Saussure as the social psychology of language (1966:16). "Pragmatics," according to van Dijk (1972:341), "is the place where linguistic, psychological and sociological parameters interact." As F. C. Grant states (117–19), the "truth" of Psalms, Job, etc., lies not in their authorship but in their psychology. G. Fohrer (1972:110) and W. Herberg (1976:110) point to experiential structures. Of course, it is possible to come to different conclusions in this as in any other area of discussion. E.g., O. Keel's interpretation of enemies in psalms as a projection, while containing a partial truth, does not recognize adequately the reality and psychology of unjust suffering (better, Seebass: 37–41; according to I. Parsons, the pattern of psalms allows the sufferer to structure the chaos). Jung's study of Job deserves the attention it has received recently; newer psychological approaches may prove helpful.

/56/   See Davitz: 128–42; Buss, 1969:38 (degree), 83–113 (positive or negative), 133–34 (active or receptive role); Berlyne: 52, 317–19; Mehrabian: 31. Compare the analysis of genres, above.

/57/   To understand an expression involves the reverse of the generative process in which a purpose (the most fundamental level of an expression) leads via conventions of language to an audible or visible phenomenon. (On these levels, cf. W. Weaver, in Shannon and Weaver: 95–96, and G. Miller, in Silverstein: 6–16.) This is part of friendship, with which M. Platt compares interpretation.

/58/   The meaning of a statement, if accepted, sets up tendencies or probabilities of action (Peirce: 5.475–76, 504; MacKay: 24, 84–91). Austin called the "force" or nature of what is immediately done by a text (e.g., promise) its "illocution," and the effect or response (e.g., a resulting trust) its "perlocution." For van Dijk (1977:174) "intention" refers to the desired act itself (as in Tucker: 16, 51–54, such as, "to explain") and "purpose" to a hoped-for consequence (with Berlo: 16 and others). Austin came to realize that *all* texts are "performative" (150–52, etc.).

/59/   This definition follows in part a suggestion by R. Carnap and Y. Bar-Hillel (Bar-Hillel: 10, 221–74). Their theory is based on negations of state-descriptions; e.g., if one person out of a group of ten is chosen for a certain task, it is implied that nine are not so chosen. Since logically there is no difference between positive and negative descriptions, their theory can be extended to include all implications for a given recipient. Such an extension enters the area of the "value" or "significance" of information (cf. Cherry: 242–43, 264, Harrah: 6, 59, 81; Hintikka and Suppes). On the relations of learning to reorganization, see also Powers: 82–204 (postulating a mystical, or religious, level as the highest level of psychological organization). Great literary works are emotionally involving in part because of their extensive implications for lived existence. Thus "existential" involvement, in the sense of human commitment and decision, is not opposed to information but rather constitutes a holistic process.

/60/   It comes in an oracle (25:23), in dreams (28:13–15; 31:11), and in an unspecified form (35:1, 10–12). See, further, below, p. 123. This divine role is not incompatible with humanistic elements of the story, as Gammie agrees (according to a recent communication), although he assigns the humanistic elements to another layer of tradition.

/61/   Acceptable uncertainty depends on particular situations, available alternatives, etc., and cannot be fully rationalized. For Schleiermacher, one extreme of understanding is to recognize something as "necessary," but this is (in relation to a text) an "infinite task" (31).

/62/   See, e.g., Pool, North, *et al.*, Holsti, Carney, and Baird. Buss, 1969:42–49, 61–69 employed correlations without formal control (cf. also the association discussed above, n. 7). The distribution noted by Verner (according to which Jacob is called Isaac's son once and Rebekah's son nine times, while for Esau the corresponding numbers are six and two) is statistically "significant" at a level below .01, as measured by both the chi-square and Fisher's exact tests; i.e., there is less than one chance in a hundred that there is no reason (other than sheer fluctuation) for the phenomenon. A well-trained judgment does not always need formal control, but it is easy to err in the estimation of probability. The formula of Fisher's exact test, for four numbers of an array in which c corresponds to d as a does to b, is as follows: $(a+b)!(c+d)!(a+c)!(b+d)!$ divided by $(a+b+c+d)!$ $a!$ $b!c!d!$ (exclamation marks designate factorials). This is now not difficult to execute with a computer or advanced calculator and requires no tables or special training. The basic reasoning of statistics, together with a number of formulas and tables, can be found in F. Williams. Statistics can also be used for examining authorship, as by Radday.

/63/   On models, see, e.g., Black. It should be noted that Black (244–57) and others question the notion that thought is determined by prior models, such as language forms. Recent experimental work suggests that perception is built up to a large extent by correlation between the elements of perception and is not altogether determined by stored patterns (Uttal). In any case, Bultmann's view that comprehension "is governed always by a prior understanding of the subject" (1955:239, 253) is incorrect. On the opposite extreme, see above, n. 15. More balanced is Peirce's concept of "abduction" as an explanatory hypothesis (2.776–77, 5.171–73, 6.475); the construction of such an hypothesis involves creativity, which is apparently based on a combinational modification (see, e.g., Taylor and Getzels: 10, 333).

/64/   Kapelrud applied a number of the procedures used in Buss, 1969, to Zephaniah and noted some differences, at least in expression (49). The hermeneutical "circle" does not oscillate between parts and a whole (to some extent against Schleiermacher: 89–90), for an understanding of the whole is a (perhaps unreachable) goal; thus the procedures of the natural sciences and of the humanities are not fundamentally distinct.

/65/   The recipient will presumably have a greater ability to predict future events (Stachiowiak: 24) and a more complex pattern of perception and action (J. Springle in Buckley: 259–80). Animals and especially human beings have facilities for a memory in which data can be stored with relative permanence and from which they may be recalled through certain triggers. A message, like thermodynamic "order," naturally decays; this decay can be counteracted only by its inclusion in a larger system. In human culture, a collective memory is preserved through oral and written transmission.

/66/   For written literature, it is usually not necessary to add much in the way of outside data for a recognition of the issue being considered. The text as a rule furnishes sufficient indication of the problem situation with which it deals (called *aitia* or *causa* in traditional rhetoric), as long as the general nature of its language system and of the community in which it stands is known. Even though the date of the Jacob stories is unclear, their meaning potential can be largely understood.

/67/   Marxists have rightly been critical of the predominance of irrationality (recently called "positivism") in "bourgeois" thought, such as in its historiography (e.g., Lukács, Kolakowski). On the other hand, if a government does not pay careful attention to the first freedom, then—through the manipulation of uncertainty (cf. Luhmann: 8)—it exerts power over, rather than gives power to, the populace. Similarly, Güttgemanns, 1978: 61, 117–19, 129 points out that, in a communicational perspective, guidelines for an ethics can be constructed.

/68/   The analysis by von Rad (1962:212–19) of the prohibition of images fails to take account of the high-god figure, well-known in the history of religion since the end of the nineteenth century (see, e.g., Eliade: 38–123, with reference also to the Near East). Apparently the Canaanite El was occasionally represented by an image, but high gods are not normally imaged concretely. For further data regarding aspects of the divine represented in Yahweh, see Stolz and Cross: 147–94.

/69/   Lonergan calls insight "the act of organizing intelligence," including the "apprehension of relations" (ix, x), so that what "was an insoluble problem, now becomes incredibly simple and obvious"(6). Similarly, according to Meyer 1973:21, "a piece of music must be seen in retrospect to have fitted together—to have been right." Insight is an express aim of the morphology of Buss, 1969:1.

/70/   Of course, one must not regard these symbols as rigid; but see above, n. 7. No matter what its etymological derivation, Yahweh functions as a name. The use of Elohim and similar general designations in Near Eastern wisdom is well known. Within Chinese religion, Shang-ti and T'ien express the individualized and general aspects of deity. In India, Ramanuja explicitly pointed to the fact that love requires an element of individuality (in opposition to a strong unitive drive in Hinduism). Zimmerli (13) is one among many who declare that the OT is primarily concerned with the particular; Heschel: 194, however, is correct in seeing that neither irrationality nor rationalism adequately represent Judaism.

Chapter 2

Structural Analysis of the Old Testament Narrative

Hugh C. White
Rutgers University, Camden

Over the past decade it has become increasingly apparent to many biblical scholars that the methods of historical criticism and form analysis do not permit an adequate illumination of the nature of the biblical narrative art (Güttgemanns, 1971a). These methods are oriented toward determining the historical milieux which influenced the content of the text. They do not provide sufficient means for dealing with the formative influences which may have flowed from the structure of the narration itself. It will be the purpose of this article to show how a mode of narrative analysis which originated in the field of linguistics offers the possibility of furthering the understanding of the nature of the biblical narrative. This new approach is generally referred to as the "structural analysis" of narratives.

The Linguistic Foundation

The structural analysis of narratives is a development which has grown up, for the most part, on the basis of structural linguistics. Whereas the largest unit treated by the discipline of linguistics is the sentence, narrative analysis deals with longer units of discourse. It is hypothesized that the same principles governing the structure of the sentence and its component parts (phrases and words or morphemes) function in the creation of these longer units. The narrative thus appears, at one level, as an extensive sentence, and at another, as comparable to a single word. The structure of the narrative is thus considered to be "homologous" (correspondent) with the structure of a sentence.

The structural approach to linguistics is an outgrowth of the pioneering work of the Genevan linguist, Ferdinand de Saussure, at the end of the nineteenth and early part of this century. De Saussure considered the linguistics of his day to be almost exclusively concerned with "diachronic" matters, e.g., the examination of historically related texts of different languages with the intention of constructing a history of the evolution of languages. When an investigator takes this approach, according to de Saussure, he "no longer observes language (*la langue*) itself, but rather a series of events that modify it" (1966:90). Language is a constant verbal system which functions as the presupposition of every act of speech (*parole*). As a system, it has the basic character of a relation between simultaneous elements. Thus, to understand *la langue*, its character as a contemporary system of mutually defined parts must be examined rather than "the substitution of one element for another in time, an event" (1966:91). According to de Saussure, linguistics can thus be divided into two major spheres: that of synchronics with its concern for the wholeness and systematic character of language as it exists in the present / 1 /, and that of diachronics, with its concern for language as a process which unfolds through acts of speech (*paroles*) in the course of time. Beyond this, he saw that nonverbal means of communication also functioned as systems of mutually defined parts in a way that was quite similar to language. He thus envisioned a larger field of investigation which he called a "general science of semiology" that would utilize linguistic models for understanding all forms of human communication (1966:16).

This Saussurian insight into the structural or systematic character of language has come to be applied to narrative analysis through additional insights gained by phonologists working under Saussurian inspiration. The horizon of the discipline of phonology is the word or the morpheme. Phonologists study the constituent elements of words, i.e., letters or phonemes. The same distinction which de Saussure made between language as a constant system vs. language as a series of speech acts was perceived by phonologists between the sound or phone and what they termed the phoneme. The phoneme was defined as that aspect of a sound which enables it to function as a meaningful part of a word, i.e., a letter (or phonological sign). A single phoneme may include a number of "allophones" or variations which do not affect its capacity to function as an understandable letter (e.g., both the phonetic clear [1] and the dark [ɫ] can be understood as the letter "1" in the pronunciation of a word). The emphasis thus shifted away from the level of the physical sound to a more abstract level on which the phoneme, consisting of a "bundle" of sounds, exists as a functional concept (Jakobson, 1971:I,285; Crystal: 177–79).

The phonologists then turned to the investigation of the system which renders each phoneme a meaningful entity. This was done by examining the relationship of phonemes to one another. It was determined that each phoneme was capable of being perceived as a meaningful entity because it stood in a necessary relationship to another contrasting or opposing sound. Roman Jakobson found that sound becomes meaningful to an infant in terms of oppositions such as tense/lax, nasal/oral, etc., and that these oppositions "are actually logical binary oppositions, and that one member of each of these oppositions includes necessarily the opposing member"(1971:I,303). The larger epistemological significance of this is indicated when Jakobson writes, "The binary opposition is the child's first logical operation. Both opposites simultaneously arise and force the infant to choose one and suppress the other of the two alternative items" (1956:47). This logical binary system which serves as a model in phonology for explaining the origin of meaningful sounds has been taken over to be used as a model for describing the logical structure of thought which underlies and gives rise to the extensive, diachronic form of the narrative, and which constitutes its deepest level of meaning.

Claude Lévi-Strauss

Lévi-Strauss has led the way in utilizing the phonological model to analyze extensive bodies of discourse. The field of his investigation has been primarily the myths and customs of American Indian cultures. The bridge between structural linguistics and myth analysis for him is the category of the "gross constituent unit," which serves as a basic unit of analysis parallel to the phoneme. Lévi-Strauss arrives at the basic material of these units by reducing the myths in all of their variations to a series of the shortest possible sentences. These are then placed on index cards and arranged in patterns according to their thematic content. As separate elements, they are parallel to allophones in phonology. When they fall into groups or "bundles" based on thematic similarity, and when these groups are shown to constitute pairs of binary oppositions, then basic units of mythic composition emerge at the semantic level parallel to phonemes at the level of sound (1963:211). These "bundles" of relations cut across the diachronic unfolding of the myth; in their synchronic relations to one another they communicate a logical "message" at the unconscious level. This mode of analysis causes Lévi-Strauss to take two decisive steps away from customary literary analysis. By reducing the myths to short sentences, he moves away from concrete "surface" characteristics of the myth to the level of semantic content, and by arranging these semantic units into thematic groups which are mutually interdefining, he breaks through the conscious diachronic level of the mythic narrative into the unconscious synchronic content.

The phonological model which generates phonemes in Jakobson's system is used here as a generative model to explain the underlying semantic content of myths. Myth then always contains in its foundations a set of opposing or contradictory ideas, and its "hidden agenda" is movement toward the resolution or mediation of this contradiction. Since the contradiction is always absolute, the resolution fails, and the failure gives rise to a new myth. The myth will thus continue in a spiral growth "until the intellectual impulse which has produced it is exhausted" (1963:229).

This method has been applied the most extensively to the OT by the English anthropologist, Edmund Leach (1969). Lévi-Strauss himself has never worked with the biblical text and has expressed reservations about the appropriateness of his method for such a task. Leach nevertheless believes that his work has been productive of results which justify the effort.

Leach sees in the stories of creation in Gen 1:1–2:4 and 2:5–3:24, as well as the story of Cain and Abel, variations which constitute the same spiral-like mythical system mentioned by Lévi-Strauss. He understands religion in general to be based on a binary system consisting of the poles:

this world vs. another perfect world.

This binary pair is meant to evade or deny the more fundamental pair:

life vs. death.

Since God must reside in the perfect world, God and man become separated. To overcome this separation, anomolous mediating creatures are needed such as fabulous monsters, virgin mothers, incarnate gods, etc. (1969:10, 11).

A further important binary pair is evidenced in laws of endogamy and exogamy. Women are thus divided into two opposing groups.

our kind vs. the other kind.

Sex relations are permitted only with *the other kind*. This presents the problem of how sex relations began when the first man and woman had to have been brother and sister (1969:11).

Leach finds tensions between such binary systems to be fundamental to the early Genesis narratives. The ultimate purpose of the narrative as a whole is to mediate the basic polar oppositions just mentioned.

The creation story in Genesis 1 consists of two sections. The first consists of days 1–3 during which the basic structure of the static, nonmoving world is outlined in terms of pairs. In day one, the basic oppositions are: heaven-earth, light-darkness, day-night, evening-morning. In day two, the water from above is opposed to the water below, mediated by the firmament. In the third day, the sea and dry land are oppositions mediated by things which grow on dry land, but need water. Days 4–6 portray the creation of moving things. First comes the sun-moon pair which establish the alternations between day and night, then the fish and birds, which stem from the sea-land opposition and constitute mediators between sky and earth and salt and fresh water, respectively. The creation next of cattle, beasts, and creeping things balances the triad of grass, cereals, and fruit trees in the third day. Creeping things occupy an anomolous mediating position. Not being fowl, fish, cattle, or beast, they are condemned in priestly texts (Lev 11: 41–42). Likewise other anomolous creatures, such as water creatures with no fins are also condemned (Lev 11:10) for the same reason.

Then the final pair, man and woman, are created together and commanded to multiply. The creation is thus presented as a progression of binary oppositions and their mediation from heaven vs. earth to man (male and female). Untouched, however, are the problems of life vs. death and incest vs. procreation, matters which pertain directly to the future of man.

In the second creation story, these problems are taken up and resolved through a new set of binary oppositions beginning with heaven vs. earth, mediated by mist, and the unity of man alone in the garden vs. the multiplicity of trees, including the tree of life vs. the tree of death (i.e., the tree of knowledge of good and evil, which represents the knowledge of sexual differences). Of crucial importance is then the opposition man vs. animals (helpmeets) which is mediated by the creation of the anomolous figure of woman. Woman is structurally parallel to the anomolous creeping things in the first story, and when Eve and the serpent come together before the tree of the knowledge of good and evil, the ingredients are present for the resolution of the incest vs. procreation and life vs. death oppositions left unresolved by the first story. By listening to the serpent, Eve "betrays Adam into incest" (18). In so doing, Eve is transformed from a sister into a wife, they are expelled from the garden, Eve becomes pregnant, and transition is made from the perfect world into the real world where sexual procreation and death are a part of the ruling order. The anomolous creatures of the snake and women are thus able to mediate the opposition incest vs. procreation, the sister becoming a wife after the expulsion. Leach sees the role of the anomolous sphinx who lures Oedipus into incest through verbal cunning as directly parallel to this.

The oppositions in the Cain-Abel story stem from the polarity in the first story between the static and moving spheres. Abel, the hunter, belongs to the mobile sphere, and is more pleasing to God than the static, agricultural Cain. Leach sees behind this conflict a primary homosexual situation, the fratricide serving as the mediating event (parallel to incest in the previous story) which causes Cain's expulsion into the east, where he finds a wife, i.e., heterosexual existence. As additional support for his argument, he points to the prevalence of incest and homosexual motifs in the remainder of Genesis.

A great many criticisms have already been made of Leach regarding his rather careless use of the text (Richard Jacobson), as well as the somewhat arbitrary way he develops his binary categories

(Chabrol: 9). The seriousness of this latter problem is best illustrated by referring to a more recent attempt by Matthieu Casalis to apply the method of Lévi-Strauss to the two biblical creation stories. Casalis limits his analysis of the creation narratives to Gen 1:1–2:4a and 2:4b–25. He argues that the ruling binary polarities of both of these narratives is that of dry vs. wet. Creation is effected in the Priestly account by a disjunction of water from land (and in turn, threatened in the flood story by their conjunction), as well as light from dark and above from below. The J account, on the contrary, effects creation by mist which moistens the arid land, thus by a conjunction of water and land, i.e., the wet and dry.

The starting point for P is the undifferentiated chaotic Tehom, whereas for J it is the arid wilderness. Creation for P is thus a process of differentiation or disjunction, and for J a process of conjunctive union.

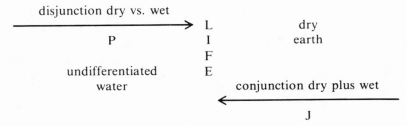

Viewed from the standpoint of mediating elements, life is the mediating force between excessive conjunction (world flooded) and excessive disjunction (world dry):

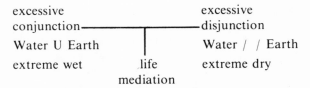

Casalis draws a parallel between this form of mediation and that proposed by Lévi-Strauss in *The Raw and the Cooked*, where, in Indian mythology, the cooking fire serves as a mediating force between the excessive conjunction of the sun with the world (world burns), and the total disjunction of the sun from the world (world rots). He concludes by suggesting that a "symmetrical" (63) relationship exists between the fire-centered myths of Lévi-Strauss' study and the water-centered Semitic myths, which would make possible a binary relation between the two bodies of myths along this semantic axis.

The rather large differences between the analyses of Leach and Casalis illustrate the subtlety and perhaps inescapable element of arbitrariness contained in this method. To choose one point of difference: Who is to say whether the mist in the J account is a mediating force between the primary heaven-earth opposition or an indication of the conjunctive action along the dry-wet axis? The decision depends upon the semic oppositions with which one begins. The semantic axis appearing dominant will, of course, depend to a large extent upon where the text is segmented for purposes of analysis. The length and intricacy of the biblical narrative makes this a very serious problem.

In spite of the lack of consistency between these analyses, both have succeeded in uncovering significant correlative structures between the P and J accounts of creation by penetrating the surface level of the narrative and attempting to deal in a systematic way with the semantic content. This method thus offers the possibility of gaining access to a much deeper level of the tradition process than has hitherto been afforded by critical literary and historical methodology. Casalis points to this when he writes: "The fact that the two Creation accounts have been kept by the biblical tradition shows how much the two opposite processes must be considered complementary" (50) /2/.

A. J. Greimas

The paradigmatic, binary model which is used by Lévi-Strauss to articulate the underlying semantic content, has no apparent relationship to the diachronic (sequential) syntagmatic structure of the mythical narrative. The lack of integration of the binary model with the surface narrative syntax has appeared to A. J. Greimas and others as a deficiency in Lévi-Strauss' method (1971:797).

In his work, *Sémantique Structurale* (1966), Greimas laid the foundation for a form of narrative analysis which grounds narrative syntax upon a binary semantic model. He begins by elaborating this binary theory. Greimas contends that it is because of our perception of differences that "...the world 'takes form' before us and for us" (1966:19); in order for us to perceive differences two term objects must be perceived as simultaneously present, one present as the logically opposing presupposition of the other. Whereas in phonology the binary terms are sounds, in semantics they are words or lexemes. For instance, the semantic content of the lexeme "high" requires the opposition "low" and the meaning of this semantic axis is revealed only within larger binary oppositions: horizontality vs. verticality, etc. (1966:33).

But a lexeme is usually understood within some context which is more concrete than its semic content. This means that the lexeme, as it functions, e.g., in a dictionary definition, is always composed of two elements, an unchanging element which provides it with semantic continuity, called the "nuclear seme" (1966:45–50), and a variable contextual component, called the contextual seme or "classeme." A word (or lexeme) in which the nuclear seme and classeme are unified is called a "sememe." A brief illustration Greimas gives of the relation between the nuclear seme and its classeme can be given by looking at the simple statement, "a dog barks." The verb "barks" might be reduced quickly to the nuclear seme of "a kind of cry." In any given discourse, one of two classes of subjects will be joined to this nuclear seme in order to provide it with its semantic content, e.g., either the classeme human or the classeme animal (1966:50).

In the study of the semantic structure of a narrative, the lexemes to be defined are *dramatis personae* or "lexeme actants." With the simple lexeme in a dictionary definition the relationship between the sememic content and the lexeme is a given; i.e., the word has established definitions. But the relation in the narrative between the lexeme actant signified by only a name and its sememic content must be established through events and qualifications in the course of the narrative. One might say that the effect of the narrative is to "define" a lexeme actant which is signified by only an "empty" name at the outset. The process of definition takes place in a series of "syntactical" operations which Greimas has attempted to express in the form of a "narrative grammar." At the deep semantic level, these operations consist of a logical process, but at the surface level of the narrative, they assume the form of a "doing" (1970:167), which can be termed a "function." Inasmuch as the doing is some kind of action, it is coupled with a human subject or "actant." The actant, however, represents only the potentiality for doing. It represents the adjunction of the classeme "human" to the otherwise impersonal function.

The missing element in the method thus far depicted is a model that will permit the diachronic, sequential narrative functions to be translated into logical operations. It is the functional analysis of Russian folk tales made by Vladamir Propp that has provided Greimas with the material for such a model. Propp made a study of the sequential patterns of several hundred Russian folk tales and reduced these sequences to thirty-one functions (e.g., absentation, interdiction, violation), which recurred in an unvarying sequential pattern in all of the folk tales analyzed. Some of these sequential functions, such as Interdiction-Violation, were treated by Propp as "paired elements" (27). Greimas noticed that many of these paired elements constituted binary oppositions at the semantic level. He submitted the thirty-one functions to a careful reexamination to determine whether the entire sequential structure possessed a semantic substructure consisting of one or more sets of binary oppositions. He concluded that the outermost perimeters of the folk tales always consisted of the rupture of a contract or agreement signifying the established order and concluded with re-establishment of that order. The contract is ruptured by the actions of a villain, who, in a series of sequences, deprives those representing the established order of something valuable; this creates a deficiency or lack remedied in the end by the return of the valued object. These syntagmatic functions can be reduced to two sets of semic oppositions:

Rupture of order   vs.   Restitution of order
Alienation   vs.   Reintegration

Since these are logical oppositions which presuppose each other for their meaning, Greimas succeeded in establishing a linkage between the synchronic, binary, semantic structure, and the diachronic, syntagmatic structure of the narrative, which Propp had delineated.

One important aspect of the narrative does not fit into this scheme, namely, the action of the hero who brings about the positive conclusion. This action can be reduced to a three-part sequential structure, called the "test," consisting of injunction vs. acceptance, confrontation vs. success, and consequence. The central element in this sequence, termed the "struggle," does not constitute an elementary semic category since it cannot appear in the narrative in its negative form and its two terms do not constitute a category of semic opposition; confrontation and success are not logically tied by a relation of presupposition (1966:205).

Further, the relation between the "struggle" and its preceding and proceeding functions is a strictly sequential relation which cannot be understood as logically necessary. Thus the sequence of the "test" and specifically the "struggle" at its center constitute an irreducible diachronic nucleus in the narrative. No distinctive, new semantic content is contributed by this sequence. Rather, it serves merely to transform the initial negative meaning into the final positive meaning. Greimas terms it a "figurative expression of the transformational model" (1966:212), i.e., the expression of an essentially logical process in the form of volitional acts by the figures (characters) in the plot.

The figurative aspect of this sequence plays a more fundamental role than in the other sequences. For instance, the freedom of the protagonist in accepting the injunction and engaging in the struggle is of fundamental importance to the operation. Greimas sees in this sequence the essential features of "historical" activity: "The elementary, diachronic sequence of the narrative then includes, in its definition, all the attributes of the historical activity of man, which is irreversible, free and responsible" (1966:211). But since meaning is not disclosed through historical diachronic processes, he describes the "struggle" as a "mythic representation of complex (i.e., binary semantic) operations" (1966:212). By "mythical" he seems to mean simply figurative, i.e., having the form of volitional acts by characters.

The synthesis achieved by the narrative between these structurally different elements indicates a mediating function between "affirmation of permanence and the possibilities of change, affirmation of the necessary order and the liberty which breaks or re-establishes this order...structure and comportment, permanence and history, society and the individual" (1966:213).

The final configurational schema which Greimas applies to the narrative seeks to reduce the relations at the figurational or actantial level to a standard model. The previous analysis bracketed out the actants and dealt with the narrative solely in terms of the binary pairs of functions. But since the "test" sequence could not be reduced to a binary model and contained a figurative, actantial element that could not be eliminated, a set of actantial relations remains in the narrative outside of the terms of the semantic analysis. It is thus necessary to attempt to describe these remaining actantial relations.

Using again the work of Propp, who found seven typically recurring personages in the Russian folk tales, and the work of E. Souriau, who found six recurring dramatic functions in his analysis of 200,000 dramatic situations, Greimas proposes a list of six typical, actantially centered spheres of action, and he diagrams their relationship to one another. The relations between these actants depict the diachronic process at the heart of the test sequence.

$$
\begin{array}{ccc}
\text{Addressor} \text{-----} \text{Object} \text{------} \text{Addressee} \\
\uparrow \\
\text{Helper} \text{--------} \text{Subject} \text{------} \text{Opponent}
\end{array}
$$

The addressor gives a mandate to the Subject regarding the desired Object Value. The Subject accepts the mandate, enters into a struggle with the Opponent assisted by the Helper, and succeeds in transmitting the Object Value to the Addressee. Only the Addressor, Subject, and Addressee are usually personages; the Object Value, Helper, and Opponent may be things, or even ideas internal to the Subject.

The heart of this scheme is the Subject-Object relationship. It is the desire of the Subject for the Object Value that gives dynamism to the narrative. Greimas suggests that the Subject is actually a sememic structure which would consist of the actor-personage (classeme) and the function of desiring (nuclear seme) (1966:177). It is the desiring subject who is capable of producing the narrative.

In illustrating the thematic investment of this model on a broad scale Greimas analyzes Marxist ideology in which the Subject would be Man; the Object Value, a classless society; the Addressor, history; the Addressee, humanity; the Opponent, the bourgeois class; and the Helper, the working class (1966:181).

A remaining question concerns the precise way in which the first actant Subject is established in the modality of desiring. Greimas does not take this up in detail, but suggests that the basis lies in the initial contract coupled with a "making to want" on the part of the original addressor (1970:179). This, of course, leads to the need to explain more fully how the original addressor "makes" the subject desire. This question points beyond the framework of semantic analysis as Greimas has defined it toward fundamental questions concerning the way in which the subject is constituted over against language itself. This is a question which constitutes the starting point of Roland Barthes' approach to narrative analysis which will be taken up below.

The method of Greimas has already attracted a great deal of interest in NT studies, but very little thus far in the field of the Hebrew Scriptures. No attempt has been made to develop a fundamental narrative grammar at the semantic level which would tie the syntax of the OT narrative to the binary structure of signification /3/.

Roland Barthes, within the context of his article on Jacob's struggle with the mysterious assailant (Gen 32:23–33), shows how the actantial model of Greimas might be applied to this story (though it should be noted that Barthes goes on to utilize the results of this analysis for his *own* distinctive purposes) (1971:36, 37). Jacob is the Subject of the action and is motivated by the Object of crossing the Jabbok river. This objective has been communicated to him by an Addressor who is God. The Addressee who receives this object value is Jacob himself. Before crossing, he is attacked by a mysterious assailant filling the role of the Opponent who attempts to prevent Jacob from crossing the river to rejoin his family. The Helper (not mentioned explicitly) is Jacob's great strength which has been illustrated earlier in the narrative. The unusual feature of this narrative is that the identity of the Opponent is revealed to be the same as that of the Addressor, i.e., God.

This briefly reported actantial analysis at least points to the applicability of the model to the Genesis narratives. The possibilities of broader application are evident at a glance, when one considers that the biblical narrative begins with a Prohibition-Violation, which is followed by a series of deprivations, the election of a hero (person, nation) who undergoes numerous tests finally climaxing in the NT with the triumph of Jesus over evil and the eschatological restoration of all that was lost at the beginning. Order is (then) restored through the concluding of a "new covenant." The general, sequential structure of the biblical narrative as a whole corresponds in a striking way with the basic outlines of the tripartite structure proposed by Greimas. Detailed work on this problem has not yet been done, however.

Hugh C. White

Roland Barthes

At the center of Greimas'analysis of the narrative is the sequence of the "test," which, in turn, has as its center the "struggle" of a Subject to obtain some valued Object. As has been shown already, the status of this Subject is very uncertain for Greimas. He describes it as a mythical representation of the process which brings about a transformation of a negative to a positive meaning at the level of the elementary structure of signification. The subject-actant itself can be reduced to a sememe consisting of the function of desire plus the classeme human being. But is this an adequate understanding of the subject which plays the indispensable, central role in the narrative structure? As Roland Barthes puts the question: "Who is the subject of the narrative? Is it or is it not a privileged class of actors?" (1966:18). It is this question concerning the status and meaning of the subject in the narrative that guides Barthes'investigations and causes his mode of analysis to differ markedly from that of Greimas and Lévi-Strauss.

Of the three levels of analysis which Barthes outlines—the functional (Propp), the actional or actantial (Greimas), and the narrational (Barthes and Todorov)—the question of the subject arises in the latter two. At the actantial level it arises from the uncertainty of the denotative reference of pronouns within the surface syntax of the narrative /4/. Barthes regards the "I," "you," or "he" who speaks in the narrative as but a mask for the "I" of the narrator. To understand the actant-subject, it is thus necessary to leave the interior of the narrative and move to that initial instance of discourse which encompasses the narrative as a whole, i.e., the act of writing or narrating. For "the personages, as units at the actional level, find their meaning (i.e., intelligibility) only if one integrates them into the third level of the description that we call here the level of narration (in opposition to the Functions and Actions)" (1966:18).

What, then, is the character of this initial instance of discourse? Who, indeed, is the subject of the narrative itself? Barthes refuses to identify the material author of the narrative with its "narrator." The significant narrator is the one whose signs are immanent to the narrative itself, since in many cases it is impossible to determine the identity of the material author: "*who speaks* (in the narrative) is not who writes (in life), and *who writes* is not who is (Lacan)" (1966:20). Barthes speaks of the narrator in the same sense as he would speak of the subject within the narrative, as a "formal person," or a "linguistic person" who is defined "only by his place in the discourse" (1966:21). He thus rejects instrumental views of language which posit a full subject that expresses itself *by means of* language. On the contrary, the subject is to be understood in purely linguistic terms, i.e., as an instance of discourse or as an instance of writing. The effect of this is to shift the narrative "to the performative order according to which the meaning of a word is the act itself which proffers it" (1966:21). The meaning of discourse would then be found not by reference to an extralinguistic reality nor by reference to a semantic paradigm which excluded the subject, but in terms of the act of writing as a language event which coincides with the structure of the subject.

To understand the meaning of the act of writing or narrating for Barthes, it will be necessary to examine briefly the way in which he utilizes Freudian theory (as developed by Lacan) to penetrate the linguistic origins of the subject. The Prohibition against incest founds the consciousness of the subject as an awareness of "difference." The union with the mother is interrupted and the subject becomes aware of itself as a separate entity, as a difference. Since it is the nature of the Prohibition, not only to interrupt the child-mother union but also to cause the object of this primary desire to be repressed, the subject's desiring, made conscious by the Prohibition, is immediately impelled toward a substitute object which is natural language. Because the initial object of desire is repressed, this "primary symbolization" is not perceived as being symbolic; rather, it is viewed as neutral, asymbolic, language. The subject constituted as an awareness of difference in the "forgotten" moment of the Prohibition becomes the conscious "I," the primary symbol of the act of speech, i.e., of the event in which desire is deflected toward a symbolic object—language.

Such symbolism which avoids direct reference to its object through the substitutionary use of a contiguous related object (e.g., as in the reference to a king as the "crown") is called, in linguistic terms, "metonymic" symbolism. Following the establishment of language itself as the primary substitutionary object, metonymy takes the form of a "slide" from word to word, each word being understandable finally only by reference to other words. As Anthony Wilden says, this infinite metonymic process "corresponds to the censorship's seeking to escape the significant term by calling up another one contiguous to it" (242). Metaphor, in contrast, uses noncontiguous imagery to bring its referent into consciousness, and illuminate it. The difference can be seen in the lexicalized metaphor in which the object of reference of the metaphor completely displaces the object *in* the metaphorical figure (e.g., as in "foot" of the bed), in contrast to the metonymic symbol in which the symbolic object may totally displace the major referent of the metonym (as, e.g., in religious symbolism when an object physically associated with a religious figure becomes an object of worship in its own right, such as the worship of relics in medieval Christianity [see also Le Guern: 32]). Metaphor thus serves to heighten one's awareness of the primary referent, whereas metonymy diverts one's attention from the primary referent and can displace it entirely. Language seen as a substitutionary object of desire which has totally displaced the original object thus assumes a closed metonymical character, but metaphor which preserves the object of reference provides an open avenue through which the primary repressions may indirectly gain access to speech and consciousness.

With this distinction in mind, it is possible to begin to see the meaning which the act of writing has for Barthes. The acquisition of natural language is experienced by the child as a necessity, and its meaning, arising out of its metonymic character, functions as a closed denotative system. Each word has a fixed reference which, as far as possible, is connected with a translinguistic object, action or state. Meaning is preserved through the repetitive use of words in the same sense. Insofar as a narrative is realistic, i.e., attempts to present an imitation of the world as it appears, it too reflects the repetitive character of metonymic language.

But the act of writing is a free act. Barthes sees its distinctive motivation as arising out of an impulse to depart from the world as it is. This impulse toward the new also accounts for the variation between sequences in the course of the narrative; as he says, "the origin of a sequence is not the observation of reality, but the necessity to vary and surpass the first form which was offered to man, i.e., repetition" (1966:26).

This sense of variation, of difference, which is at the basis of the narrative, reflects the repressed sense of difference which characterized the initial form of self-identity formed in reaction to the Prohibition. In the free act of narrative writing, this forgotten self thus emerges in the form of the open undefined characters, which stand in contrast to the closed structure of the post-Oedipal self. The reality that is represented in the narrative thus does not imitate the self and world beyond the text. In fact, "'that which transpires' in the narrative is, from the referential (real) point of view, literally, nothing" (1966:27). That which occurs in the narrative is language itself: "'what arrives' is language alone, the adventure of language, the coming of which never ceases to be celebrated" (1966:27).

The ultimate "reference" of the narrative is thus to this forgotten self, experienced as an unutterable sense of difference. It cannot be expressed in language since the establishment of the subject in language by means of the Prohibition was contingent upon the repression of this form of the self. The narrative can thus only create a second "language" consisting of lexeme-actants which meta-phorically portray the open, desiring form of the repressed self. Since the classical narrative depicts the process through which the initially open subject encounters those systems which impose closure upon him, the classical narrative structure itself re-portrays, in the form of sequential events having duration, the primordial process (which lacks duration) through which closure is imposed upon the subject by the Prohibition.

Writing in its origin thus returns to the profound silence which enfolds the primal experience of self, and records the advent of a new metaphorical language which eludes the primary Oedipal determination. By providing a way for the alienated self to enter the social world of language, writing thus offers the possibility of the reconciliation of the divided self. This type of meaning is explained by Barthes in a general discussion of signs, as arising from the "zero degree of opposition, i.e., the power held by any system of signs, of creating meaning 'out of nothing'... an opposition of something and nothing (Saussure)" (1967:77). In rhetoric, this refers to a "significative absence" in which the absence of a signifier or sign has its own meaning. If one applies this to the narrative, the poles within which the free act of writing acquires meaning could be identified as: word vs. silence. Within the context, the way in which the narrative constitutes the "arrival" of language, and why its arrival is an occasion for celebration, become understandable.

It is clear that the open meaning signified by this "arrival" of new language does not stem from the binary model of Greimas' elementary structure of signification. In that model, meaning originates from logically contradictory oppositions, not from contrasting (or contrary) ones, whereas here meaning is disclosed at the narrational level by means of a contrasting variation of given narrative patterns. Meaning disclosed along a sequential axis of contrast stems from a free substitution of one term for another. Since there is no necessary relation between the terms, the meaning disclosed by the contrast is open, metaphoric meaning. The relation between binary terms on an axis of contradiction is one of logical necessity. Meaning in such a case is generated by one term's totally displacing the other in the present; it is thus closed, metonymic in nature. By focusing upon the element of variation within the narrative, Barthes understands the narrative as a product of the narrative situation which embraces the writer and reader. Thus, rather than seeking to reduce all narratives to a single paradigmatic model which eradicates differences, he seeks to understand the text precisely in its difference, and to ground that difference not in the existential uniqueness of the author, but in the "paradigm of the difference" which accounts in linguistic and psychoanalytic terms for the birth of the subject. A correspondence is thus drawn between the way in which the subject is structured vis-à-vis the Prohibition, the structuration of the narrative that occurs in the process of writing (and, consequently, also reading), and the structure of the subject internal to the narrative.

But the freedom of the act of writing is not absolute. It occurs between the constraints of the closed, metonymic, linguistic and translinguistic codes. The linguistic code embraces not only the phonological and grammatical rules of word and sentence construction, but extends to the structure of the whole narrative which Barthes sees as corresponding to the structure of a sentence: "To narrate (in the classic fashion) is to raise the question as if it were a subject which one delays predicating; and when the predicate (truth) arrives, the sentence, the narrative are over, the world is adjectivized (after we had feared it would not be)" (1974:76). The narrative subject is thus "based on the expectation and desire of its imminent closure" (1974:76). The text then appears as a meaningful duration oriented toward the "definition" (nomination) of a name (lexeme) which resembles the predication of the subject in a sentence. When the defining predicate has been attached to the named subject, the result is the "figure," i.e., a name with a fixed definition which is now beyond the changing, temporal process (1974:68). The sentence structure of the narrative thus produces semantic closure.

The translinguistic code consists in part of the social structures and historical conditions which dictate the literary forms in which a work is produced and consumed. The alienation which may be found in the society is thus indirectly transmitted into its literature. So powerful and inhibiting are these social codes that Barthes has said: "Writing, free in its beginnings, is finally the bond which links the writer to a History which is itself in chains: Society stamps upon him the unmistakable signs of art so as to draw him along more inescapably in its own process of alienation" (1970:40). Greimas, as well, in his description of the syntax of the narrative as leading from the rupture of a social contract to its reinstatement, points to the strong tendency of the narrative to serve as a support for the social status quo.

Yet the origins of the narrative in the free act of writing, together with its reliance upon metaphor, allow the possibility of genuine openness between the closed linguistic and translinguistic codes. In its use of languages, literature is caught up in the oppressive social divisions and alienation which those languages embody and support, but "as Freedom, it is the consciousness of this division and the very effort which seeks to surmount it" (1970:87, 88). For this reason, Barthes can speak of writing as "essentially the moral of form, the choice of that social area within which the writer elects to situate the Nature of his language" (1970:15). As a critic he thus supports that literature which "hastens towards a dreamed of language whose freshness, by a kind of ideal anticipation, might portray the perfection of some new Adamic World whose language would no longer be alienated" (1970:88).

The "meaning" of the narrative thus flows from the emancipating power of its metaphorical language to open up the closed systems of meaning, both personal and social, in which man exists. Those narratives which were themselves determined almost totally by linguistic and translinguistic codes would border on the "meaningless" from this viewpoint, whereas those narratives in which the meaning "flees" (1964:264) would paradoxically have the most significance for human life. A narrative typology based on the degree to which the narrative is subservient to closed systems of meaning thus becomes possible.

As a critic, Barthes writes so as to expose the fixed codes which operate in narratives and to illuminate the open dimension of the narrative by describing its structure from the viewpoint of the open subjective process of writing (and reading). In *S/Z*, his analysis of Balzac's novella, *Sarrasine*, Barthes reads the text as a complex tissue of various fixed codes. Each code constitutes its own closed system of meaning which vies with the other codes for the attention of the writer (and reader). Barthes depicts these codes as personal voices which continually pull the writer into their sphere of meaning from which he must return to pursue the consistent unfolding of the course of events. This movement, generated by the tension between the open movement of the narrative toward the new and the imposing force of closed systems of meaning or codes, re-enacts the primordial tension of the self in its relation to language beginning with the Prohibition. The role of the critic is then to probe into the open dimension of the narrative, exposing the tensions and frictions which are signs of the open process of its production, and thus also of its deeper meaning.

By taking the occurrence of language in the act of writing as the generative source of the meaning and structure of the narrative, Barthes clearly elevates the significance of *la parole*, the actual word, above that of *la langue*, the synchronic, systematic aspect of language. Since writing is a free act which metaphorically reveals and opens the structure of subjectivity, its deepest semantic level does not rest upon atemporal necessary, logical, binary oppositions, but arises from the meaning of the primary temporal *contrast*: word vs. silence. This meaning is not opposed to history, but rather is the primary paradigm which gives meaning to history as an open process. "Writing," as Barthes understands it, is thus historic in the deepest sense.

To what extent can Barthes' approach be used fruitfully to analyze the biblical narrative? Barthes himself has shown the way in his article on Jacob's struggle with the divine assailant (Gen 32:23-33), reported in part above, and discussed more fully by this writer elsewhere (1975). There he gives a provocative suggestion of how his own semantic paradigm might illuminate the deepest level of meaning in the biblical narrative. In his interpretation of the meaning of the limp with which Jacob was marked as the result of his divine encounter he writes: "in marking Jacob (Israel), God (or the narrative) permits an anagogical development of meaning: he creates the formal conditions for the function of a new 'language' of which the election of Israel is the 'message.' God is a logothete, Jacob is here a 'morpheme' of the new 'language'" (1971:35). Thus, to the extent that election in the biblical narrative consists of word events through which new, open subjects are created, there may be a convergence between the meaning and structure of biblical history and Barthes' understanding of "writing." God appears as a "logothete" (language founder).

Conclusion

If it now can be assumed that a structuralist approach to the biblical narrative is possible and desirable, the central question which emerges from a comparison of the approaches of Lévi-Strauss, Greimas, and Barthes concerns which paradigmatic model corresponds to the underlying generative structure of this narrative. It cannot be assumed that one can use the structural method of narrative analysis on the surface of the narrative, and that the conclusions can then be transferred into another semantic context (e.g., an existential, theological, or religious context) for interpretation, because the generative models are global and operate at the semantic level. If the generative model validates itself in disclosing the structure of the narrative, it is logically impossible to transfer conclusions of that analysis into another system of meaning without the second context appearing unrelated and logically ungrounded. In fact, the second context would appear meaningless in the absence of its own semantic paradigm. Thus structural analysis should not be viewed as a neutral method, since the structure of the text uncovered by the analysis already coincides with its semantic content.

It exceeds the scope of this article to enter into a serious examination of the relative merits of the paradigmatic model of Lévi-Strauss and Greimas vs. that of Barthes for biblical studies. The capacity of these methods to illuminate the art of the biblical narrative would, however, seem to dictate a thorough exploration by biblical scholars. Such an exploration cannot avoid the deeper problems posed by the paradigmatic, semantic models which are fundamental to this approach.

Hugh C. White

Notes

/1/   The term "system" was used by de Saussure rather than "structure," which came much later.

/2/   For another example of the application to an OT text of a method of structural analysis heavily influenced by Lévi-Strauss, see Polzin. Polzin develops a method of structural analysis, inspired in part by Lévi-Strauss, which he applies to the Book of Job. He also gives a very complete annotated bibliography of works concerned with the structural analysis of OT texts.

/3/   In an article by G. Vuillod, texts are only referred to in a rather casual manner as illustrations and variations of Greimas' syntagmatic units; e.g., the beginning of the story of Jonah depicts the refusal of a mandate by the subject followed by nonrealization and recompense, the story of the stoning of Achan for the violation of the ban against Jericho in Josh 7 illustrates the recompense that follows the violation of the prohibition, etc.

/4/   Here, Barthes turns to studies of the pronoun by Benveniste (also Jakobson, 1971:esp. 131–35), which have shown that the personal pronouns can be understood only as ciphers for the instance of discourse rather than as having some relation to reality.

Part II

Structures in History: Historiography and Historical Criticism

Introduction

Martin J. Buss

Structures play a significant role in history. For the essays by Gottwald, Willis, and Melugin, the primary framework is that of historiography, but within that frame the examination of structures is prominent. One can leave open the question whether the authors consider history (or the particular) primary in relation to form (or the general). No matter what ontology is held, it is appropriate to give priority to one facet for certain purposes.

In the field of sociopolitical historiography—the topic of Norman Gottwald's paper—structural aspects include forms of social organization and of interactions between different elements within a society. Social history involves extensive interrelations and reflects processes which occur in more than one time and place. For the study of Israelite history, such matters can be given more extensive and more careful attention than they have received already. Gottwald lays out some of the basic issues and procedures for an incisive sociological understanding of ancient Israel, with special attention to the oldest period. He seeks to describe Israelite society in its particularity, but necessarily uses general categories in doing so. He also shows how superficial comparisons may mislead.

In the history of literature, structures appear in the forms of tradition, including the organization of the text as it stands. Early in

67

the present century, considerable interest in a study of the early stages of oral tradition emerged; detailed attention to the final shape of the text is more recent. John Willis offers here an outline of the major concerns and problems of redaction and tradition criticism. He gives room to the possibility of historical reconstruction and points to the need of examining the structures of the textual data for recovering earlier stages as well as the intent of redactors.

An important aspect of tradition is constituted by culturally defined genres, or established patterns of expression. A crucial issue, then, concerns the way in which a particular text is governed by conventions. Roy Melugin argues that J. Muilenburg, in describing the aesthetic ("rhetorical") form of a text, paid insufficient attention to conventional style. Melugin's interest in genres does not mean a de-emphasis of history. On the contrary, he understands genres as conventions within a culture; they provide a link with history, seen as a human process. He illustrates his view by describing the story of Rebekah at the well in relation to similar narratives, with special attention to the account's own structure and purpose. He concludes by expressing a theological concern for particular history.

Chapter 3

Sociological Method in the Study
of Ancient Israel

Norman K. Gottwald
Graduate Theological Union, Berkeley

Historical method and sociological method are different but compatible methods for reconstructing ancient Israelite life and thought. Historical study of ancient Israel aims at grasping the sequential articulation of Israel's experience and the rich variety of its cultural products, outstandingly its literature and religion. Sociological study of ancient Israel aims at grasping the typical patterns of human relations in their structure and function, both at a given moment or stage (synchronics) and in their trajectories of change over specified time spans (diachronics). The hypothetically "typical" in collective human behavior is sought by comparative study of societies and expressed theoretically in "laws," "regularities," or "tendencies" that attempt to abstract translocal and transtemporal structural or processual realities within the great mass of spatiotemporal particularities. In such terms, the tribal phase of Israel's social history is greatly illuminated by a theoretical design of social organization (as developed by Sahlins and Fried, among others).

Historical method embraces all the methods of inquiry drawn from the humanities (e.g., literary criticism, form criticism, tradition history, rhetorical criticism, redaction criticism, history, history of religion, biblical theology). Sociological method includes all the methods of inquiry proper to the social sciences (e.g., anthropology, sociology, political science, economics). Sociological method in data collection and theory building enables us to analyze, synthesize, abstract, and interpret Israelite life and thought along different axes and with different tools and constructs from those familiar to us from historical method. Sociological inquiry recognizes people as social actors and symbolizers who "perform" according to interconnecting regularities and within boundaries or limits (social systems).

If we wish to reconstruct ancient Israel as a lived totality, historical method and sociological method are requisite complementary disciplines. Historical method has long recognized the need for collaboration with archaeology, which as a discipline does not fi, immediately or comfortably into the molds of the humanities. It is increasingly clear that the need of historical method for sociological inquiry into ancient Israel is just as urgent as its need for archaeology.

The social system of ancient Israel signifies the whole complex of communal interactions embracing functions, roles, institutions, customs, norms, symbols, and the processes and networks distinctive to the sub-systems of social organization (economic production, political order, military defense, judicatory procedure, religious organization, etc.). This social system must be grasped in its activity both in the communal production of goods, services, and ideas and in the communal control of their distribution and use.

We must resist the tendency to objectify Israel's social system into a static and monolithic hypostasis. It developed unevenly, underwent change, and incorporated tension and conflict. It was a framework for human interaction in which stability struggled against change and change eroded away stability. To call this complex of human interaction a social system is meaningful in that it was something more than an aggregation of discrete interhuman relations. There were regularities in the ways that Israelites organized their actions and thoughts, cooperated and contended with one another and with outside groups. These regularities form an analyzable system in the additional sense that they placed Israelite behavior and valuing under impulses and pressures toward normativeness or standardization. The social system tended to validate particular uses and distributions of natural and human resources and to delimit the exercises and distributions of personal and public power. The social system supplied the constraints of physical coercion and symbolic persuasion. By carefully noting the regularities and normative tendencies, it is possible to identify deviations and idiosyncrasies, both those that appear to have been "social waste" and those that augured "social innovation."

The materials for sociological study of ancient Israel are the biblical text and all available extrabiblical evidence, written and material. In addition, the contents, structures, and developmental trajectories of other social systems—whether in Israel's immediate milieu or far beyond in time and space—are potentially relevant for comparative study. What is vital is that those contents, structures, and trajectories be examined in their total contexts and that they be compared with Israel in its total context. Alleged comparison of isolated social data torn out of systemic context is not comparison at all, but superficial juxtaposition lacking criteria for evaluation.

Sociological method works as a totality with its own analytic tools and theoretical perspectives quite as much as does historical method. Since historical method has already "staked out" the field of biblical study, sociological method tends to arrive on the scene as a "tacked on" adjunct to the customary privileged methods. As long as it performs in the role of supplying addenda or trying to do "rescue work" on texts and historical problems that are momentarily resistant to historical methods, sociological method in biblical study will appear tangential and quixotic, as a problematic interloper (Frick and Gottwald, I:165–78).

In any given text the sociological data may be no more than traces or shattered torsos. What are we to make, for example, of the kinship and marriage patterns attested in the patriarchal accounts? When sociological method is called in to assist on this problem, it must try to contextualize the fragments within their larger complexes. So far, what is loosely called "sociological" inquiry in this instance is a ransacking of ancient Near Eastern societies for parallel social phenomena. As in the appeal to Nuzi parallels to patriarchal kinship and marriage practices, insufficient attention is paid to the nature of the compared texts and to the social systems presupposed by the texts.

We are becoming freshly aware of the scandalous imprecision of such "sociological" dabbling in the patriarchal traditions. The historical and social loci of the patriarchal traditions are simply not specifiable with any degree of confidence, and, in fact, there is every reason to believe that the historical and social horizons of the separate units and cycles of tradition are highly diverse /1/. In this stalemated situation, sociological inquiry can be most helpful when it extends the examination of how biblical texts with similar social data function in relation to texts or traditions of a similar nature among other peoples, whether literate or preliterate. Working on its own ground, sociological method will try to build up a body of knowledge about types or families of texts and traditions containing social data of certain kinds. How do these tradition types reflect or refract social reality in various types of social systems? How, for example, do genealogies function in oral and written traditions, as separate pieces and as elements within larger compositions, in tribal and in statist societies, etc. /2/?

In other words, a sociology of ancient Israel can be a proper complement to literary and historical inquiry only as it pursues its own proper object of reconstructing the Israelite social system as a totality, without prejudging which of its results are likely to be germane to understanding specific texts or historical problems and without diverting too much energy at the start to narrowly or obscurely framed "social puzzles" in idiosyncratic literary and historical contexts.

In order to approximate comprehensive reconstruction of the Israelite social system, sociological method depends upon literary and historical criticism to undertake their tasks in a similarly comprehensive and systemic way. It also relies upon archaeology to break loose from the domination of historically framed orientations and to become an instrument for recovering the total material life of ancient Israelites irrespective of immediate applications to texts or to historical and sociological problems.

We may illustrate the way the integral projects of sociological method intersect with historical methods by noting the impact of the introduction of a new model for understanding the origins of Israel within its Canaanite matrix. The proposal that earliest Israel was not an invading or infiltrating people but a social revolutionary peasant movement within Canaan is at least a quasi-sociological model /3/. This heuristic model gives a new way of looking at all the old texts, biblical and extrabiblical, and the material remains /4/. Its effect has been to shift attention away from the precise historical circumstances of Israel's occupation of Canaan and toward the social processes by which Israel came to dominance. The effort to reconstruct a history of the occupation has long been deadended by the sparse historical data. A sociological model in this case provides a way of re-viewing the fragmentary historical data and in the end may help us to understand why the historical data are as obscure as they are. Finally, the specifically historical project of identifying the agents and spatiotemporal course of the emergent dominion of Israel in Canaan may be freshly facilitated by the working out of a different conception of the process at work in that achievement.

The effect of the peasant-revolt model of the origins of Israel has been to replace uncritical cultural assumptions about Israel's alleged pastoral nomadism with sharper sociological inquiry into the internal composition of early Israel, demographically and socioeconomically (Gottwald, 1974:223–55; 1976a:629–31; in press: 464–92). What exactly was this formation of people called Israel which took control in Canaan and whose social system took form as it gained the upper hand in the land? From what social spaces in Syro-Palestine did these people derive? What brought them together, enabled them to collaborate and to succeed? What were the goals these people shared and what social instrumentalities and material conditions contributed to their accomplishment? How does this social system of earliest Israel relate to those that preceded it and those against which it was counterposed? In other words, a proper model of the Israelite emergence in Canaan is not attainable apart from a proper model of the social system of the people who gained dominion in the land (Gottwald, in press: 493–587). And of course neither the historical course of Israel's coming to power nor its emergent social system can be grasped without an understanding of the cultic-ideological process of tradition formation.

Up to the present, biblical studies have grappled with a model of the settlement and with a model of the cultic production of traditions, but there has been no adequate mediation between these two forms of inquiry within a larger analytic model of the social system involved in the twin process of taking power in the land and of building its own traditions. Martin Noth and George Mendenhall have made suggestive, incomplete, and at times mistaken attempts at an encompassing societal model. By drawing together the seminal contributions of Noth and Mendenhall, while weeding out their errors and false starts, we have the beginnings of a comprehensive social model for early Israel—or, more precisely, we have an inventory of the questions to be pursued and a general sense of the appropriate range of model options /5/.

A theoretical model of the origins and operations of early Israelite society will entail two axes of investigation: 1) the analysis of Israel's internal composition and structure at its several organizational levels and in its sectoral subsystems; 2) the characterization of Israel's social system as an operational and developing totality in comparison and contrast with other social systems. Both types of inquiry have synchronic and diachronic dimensions, and both types of inquiry will proceed dialectically in movement back and forth between concrete data about specific social systems and more abstract heuristic models, such as a theoretical design of "tribalism" /6/.

As for the first task, evidence of the internal composition and eclectic structure of early Israel is largely biblical, but there are significant checkpoints in the Ugaritic, Alalakh, and Amarna texts, as well as rich resources concerning the material culture which have yet to be sufficiently mined. These immediate social data must be reflected upon against the backdrop of the large body of information and theory we now possess as a consequence of anthropological field studies, work in pre-history, and theorizing about social organizaton.

To what levels, ranges and functions of social organization do the designations *shēveṭ, mishpaḥāh,* and *beth-ʾāv* refer? To date it has seemed sufficient to give them the naïve meanings of "tribe," "clan," and "household" or "extended family," without further ado. If early Israel is conceivable as a form of "retribalization," what were the bonding organizational elements for holding together the segmented "tribes" of diverse origin? Noth provided the summary answer of "a sacral league," but his analogy between the Greek amphictyony and the intertribal league of Israel holds good at such an abstract level that it is of doubtful value in illuminating the crucial features of Israel's retribalization process. If Israel was a revolutionary movement within Canaanite society, how did matters develop from the uncoordinated restiveness of peasants and ʾapiru in Amarna days into the coalition of Israelite tribes? So far only Alt has offered a bare sketch of diachronic possibilities (1966: 175–204). Merely appealing to Mosaic traditions and Yahwistic faith as "explanations" for this coalescing process does not clarify and reconstruct the arduous struggle by which Israel put itself together in Canaan.

As for the second task, what was the over-all character of Israel's social system in comparison with other preceding and contemporary social systems? Such a comparison depends upon prior analysis of the social systems compared, and this analysis must follow an inventory of social desiderata so that we do not simply accept at face value either the form or the preponderance of specific social data as they happen to appear to us in texts. The comparison of social systems must constantly contextualize social systems and subsystems within the systems as a whole and in terms of the direction of their movement (e.g., expansion, differentiation, decline, transition to new systems, etc.).

Whether two different social complexes can be meaningfully compared is of course a matter of much discussion (see Goldschmidt). In biblical studies there has been an abundance of hasty and superficial cross-cultural comparisons. With each new discovery in the ancient Near East—such as the Amarna, Mari, Ugaritic, or Ebla texts—there has been a rush of claims for direct correlations between them and the biblical text, or for wholesale borrowings of systems or institutions or offices by Israel. On more careful analysis these "parallels" either vanish or are greatly scaled down and nuanced. Such defaults establish the urgency of developing more reliable ways of comparing and contrasting social data and systems. If we wish, for example, to compare early Israelite society with its Canaanite counterpart and matrix, we face serious gaps in our knowlege of aspects of both entities, but these difficulties need to be brought out more systematically so that we will be clearer about the explanatory strength or weakness of our theory and thereby more aware of the kinds of research needed to test and improve theory.

It is evident that comparison of early Israel with other contemporary social systems entails diachronic and synchronic approaches. The social systems under comparison were not static, isolated entities; they developed internally and stood in varying relations to one another over spans of time and in different regions. A great deal of nuancing in treating these societal interfaces is required, often dismally lacking, for example, in the way "Canaan" and "Israel" are counterposed by biblical scholars, like characters in a morality play. According to all known analogies of revolutionary movements, we should expect that by no means all of the people of Canaan will have been "polarized" by the nascent Israelite movement. It should be expected that as the Canaanite and rising Israelite social systems collided and conflicted, there will have been many people—probably a majority at first—who were conflicted in their own feelings and stances toward the two options. We should expect to find those who strove for neutrality, by choice or necessity, some who were half-hearted converts and those who switched sides, others who were secret supporters and yet others who were opportunist in their allegiances /7/. A re-examination of Israel's early traditions in terms of these dynamics of social revolutionary movements will reveal unexpected results toward a clearer conception of how Israel arose. The result is likely to be that the initially simplistic-appearing peasant revolt model will turn out to be even more complex and nuanced than the previous conquest and immigration models of Israel's origins.

In pursuing the comparative approach to Israelite society a major issue is how we are to decide which social systems should be compared with Israel's. Here we encounter the vexed problem of determining the boundaries of social systems in relation to the boundaries of the various historic state, tribal, and cultural formations which appear under various, vaguely depicted proper names and gentilics in the biblical and extrabiblical texts. No doubt we should identify the Canaanite city-state system as the dominant and definitive social system within earliest Israel's horizon (Helck; Mohammad, 105–37; Buccellati). But do the ʾapiru of the Amarna period form another such system? Here the time trajectory enters into consideration. The ʾapiru appear as a sub-set within Amarna "feudalism" or "Asiatic mode of production" (Gottwald, 1976b:145–54), but insofar as the ʾapiru are seen as forerunners and one of the contributors to early Israel, they may indeed merit attention as another social system in embryo or as one trajectory along which the Canaanite social system declined and the Israelite social system rose. And it would be a grave methodological error to assume that early Israel arose along only one such trajectory. More often than not, the relation of the ʾapiru to early Israel has been examined as though it was the only or the primary pertinent relationship and that, if the ʾapiru data could not account for all or most of the features of early Israel, then they were irrelevant.

Pastoral nomadism as the supposed socioeconomic condition of early Israel might be viewed as another social system, but we now see how doubtful it is that we can locate an autonomous pastoral nomadic system in the immediate environment of Canaan contemporary with early Israel. The transhumant, village-based pastoral nomadism of Israel's environment was a minor sub-set of village tribalism subordinated socioeconomically and politically to sedentary Canaan. This pastoral nomadism was at most a minor contributor to early Israel. Nonetheless, it is necessary that this pastoral nomadic sub-specialization of village tribalism be carefully analyzed in order to reassess properly its vastly overstated role in Israelite origins /8/.

Other possible social systems in Israel's milieu come to mind. Do the Philistines constitute a new social system or are they merely heirs of the Canaanite system with new organizational twists, mostly of a political and military nature? (Cf. Alt, 1953:216–30; Kassis: 259–71). And what are we to make of the Ammonites, Moabites, and Edomites, whose origins were roughly contemporary with Israel and yet who did not become a part of Israel? Did these people feel the tug of Israel's social mutation, did some of them actually engage in social revolution, and if so, why did they accept kingship earlier than did Israel itself? (Cf. Horn: 20; Bartlett, 1972:26–37; 1973:229–58).

Against this methodological sketch, we can see why the patriarchal traditions are particularly resistant to sociological analysis. From all appearances, those traditions belong to any number of peoples moving along various trajectories toward their convergence in early Israel. The patriarchal groups are proto-Israelites. Just as Noth recognized that the patriarchal traditions can only be approached backwards, working out of the congealing traditions of united Israel in Canaan, so the sociological analysis of the patriarchal communities must be approached backwards from the coalescing peoples of the intertribal community in Israelite Canaan. No sociological wonders will be workable on the patriarchal traditions until much more is known of their literary form and function, of their temporal horizons, and of their rootage in one or another of the social trajectories along which sectors of the Syro-Palestinian peoples converged toward their unity in Israel (Gottwald, in press: 32–44, 105–10).

An instance of the great difficulties in precise sociological analysis of the groups represented in the patriarchal traditions of Genesis 25–35 is the practice of using the connubium reported in Genesis 34 between Shechemites and Israelites as evidence for clan exogamy, a habit that goes back at least to the nineteenth-century anthropologist E. B. Tylor.

Genesis 34 tells us only that the two parties began to reach agreement on an alliance that was to include the exchange of wives. It does *not* tell us that a presupposition for the proposed wife-exchange was that Israelites or Shechemites could not marry among themselves and thus were obliged to get wives from outside. It does *not* tell us that the wives to be exchanged between the group constituted all or most of the marriage arrangements to be made by Israelites and Shechemites, thereby sharply reducing or excluding intragroup marriages or intermarriage with other groups. In other words, since we do not know the actual scope demographically or the internal social structure of the two contracting entities in Genesis 34, we have to try out various hypotheses to see how clan-exogamous they look on close examination. The results are not reassuring.

If, for example, "Israel" in Genesis 34 was actually only a relatively small social group (still proto-Israelite), the connubium formula might be read—especially noting the phrase "we will become one people" (v 16)—as alluding to an early endeavor to meld together two groups of people into one tribal formation as complementary moieties. We might in that case be witnessing an initial act by which a member of later Israel (Manasseh or a section of Manasseh?) was formed from two originally separate groups that become segments practicing exogamy and thus exchanging wives within the newly shaped tribe. Granted that the formation was not carried through according to Genesis 34, it could at least be construed that connubium covenant was a means by which some peoples did come together as tribal entities within Israel, the tribes being built up by exogamous clans.

If, on the other hand, we imagine (as the final state of the text certainly does), that many Israelite tribes are present and that this is an "external" arrangement between autonomous entities, a matter of intertribal "foreign policy," we could say that Israel developed, or sought to develop, peaceful relations with some surrounding peoples by connubium covenant. But would a tribal organization (Israel) and a city organization (Shechem) be likely to enter into such an exogamous connubium? Would a large assemblage of tribes be able to get enough wives from one city for an exclusive connubium if exogamy forbade marriage of Israelites to fellow Israelites? The anthropological evidence is that whole tribes are not exogamous; it is clans within a tribe that are exogamous and that take wives from and give wives to other exogamous clans, the tribe as a whole remaining endogamous (although marriages may be allowed or prescribed outside the tribe in certain cases). The more large-scale the Israelite partner in the proposed connubium is conceived to have been, the more likely it becomes that the group already would have worked out marriage patterns, exogamous or otherwise (that cannot be known from the text), among its member units, and thus the more peripheral the connubium with Shechem would become as a wife-exchange mechanism and the more it would look like an alliance sealed with limited intermarriage bearing no correlation whatsoever with exogamy rules. Maybe the difficulties can be eased by conceiving the proposed connubium as an arrangement involving only a single clan or group of clans (of Manasseh?) located in the vicinity of Shechem. In that way a possible symmetrical, exogamously based exchange of wives could be made plausible, but that hypothesis still fails to deal with the issue of whether a city would be interested in, or capable of, wholesale exogamy.

The farther our analysis and speculation about alternatives runs, the more evident it becomes that even if Genesis 34 goes back to early times, the obstacles to perceiving its exact sociohistoric context, the parties involved, and the mechanisms posited, are insuperably opposed to any reasonable confidence that this tradition shows the existence of exogamous clans in early Israel. A careful examination of other early biblical traditions thought to attest to clan exogamy yields similarly doubtful or flatly negative results (Gottwald, in press: 301–15).

A main sociological task in the study of early Israel is the development of an adequate socioeconomic and cultural material inventory. This will require further historicoterritorial and topological studies (of the sort begun by Alt and carried on by Rowton). Archaeology will have to attend not only to fortified cities but to the agricultural village/neighborhood complexes that included settlements, roads, fields, springs, irrigation, terrace systems, etc. Renewed attention will have to be given to population size, density, and distribution. The role of technological factors taken in combination will have to be explored more thoroughly: the introduction of iron, waterproof cisterns, improved terracing, and irrigation works. The archaeology of biblical Israel, previously overwhelmingly oriented to direct synchronizations with biblical literature and history (e.g., who were the kings of Genesis 14:1?), will increasingly offer a wider spectrum of data for the social and cultural reconstruction of the early Israelite movement. More and more we can hope for the collaboration of all methodologies in clarifying the material and socioreligious processes by which the Israelites came into dominance in the hill country of Canaan (Gottwald, in press:642–63).

The sociological inquiry which I have here illustrated in the instance of Israel's origins will equally apply to the major social transition to the monarchy and the resulting tensions and conflicts between state, empire, and tribe, as well as to the later period of the disintegration of the Israelite states and the survival and reconstruction of social forms into the postexilic age. It is obvious that in this task it will be necessry to call upon a host of specialists so far only sporadically enlisted in the task of reconstructing ancient Israel, e.g., agronomists, botanists, hydrologists, geologists, demographers, etc. The reconstructed cultural-material complexes will bear important indicators for social, military, and religious organization, especially when contextually compared with agrarian complexes and urban center/rural periphery complexes of similar sorts that can be studied at first hand by contemporary ethnologists.

In sum, it is essential that we devise a constructive model of the Israelite social system in its own right, firmly rooted in its material conditions, a model which delineates the major subsystems and segmented organization, as well as a model that grasps the integrating mechanisms and the solidifying ideology of the social whole /9/. This model will necessarily be viewed genetically in order to show how Israel arose, achieved its first cohesive form, and then passed over into other forms in the course of time through a combination of internal and external pressures. Synchronics and diachronics, internal dynamics and external interfaces and interpenetrations will be drawn together under the principle or law of internal relations whereby an alteration in any element of the whole will be seen to bring about alterations in the entire system.

A model of the Israelite social system will incorporate the highly centralized and richly articulated religion of Yahweh. But it must do so sociologically by understanding the religion as a social phenomenon (institutionally and symbolically) and therefore related to all the other social phenomena within the system by the law of internal relations. This socioreligious inquiry must proceed without simplistic recourse to the tautological, philosophically idealist claim that because religion was central to the social system, it can be posited as the unmoved mover of the Israelite mutation (Gottwald, in press: 591–691).

The sociological contribution to biblical hermeneutics is that the Israelite traditions must not only be interpreted within their original matrices, but must be interpreted from out of the social matrix of the interpreter. In the end it will be learned that an adequate biblical hermeneutics will require the investigation of the evolution of social forms and systems from biblical times until the present (Gottwald, in press: 692–709)! Any interpreter who claims continuity with the biblical texts must also assume the continuity of the history of social forms as an indispensable precondition of the hermeneutical task.

Notes

/1/   The precariousness of attaching the patriarchal traditions to Bronze Age historical and social settings is independently demonstrated by Thompson, 1974, and Van Seters.

/2/   Renger, working from Amorite texts in which he finds exogamous clan organization, posits patriarchal exogamy for the biblical patriarchs, but can only succeed by capriciously regarding the biblical genealogies sometimes as actual descent lineages and sometimes as fictitious or eponymous constructs. Much more sophisticated in using comparative method and thus in advancing our comprehension of biblical genealogies are Malamat and Wilson. See also Gottwald, in press: 308–10, 334–37.

/3/   See Mendenhall, 1962 and 1973. The same broad conclusion that early Israel was "the *first* ideologically based socio-political revolution in the history of the world," was reached independently by Dus (28). See also the discussions by Hauser, Thompson, and Gottwald in *JSOT*, 1978.

/4/   A striking example of heuristic value of a sociological model for textual criticism and historical reconstruction is Chaney.

/5/   My critiques of Noth's and Mendenhall's societal models for early Israel will be found in Gottwald, in press: 220–33, 345–57, 376–86, 599–602.

/6/   For an elaboration of this programmatic statement see Gottwald, in press: 228–33, and for my provisional conclusions on the content see 237–587.

/7/   For an analysis of Israel's Canaanite converts, allies, and neutrals, see Gottwald, in press: 555–83.

/8/   On classificatory typology of pastoral nomadism, see Johnson, and for ancient Near Eastern pastoral nomadism, see Rowton, 1973a and 1973b.

/9/   Gottwald, in press: 191–663.

Chapter 4

Redaction Criticism and Historical Reconstruction

John T. Willis
Abilene Christian University

Attempts to reconstruct historical events and sequences of events reflected in OT literature face major difficulties. Since OT books are the end product of a long oral and written transmission process and in their final form represent the work of a redactor or redactional school, the historian is obliged to deal with the nature and structure of the final redaction as well as with the transmission of the material. Realistically, one must begin with the position and form of a pericope in the completed OT book, determine its meaning and function there, and then work back meticulously and cautiously to earlier stages (with Koch: 57; Tucker: 48–50).

Of course, this task is extremely hazardous and difficult, for one cannot understand the theological emphasis of an entire book without a careful study of each unit within it. Nevertheless, the first task of the redaction critic or historian is to understand each part of a book in relation to the other parts and to the whole; after that step, he can seek to go behind this final stage to earlier levels in the transmission process.

The Activities of Redactors

Redactors preserved traditions that were handed down to them by their predecessors. But it is always difficult to know the extent of the redactor's fidelity to the *ipsissima verba* of the traditions with which he is dealing (see Ringgren). Often, redactors are depicted as individuals who felt duty-bound to pass on traditions just as they were handed down to them, either because they felt these traditions were too sacred to be altered or because they feared criticism from their contemporaries if they changed community property /1/. It is frequently assumed that this procedure provides a major explanation for the discrepancies, incoherencies, and inconsistencies in the various biblical books. Accordingly, redactors are pictured as well-meaning, but ignorant of the significance of the traditions that they propose to transmit /2/. The creative spirits in the traditio-historical process are often believed to be earlier figures, such as the Yahwist in the Pentateuch or a great prophet, and not the redactors (cf. Rast: 16). Still, there have always been scholars who have proposed a more constructive role for the work of redactors.

In addition to preserving material, redactors commented on it so that their audiences might understand their interpretation of that material, or they explained words or phrases in the tradition. For example, at the end of the account of Jacob's struggle at the Jabbok, the redactor explains to his audience: "Therefore to this day the Israelites do not eat the sinew of the hip which is upon the hollow of the thigh, because he touched the hollow of Jacob's thigh on the sinew of the hip" (Gen 32:33 [Engl. 32:32]).

Redactors frequently deleted material which existed in their tradition, as is clear from a comparison of parallel accounts in Kings and Chronicles. There are several reasons why a redactor may have deleted items: it was already so well known to his audience that it was unnecessary to record it; it was not relevant to the needs of the redactor's audience at the time of its compilation or arrangement; it did not fit the author's theme or purpose. For instance, the inquisitive historian would like to know many details concerning Jacob's stay with Laban which the biblical narrative passes over lightly, such as the events which transpired during the month before Laban drove a bargain with Jacob (Gen 29:14) or during the seven years Jacob labored for Rachel (Gen 29:20). But other matters took precedence either for the earlier tradents or for the final redactors.

Finally, redactors often gave coherence or sequential arrangement to traditional materials they received, materials which originated and were preserved in varying localities at different times. In order to accomplish this, they made at least four kinds of contributions: (a) They composed comprehensive introductions to the traditional materials they inherited in order to prepare their readers to understand those materials in a specific way; the birth story of Jacob and Esau may function in this way (cf. the roles of Judg 2:11–23 [Wharton: 730–31]; Isa 7:1–2; and possibly I Sam 16:14–23 [Willis, 1973:294–314]). (b) They composed summary statements at the end of blocks of material to highlight some of the main emphases they desired their own audiences to see in the material (e.g., Gen 26:35; 30:43; 33:16–17). (c) They inserted words, phrases, verses, or paragraphs to link together disparate material, or to make a sweeping transition from one unit or complex to another (such as Gen 26:15; 29:24; 31:32c), a procedure which frequently forms a structural pattern for a whole complex or book (as the recurring introductory and concluding formulas providing the framework for the books of Kings). (d) They constructed, in many cases, well-ordered compositions. In Genesis, for example, Jacob's departure from Esau and his mysterious meeting with Yahweh at Bethel correspond to a similar encounter with the divine upon his returning and to the reunion with Esau (cf., further, Gammie, below); the places where Jacob is said to have traveled fit the geographical situation well.

The Functions of Redactors in the Development of the Biblical Tradition

In view of the types of work in which redactors engaged, it is possible to make some specific proposals in regard to their operation. First, there is good evidence that the same block of traditional material was subjected to more than one redactional or editorial reworking during the course of its transmission. In other words, redactors are not always to be identified with the final editors of biblical books.

Second, special studies approaching the biblical text from different viewpoints are building a strong case for the proposition that the final forms of OT books are much more coherent in their structure and much better organized in their thought patterns than was often thought previously. (See Walker and Lund, for Habakkuk; Buss, 1969:116–40, for Hosea; Willis, 1969, for Micah.) Such insights support an appreciation for ancient thought patterns and arrangements of literary material as viable for that day and for those particular cultures. Redactors, on the whole, were not passive, unthinking recipients and transmitters of ancient traditions, but theologians in their own right. It is reasonable to believe that tradents or redactors of traditional material preserved what was handed down to them because they believed it met the contemporary needs of their own audiences and that it conveyed their own religious message in the most effective manner to those audiences.

Third, redactors usually depended on a tradition without being rigidly bound by it. Budde and Wolfe apparently assumed that redactors approached the text with theological biases gained from sources other than the texts which they transmit, with the purpose of deleting or adding material so as to convey their various theological positions. At the other extreme, Boling (11, 29–38) argues that the redactors of the book of Judges considered the traditional material which was handed down to them as "already fixed and inviolable in all essentials," so that the most they contributed to this work was connectives between existing narratives, stylistic adjustments, lexical substitutions, and the like.

A mediating position seems to reflect best the reality of the transmission of OT material. The redactors were indeed theologians, but their theology was not created out of a vacuum. Instead, it was shaped largely by those people and works which especially impressed them. Since they preserved the materials which they did (and not other materials), it is reasonable to believe that these materials functioned as the dominant force shaping their theology. But that theology was expressed in light of the needs of the particular audience for which a certain redactor (or group of redactors) composed his work. Hence a redactor did, in fact, pass on traditional material, but in doing so he selected those portions which he felt spoke to the needs of his audience. He did not hesitate to rearrange or interpret the material or to place emphasis on a certain thought which he believed his readers needed or might otherwise overlook, in order to "reapply" the message of the tradition to the new situation (cf. Willis, 1974:64–76). To insist that a redactor did not create something new, and therefore was not an author, can in most cases be true only if one defines the terms "new" and "author" (cf. Tucker: 19) in a very restrictive sense. Yet von Rad is correct in saying that the continuing reapplication of earlier prophetic oracles to new situations demonstrates the vitality inherent in the original oracles themselves (1965:46). In the Jacob stories (Genesis 25–36) at least two major religious themes stand out: (1) Jacob's "struggles" (encounters, confrontations) with Esau (25:19–26, 27–34; 26:9; 32:4–21 [Engl. 3–20]; 33:1–17; 36), Laban (29–31), Hamor (33:18–34:31), and God (28:10–22; 32:2–3, 23–33 [Engl. 1–2, 22–32]; 35); and (2) God's presence with and promises to Jacob (25:23; 28:3–4, 12–22; etc.). Both are inseparably intertwined with the portrayal of Jacob as a character who deceives and is deceived (25:26, 31–33; 27:18–29, 34–36; 29:15–30; etc.). It seems clear that these themes were part of the warp and woof of the traditional material, but also that they were important to the redactor(s), who selected and shaped them.

Redactional Activity and Recovering Historical Data

Biblical authors (redactors, tradents) did not preserve historical data simply in the interest of relating historical facts, but in order to cast certain (well-known?) historical events in a particular theological light. Historical event and theological interpretation go hand in hand in the Bible. Thus the reader of the Jacob narrative is repeatedly reminded that the hero survived Laban's connivings because Yahweh was with him (Gen 30:27, 30; 31:3, 5, 7, 9, 11–13, 16, 24; etc.).

In selecting and arranging the stories that best suited his purposes, it was inevitable that an author (redactor, tradent) would destroy or obscure the actual cause-effect relationship that helps explain events in human history. Thus the scholar should not be too quick to criticize the arrangement, lacunae, wording, etc., of the biblical text for lack of sequential historical information, because this may not be the author's purpose.

Nevertheless, a text can furnish historical information. Even a late tradition may be historically valuable. In any case, it is not necessary to recover the *ipsissima verba* of a speaker in the Bible to get a correct impression of his message or position (with Engnell: 22; cf. J. Miller, 1976:11–39).

In reconstructing a particular tradition preserved in a specific text, it seems likely that in most cases a minimum of five stages must be considered. The first one in time (which is frequently given inadequate treatment) is the larger background into which a "new" tradition was introduced. All biblical material (like all material produced by man) was occasioned by prior events and thoughts; it did not emerge in a vacuum, nor was it preserved and transmitted in a vacuum. The tradents of biblical tradition were bound naturally and ethically to employ forms that their respective audiences already used and understood (Gunkel, 1915:xxxvii).

Second, it is helpful when one is able to recapture, if possible, a crucial event. This may be a political happening, but it may also be the first public utterance of a prophetic oracle or wisdom maxim, or the initial creation of a song or prayer.

Third, one may consider the early preservation of that event in memory. At this point, the interests and concerns of tradents lead to omissions, additions, and the shaping of the material, as at a written stage.

Fourth, it is important to take into consideration the complexes which emerged from the combination of early traditions prior to the creation of the OT book in which they now appear. Such complexes were formed deliberately, for practical reasons. For instance, Jeremiah dictated his oracles to Baruch when he was debarred from going to the temple (Jer 36:5), so that Baruch could read them to the temple worshippers on a fast day in hopes that they might repent (vv 6-7). Most likely, cycles of Genesis stories were formed for similarly concrete purposes. Possibly the Jacob-Esau cycle was intended to promote more positive relationships between Israelites and Edomites in a period of harsh tension between the two groups.

Fifth, one may deal with the intention of the author(s) of the entire book in which a particular tradition now appears, and with the function of that tradition in the over-all scope of the book. This intention and function can be deduced with some confidence from the text as it is available or as it can be reconstructed by textual criticism. Indeed, the initial task of the interpreter is to look at the final form of biblical books with a hope of discovering purpose and coherence.

Notes

/1/   Gunkel was extremely skeptical about finding any sort of meaningful or coherent arrangement in the prophetic books. He writes (1915:XLI): "Wer ein solches 'Buch' zusammenstellte, hatte kaum die Empfindung, ein irgendwie gegliedertes Kunstwerk zu verfassen, sondern er schrieb zusammen, was und wie er es vorfand."

/2/   In response to Elhorst's attempt to explain the supposed incoherence of the book of Micah by arguing that a copyist or redactor incorrectly arranged the material of the book, Pont (338) and Kosters (258) argue, respectively, that if this is really the case, this redactor was "extremely dumb" (*oliedomme*) and a "poor stupid wretch" (*aartssukkel*).

Chapter 5

Muilenburg, Form Criticism, and Theological Exegesis

Roy F. Melugin
Austin College

Rhetorical Criticism and the Limits of Form Criticism

Several years ago James Muilenburg developed a thesis about the limits of form criticism in an essay entitled, "Form Criticism and Beyond" (1969:1-18). He argued there that the preoccupation of form criticism with typical patterns of speech has often meant that "the individual, personal, and unique features of the particular pericope are all but lost to view" (5). Although form criticism has made a significant contribution to biblical studies, Muilenburg contended that form criticism needs to be supplemented by methods which are better suited to illumine the particularities of individual texts. He argued in this way because of his belief that many texts display a considerable degree of individuality in form. For example, Muilenburg considered Jer 2:1-4:4 to be a sequence of units of the *rîb* genre; but their structure is varied, and most of them are but "excerpts and extracts" of the genre, reformulated in such a way that they are artistic *imitations* of the real genre (5). Form criticism as traditionally practiced, said Muilenburg, does not adequately take account of the artistic creativity of the individual poetic unit.

Muilenburg proposed as a supplement to form criticism a method which he called "rhetorical criticism" (8). Rhetorical criticism focuses on the particular linguistic features which constitute structural features of a given text, regardless of whether any of these word patterns are rooted in the conventions of a genre. Muilenburg was

91

aware of the influence of typical forms of speech upon structure in individual texts, but the method of rhetorical criticism as he used it concerns itself primarily with the structure of *particular* texts. In the study of structure in individual texts, he suggested that we look for literary devices such as word repetition, e.g., *šûb* in Jer 3:1–4:4, *nilḥāmû* in Judg 5:19–21, *qôl qôrēʾ* / *qôl ʾōmēr* and the imperative of *qrʾ* in Isa 40:1–8, or *lᵉkû* in Isa 55:1. Sometimes a recognition of strophes illuminates structural patterns in a particular text, as in Psalm 29 or Isa 40:1–11, and key words frequently serve as signals for the beginning and ending of strophes, e.g., *hinnēh, lākēn, wᵉʿattāh,* and the like.

Muilenburg intended rhetorical criticism as a supplement rather than a substitute for form criticism (4,7), yet in practice his exegesis shows little regard for serious form-critical work /1/. Why he neglected form criticism, despite acknowledging its significance, is not clear. In some cases, as in his commentary on Deutero-Isaiah, he dealt with texts which he considered to be rather freely-formed poems rather than examples of traditional *Gattungen* closely tied to their conventional *Sitz im Leben* (1956:384–92). We may not be certain, however, whether he would also have largely avoided detailed form-critical study of literature which he considered to be more traditional in form, such as the psalms /2/.

Although we cannot be certain how Muilenburg saw the precise relationship between rhetorical criticism and form criticism, it is not difficult to see that his *method* of analysis leads us in directions which are quite different from form criticism as it has usually been practiced /3/. In the first place, Muilenburg's approach is more synchronic than diachronic. The kind of rhetorical criticism which he practiced tends to treat the text as a unity rather than focusing on the historical processes of its development and the social settings in which it was used. Admittedly we must speak of tendencies of the method, for much of Muilenburg's work is so programmatic that we cannot be sure how he would have dealt with methodological questions about the historical development of the text and its societal function. In some instances he practiced rhetorical criticism on texts which he considered to be essentially in their original form, e.g., Deutero-Isaiah (see his commentary of 1956). On other occasions, however, such as his discussion of Jer 2:1–4:4 (1969:5), it is not clear whether he viewed the text as an original composition or as the product of a process of redaction. In any event, his method is primarily designed for the analysis of texts in the form in which they presently exist; the rhetorical critic constantly searches out the linguistic structure of the text *as it presently lies before him* /4/. To be sure, Muilenburg considered it important to delineate units (1969:8–10), but he characteristically approached the problem of the juxtaposition of units in accord with the synchronic methodology of rhetorical criticism, as illustrated by his commentary on Deutero-Isaiah /5/. Form criticism, by way of contrast, has been in part a method of historical analysis. Form critics have typically probed behind the text in its present form, looking for earlier (usually oral) stages of development. Moreover, even when scholars trained in form-critical methodology have been interested in written literature in the form of biblical books, they have generally inquired about the historical process of the growth of those books.

Muilenburg's approach leads in a direction different from form criticism in a second important way: his method emphasizes the text itself and its artistry more than questions about its social setting (*Sitz im Leben*) and function. Muilenburg was, of course, not oblivious to the setting in which a text arose and was used, but his method is not especially geared to address such questions. Form criticism, on the other hand, has been vitally interested in the relationship between a text and the life setting in which it was used.

Form Criticism and the Limits of Rhetorical Criticism

Muilenburg has indeed made an important contribution in supplying a corrective to form criticism. He is quite right that many texts are characterized by unique structural features as much as they are by typical patterns of speech. The degree of typicality and uniqueness differs from passage to passage /6/, but it is safe to say that virtually every text has features which are not shared with any other text.

Muilenburg's dialogue with form criticism is important for another reason as well: his method serves better than genre analysis as the starting point in exegesis, particularly for texts which exhibit artistic formulation. Analysis should begin by examining structure in particular texts rather than by starting with typical patterns of expression. This is methodologically preferable because in actuality we are confronted by individual texts with particular structures; statements about general patterns are the result of processes of abstraction which are derived from a comparison of particular texts /7/. Rhetorical criticism as Muilenburg employs it is designed to explore structural features of individual texts, for the method intentionally focuses on the particular. Repetition of words or phrases, strategic placement of particles, the use of parallelism or chiasmus—all these devices and still others are means by which individual texts are often given shape /8/.

Even though we begin with the structure of particular texts, it would be a serious mistake to underestimate the role of conventional genres in the shaping of individual texts. The truth is that a given text is almost invariably a mixture of the typical and the unique. The author or speaker used conventional forms of speech, to some degree at least, so that his words would have a frame of reference understandable to his audience; without the use of such conventions the audience would lack the signals needed to appropriate his language. At the same time, the writer/speaker wanted to do something *particular* with the inherited speech pattern as he fashioned the individual unit of tradition; invariably each example of a genre is in some sense a unique formulation of the genre. Good exegesis, then, will study both the typical and the unique (see Melugin, 1974). Questions such as the following should be asked: Which elements are typical and which are unique? Does the particular formulation stay within conventions normally expected for the genre? Or has the author gone so far beyond the conventional options that the genre is no more than background in the formulation of the text? Unless we ask these questions and others designed to explore the relationships between (1) the particular structure of a text and (2) its generic features, we shall have missed two important elements in the formation of a text. It is for this reason that Muilenburg's fine work must suffer criticism; for despite his announced intentions, he neglects the study of genre.

Thus far we have concerned ourselves primarily with synchronic matters. To be sure, our insistence on genre analysis has had an element of the diachronic, for any recognition that the structure of a text is to some degree shaped by a certain genre necessarily involves inquiry into the history of the community's conventions of speech. Yet it is quite possible to undertake genre analysis, not primarily for the purpose of understanding preliterary settings and functions of such typical language, but in order to comprehend structural features of the text *as it presently stands before us.*

Now we must ask whether theologically oriented exegesis ought to have a higher level of interest in diachronic matters than the purposes indicated in the preceding paragraph. This question is of particular relevance because rhetorical criticism exhibits little methodological concern for the process of the growth of a text. If one takes seriously the concern of scholars such as Brevard Childs that the canon should be the primary context for exegesis in the church, might that not suggest that our goal ought properly to be the interpretation of the final and canonical form of the text? Might not the prevailing interest of biblical research in the history of the literature prior to its canonical shape take on lesser significance?

Without doubt the canon should be the primary context for interpretation in the church, for it is the canon which the church confesses as sacred scripture (Childs: 99). Thus the structure and message of the text in its completed, canonical form should have the highest priority. This need not mean, however, that earlier contexts in which pericopae were used are theologically irrelevant (see Childs: 103, 107–8). Indeed, the canon itself prompts us to study such precanonical usages, for the canon bears witness to the fact that God has spoken to Israel throughout the various periods of her history. In this way, then, the canon legitimizes a concern for the ways in which the divine word was spoken and received in precanonical stages in the use and development of the text. Therefore, the theologically oriented exegete has yet another reason for supplementing rhetorical criticism with diachronic methods such as form criticism, tradition history, and redaction history. These historical methods should be kept in perspective, however, for ultimately precanonical meanings and usages should be secondary to the text in its canonical form.

Muilenburg's work prompts us also to inquire afresh whether it is critically important for theologically oriented exegetes to emphasize questions about *Sitz im Leben.* To begin with, a survey of form-critical studies would show how tenuous the reconstructions of *Sitz im Leben* often are. Sound exegesis surely ought not to rely heavily on speculative reconstructions of settings in which certain units of tradition were used. Muilenburg's emphasis on the *text* has indeed a certain appeal when one cannot describe with confidence the life situation outside the text in which that passage was used. Moreover, the common understanding of *Sitz im Leben* is somewhat oversimplified, as Douglas A. Knight has shown /9/. The setting (or context or matrix /10/) for a unit of linguistic expression is not necessarily limited to a sociological context. For example, a passage may have a literary setting rather than a clear societal context. Or the generating context may be the prevailing cultural ideology of a certain period or group rather than a particular social institution. Knight's demonstration that a whole variety of matrices are to be considered means that traditional concepts of *Sitz im Leben* in form criticism must be reevaluated.

A comprehensive discussion of setting or context lies beyond the scope of this essay. Two brief statements must suffice: (1) The incarnational emphasis of the Christian faith prompts us to pay attention to the human contexts in which the biblical traditions were employed. Indeed, the Bible again and again bears witness to God's activity in the specific circumstances in which human beings live in the world. We must therefore guard against the tendency in rhetorical criticism to pay insufficient attention to this matter. (2) Because the contexts or settings in which biblical traditions arose were not only sociological contexts, we must be open, as Knight bids us to be, to consider a variety of contexts, not the least important of which is a *literary* context. At this point rhetorical criticism has had insights to which form critics have sometimes been oblivious. Yet literary contexts need to be examined according to their *kinds*. Genre analysis and redaction criticism deal with certain questions about the nature of literature in ways which are unknown to rhetorical criticism.

The Well Narration in Genesis 24

For a brief illustration of the methodological issues raised above, I have chosen the story of the journey of Abraham's servant to procure a wife for Isaac (Genesis 24), with primary attention to the scene at the well.

A.   We begin, as indicated by the procedure set forth, with the structure of the particular text which lies before us. A few observations must take the place of a comprehensive analysis of structure. Genesis 24, in contrast with the majority of the Abraham narratives /11/, is involved and complex. It is characterized by lengthy speeches, and there is a great deal of repetition: vv 1-9/34-41; vv 10-27/42-48. In comparison with most other narratives there is considerable interest in details, e.g., the number of camels (v 10) or the nature of the jewelry which is given to the girl (vv 22, 47, 53). Moreover, the narrator's descriptions are extended and detailed (e.g., vv 11, 15, 16, 20). The uncharacteristic complexity of the narrative can be seen in the interweaving of several motifs, such as the oath, the question of the girl's willingness to leave her homeland, the asking and receiving of a sign, and the elaborate display of the servant's piety and loyalty.

The scene at the well is an integral part of the story of Genesis 24. The occurrences at the well and the servant's later narration of these constitute a large part of that chapter. Furthermore, the sign associated with the servant's prayer (vv 13-14) is an important prerequisite for the entire narrative. In addition, the servant's bowing before Yahweh at the well (v 26) is consistent with his activity elsewhere in the story (v 52).

B.   It is important to recognize that when the narrator of Genesis 24 had the servant meet Rebekah at the well, he employed a narrative pattern which was already familiar to his audience (cf. Gen 29:1-14; Exod 2:15-22). Our intention is to discover what the narrator of Genesis 24 has done with this familiar storytelling convention.

To achieve this goal we must first recover the features of the conventional narrative pattern. These include the following elements (Gunkel, 1910:324-27; Culley, 1976:42-43): (1) The hero (or servant) arrives in a foreign land. (2) He reaches a well. (3) Shepherds play a role at the well (in Gen 29:1-14 and Exod 2:15-22 only). (4) A girl (or more than one) appears at the well. (5) The man does something for the girl. (6) The girl returns to her home and narrates what has transpired. (7) The father (brother) of the girl sees to it that the man is brought to the house of the father (brother). (8) The girl marries the man (or the person on whose behalf the man has come).

The similarities between Gen 29:1-14 and Exod 2:15-22 are particularly apparent (Culley: 43). The main character has fled to the foreign land, and his behavior at the well is heroic. Moreover, in both Gen 29:1-14 and Exod 2:15-22 shepherds are involved in the narrative, although their role is different in each account. Gen 29:1-14 and Exod 2:15-22 are similar also in that each of these narratives is a bridge between two originally independent blocks of tradition (Gunkel, 1901:81; Noth, 1972:221), while the well narration in Genesis 24 is tightly integrated into the chapter as a whole.

There are, however, correspondences between Genesis 24 and Gen 29:1–14 which are not shared by Exod 2:15–22 (Culley: 43). In the two Genesis narratives the foreign land is the original home of the man who marries the girl. Indeed, the girl is a relative—the daughter or sister of Laban. Also, in both these texts Laban comes out to meet the stranger (compare the activity of the father in Exod 2:15–22).

Is the well narrative in Genesis 24 simply an additional example of the genre found in Gen 29:1–14 and Exod 2:15–22? In my judgment Genesis 24 does not reflect an independent usage of the conventional narrative pattern. Whereas Gen 29:1–14 and Exod 2:15–22 appear to employ the same genre without dependence of one text upon the other, Genesis 24 seems to be dependent upon the Jacob traditions. The well narrative in Genesis 24, unlike Gen 29: 1–14 and Exod 2:15–22, is not a narrative bridge to connect already-formed blocks of tradition with geographically distinct settings. The journey in Genesis 24 is prompted rather by the need to show that Isaac, like Jacob, did not marry a Canaanite woman.

Two arguments support the view that the well narrative in Genesis 24 is a later modification of an earlier narrative pattern: (1) Genesis 24 does not have the motif of the heroic deed to impress the pretty girl (Gen 29:10; Exod 2:17). To be sure, recent research indicates that narrative genres readily allow for considerable variety (see Culley: 1–32, for a summary of several important studies). Still, the absence of the folk motif of the heroic deed suggests the likelihood that Genesis 24 comes out of a different kind of consciousness and thus reflects a recasting of a more primitive type of narrative art. (2) The more complex and developed style of Genesis 24 (see above; also Gunkel, 1901:82–87) indicates that we are dealing with a *Geistesbeschäftigung* which is somewhat removed from that of Gen 29:1–14 and Exod 2:15–22.

The author of Genesis 24, then, has used a conventional type of narrative but has remolded it considerably for his own particular purposes. In particular, his intent was to model the origin of Isaac's wife after that of Jacob so that no patriarch would have a Canaanite wife. Moreover, a theology of Yahweh's providential activity (vv 7, 40) is worked out in the way in which the events show the servant the young woman whom Yahweh has chosen.

C. The most obvious setting or context for which the well narrative in Genesis 24 was designed is a *literary* context. These verses were never used independently in an oral setting but were designed specifically for the narrative of chapter 24 as a whole and, beyond that, to give to the Abraham, Isaac, and Jacob traditions a literary and theological unity with regard to the non-Canaanite purity of "the great and mighty nation" promised to Abraham. Indeed, the context in which Genesis 24 arose is one in which the process of canonization is well on its way. Though the present Book of Genesis was not completed until centuries later, Genesis 24 was created in circles whose aim was to provide a full and normative literature for the Israelite community, taking into account the particular traditions of various segments of the community and providing a full and systematic order for those traditions. This "canonizing" context represents a distinctive period of Israel's life in which God's activity among his people was understood and expressed in a particular way and in a particular literary form.

Conclusion

This essay has affirmed Muilenburg's emphasis of taking seriously the particular features of a biblical text; indeed, exegesis should begin by analyzing particular structural patterns of individual texts. As a next step, however, careful genre analysis may be undertaken to a degree not envisioned by Muilenburg. Moreover, the synchronic emphasis of rhetorical criticism should be supplemented by diachronic concerns. Finally, the theological value of exploring the context(s) in which the text was used requires questions which go beyond the methodology of rhetorical criticism and reflects the canon's concern for the history of God with his people in particular events and social settings.

Notes

/1/   Muilenburg understandably neglected form criticism in his Deutero-Isaiah commentary (1956:384–92) because he did not believe that the prophet was tied to traditional *Gattungen*. Why Muilenburg virtually ignored form criticism in the application of his method in "Form Criticism and Beyond" is not quite so clear.

/2/   Muilenburg indicated that laws, wisdom utterances, and psalms are generally more conventional in form than certain other types of literature, notably prophetic books (1969:5).

/3/   See, however, scholars such as Tucker (1–21) and Knierim (458–66) for newer approaches to form criticism which differ in some respects from earlier form criticism.

/4/   An especially good example of a rhetorical critic who deals with only the final form of the text is J. Ackerman (see Gros Louis *et al.*: 74–119).

/5/   Although Muilenburg speaks of a number of "poems" in the composition of Deutero-Isaiah, the juxtaposition of these "poems" shows "continuity of the prophet's thought" (1956:385). Thus Muilenburg deals with the juxtaposition of the poems on a synchronic rather than a diachronic level.

/6/   See Melugin: 301,311.

/7/   We begin with the particular, not because the particular is more basic in human language than general patterns of expression, but rather because our knowledge of general patterns in a culture is dependent upon a comparison of many particular texts.

/8/   Muilenburg's use of rhetorical criticism is geared toward artistically formed texts. Many individual texts, however, were not structured with aesthetic purposes in mind. Study of linguistic patterns which give structure to a text should therefore not be limited to artistic uses of language.

/9/   Knight: 105–9. Knight's article contains a useful discussion of recent scholarly writings on the subject.

/10/   Knight prefers the term "matrix" over "setting" or *Sitz im Leben*. "Matrix," however, has a jargonistic ring, so that I would suggest "context" instead.

/11/   For a discussion of the briefer and less complex narratives in Genesis, see Gunkel, 1901: 37–78.

Part III

Structure and History:
Linguistic and Literary Studies

Introduction

Martin J. Buss

History and structure can be treated as balancing each other, so that neither is primary. Such an approach is highly appropriate for a study of language and literature, as the contributions of Wolfgang Roth and John Gammie show. Roth puts emphasis especially on a linguistic model, following Ricoeur. Gammie's method is primarily literary. The linguistic and literary paths, however, cannot be sharply distinguished from each other.

Roth's discussion takes for granted the documentary analysis previously carried out within the field and shows how source division adds to the perception of richness of patterns. It is true that such a procedure is somewhat hypothetical, but it is based on the insight that structural analysis is not limited to redaction criticism. Indeed, a good reason for source criticism, besides the recovery of history, is to increase an appreciation of form.

Roth does not make a sharp break between nature and history; on the contrary, he compares linguistic with other structures. His central thesis is well summarized in this sentence: "The word is not only the place where system and event encounter each other, where structure and genesis meet, but also and basically the place where self-disclosure of being is fixed into the enclosure of the word responding to it" (p. 113). He is confident that the word contains a revelation of being, which can reach hearers at different times and places through fresh actualization. The text, then, invites the reader to participate in its creative possibilities.

Gammie similarly seeks to combine a number of procedures. His essay pursues the arrangement and internal relations of Genesis 25–36, together with a synchronic survey of motifs. In addition, it deals with the history of the text and with its function in social situations. The analysis pays attention to humor, including ironic reversal, and to the evocative power of language. On the basis of these observations, conclusions are drawn about what is said theologically by the text.

The theological perspective delineated by Gammie is not a purely theoretical one. Rather, it is closely tied to the way in which the texts operate in human life. Since many individual and group conflicts of the present are similar to those of the past, indications of how to deal with them can be found in the tradition. Gammie finds in the Genesis stories a worthy model for self-transcendence and reconciliation.

Chapter 6

The Text Is the Medium
An Interpretation of the Jacob Stories in Genesis

Wolfgang M. W. Roth
Garrett-Evangelical Theological Seminary/
Northwestern University

The plurality of our exegetical methods leads to fragmentation. Many an insight goes abegging for want of integration. This is why reasoned syntheses of interpretive approaches are welcome. In 1971 Paul Ricoeur proposed such an integration by relating three levels of interpretation to each other: (1) structural linguistics, in which he approaches language through the study of its forms; (2) a phenomenology of speech, in which he studies the use of language in its intention to say something about something; and (3) an ontology of discourse, in which language is approached as a mode of being (1971:304).

In this paper I apply Ricoeur's methodological synthesis to an interpretation of the Jacob tradition of Genesis.

The Text as Frozen Language

For the first level, that of structural analysis, Ricoeur outlines four methodological factors: (a) to distinguish between "language," a social institution in which one has competence (*langue*), and "speech," an individual utterance (*parole*); (b) to distinguish between the text as a system in its own right, comparable to the state of a chess game at a given moment (a synchronic approach), and its changes and developments (a diachronic approach); (c) to interpret the constituent words and phrases in their mutuality and interdependence, by which they constitute themselves in relation to, or differentiation from, the other constituents, forming the "structure" of a system; and (d) to recognize that a language system as such (*langue*) has no external relations, that is, neither source nor addressee nor referential content; Ricoeur here notes that structuralist analysis is not concerned with the text as "saying something about something" (307).

The Jacob stories, as contained in the Bible, mention neither their originators nor their addressees; they are monological. They do not expressly set forth an appeal, a message, as a prophetic word or a literary collection of prophetic words does. With reference to the Jacob and Abraham stories, Gerhard von Rad noted: "In most of the patriarchal stories—to a certain extent in the Abraham stories and altogether in the Jacob stories!—the reader feels left by the narrator without direction. He would urgently like to know what was good and right, what bad and evil in what the actors did or failed to do. But the narrator remains 'silent'" (1970:13, author's translation).

These narratives were of course not conceived in a vacuum or designed to exist without relationships. Yet, whatever these relations were, they cannot simply be surmised and directly introduced into the interpretation by the exegete. He must first of all reflect on the monological character of the writing and take its scripturality seriously. Monological narratives do not call for any response in particular. Their existence in written form gives (limited) permanence to that which they set forth, and their scripturality makes them approachable from various perspectives. However, this does not imply that one must view such a text without internal differentiation. Thus, rather than approach the Jacob tradition of Gen 27–35 (parts of Gen 27—Exod 1,P) as it stands, I propose to begin with the hypothetical historical layers of the text, that is, of the Priestly, Elohistic, and Yahwistic strata. A similar procedure is adopted by Casalis (see above, p. 51, and Detweiler: 128–30). The course of our exegesis will then lead to the interaction of these layers within the Jacob tradition and come to a climax in the analysis of the Jacob tradition as an integral whole, in which all constituents are interdependent.

The Priestly Jacob story can serve as the first example. Its Jacob is the one whose name is changed to "Israel" by the very God who had changed Abram's name to Abraham (Gen 35:10; 17:4–5). That Jacob is also the one to whom God reintroduces himself as El Shaddai, as he had first introduced himself to Abram under that new name. The promises of numerous descendants and of the possession of the land, given to Abraham as part and parcel of the Abrahamic covenant, are renewed (Gen 35:11–12; 17:1–2, 8). The divine speech, the central section of P's Jacob tradition (35:9–13), is summarily introduced as appearance and blessing: "God there [at Bethel] appeared to Jacob . . . and blessed him" (35:9).

The structure of the Priestly Jacob story has been analyzed recently by Peter Weimar. It is a three-part symmetrical compositon. Part II is the center. Part I and III are the frames, corresponding to each other. Each frame is divided into two sections; each of these four sections begins with the "toledot" formula ("These are the generations of") as structuring signal. The opening frame deals with the descendants of the two sons of Abraham in the order of their birth (I/1, Ishmael: 25:12–17; I/2, Isaac: 25:19, 20. . . . 26b; 26:34–35; 27:46–28:9) and the closing frame with the descendants of the two sons of Isaac in the order of their birth (III/1, Esau: 36:1a–37:1 in part; III/2, Jacob: P texts in Gen 37:2–Exod 1:7).

Part II is centered on the appearance of El Shaddai to Jacob at Bethel with a blessing. Two divine words reinterpret the Yahwistic change of name tradition (compare 35:10, P, with 32:23–33, J) and the promise of land and descendants (compare 35:11, P, with 28:13–14, J). Jacob's renaming of Luz as Bethel (35:15, P) and the listing of his twelve sons (35:22b–26, P) demonstrate the (preliminary) fulfillment of both promises. This core of P's Jacob story (II/2) is surrounded by II/1, Jacob's wandering toward the place of revelation (31:. . . 18aβb; 33:18a), and by II/3, his move from there onwards (35:27–29). It is prepared in 28:1–4, P, and recalled in 48:3–6, P, both referring to the blessing given to Jacob yet put (only) into the mouth of humans (Isaac/Jacob).

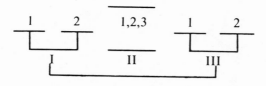

Figure A   P's Jacob Story (Weimar)

The Yahwistic Jacob story is a system within the Yahwist's etiology of Davidic-Solomonic Israel. On the surface it is less structured than P's Jacob story. While P *centered* the Jacob story in the divine appearance and blessing, condensed into brief divine statements (Gen 35:10, 11–12), J structured the Jacob story as *two arches*, more exactly, as one arch (the Jacob-Laban series) set within another (the Jacob-Esau series). The rivalry of the unborn twins Esau and Jacob (25:21–26a) is the tension which sets the narrative series Jacob-Esau (the first or outer arch) in motion toward its eventual solution (32:29: ". . . and with men . . . "; cf. 32:4–14a; 33:1–3, 6–7, 12–17). Jacob's encounter with Laban (especially 29:15) is the tension which sets the Jacob-Laban narrative series (the second or inner arch) in motion toward its solution (32:1–2a). The potential threat to Jacob coming from the first-born brother Esau and from the maternal uncle Laban are overcome in settlements which assure life to Jacob through the possession of Canaan and through numerous descendants.

The two arches, however, do not exhaustively diagram the Yahwistic Jacob story. Where they touch each other, Jacob's encounters with the divine intervene: this occurs first at Bethel, after the Jacob-Esau tension had become so unbearable that Jacob had to flee and before Jacob reaches Laban (28:13–15). It occurs a second time at Penuel, on Jacob's return journey after the Jacob-Laban tension had been settled and before the crucial meeting with Esau was to take place (32:23–33). The divine words addressed to Jacob interpret what happens to him by pointing beyond the beginning and end of the Jacob cycle itself. What happens to Jacob is the manifestation of the will of the God of Abraham and of Isaac (28:13–15) who now blesses also Jacob and bares his future name "Israel,"

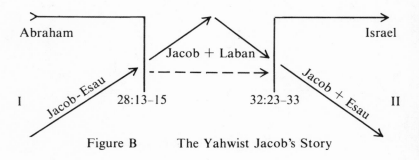

Figure B   The Yahwist Jacob's Story

but who withholds the secret of his own name (32:23–33). The two divine-human encounters open the otherwise closed structure of the Yahwistic Jacob story toward past and future. More, they introduce into the Jacob story itself a dialectic that pits Jacob against both men and God (32:28!).

The fragmentary character of the Elohistic Jacob story does not permit a structural analysis (for this and the following, cf. Wolff). However, there are two units where the Elohistic component is dominant, both revolving around Bethel: 28:10–22 (E: 11b–12, 17–18, 20–22) and 35:1–8 (only v 6 is not Elohistic). The Elohistic Jacob interprets his relationship to the sacred place in direct speeches: first, his exclamation which affirms Bethel as fear-inspiring and hence as a unique place of divine presence (28:17); secondly, his vow which focuses only on his safe return and the ensuing recognition of Bethel as "house of God," to be supplied by Jacob with his tithe (28:20–22); and thirdly, his demand that his clan strip themselves at Shechem of foreign gods in preparation for the pilgrimage to Bethel (35:2b–3), where he fulfilled his earlier vow.

The initial narrative tension created by the vision (28:11b–12) is brought to a solution in the erection of an altar after the conditions of the vow had been fulfilled (35:7). The narrative is quite complete; while it presupposes Jacob's flight and return, it almost ignores them and their circumstances in that merely the character of Jacob's response to them in relation to Bethel is in focus. The story is self-sufficient in its relative closedness and completeness. It is like a link of a chain; each link is comparable to the others in that it stands for a divine address and a human response, mediated in space and time.

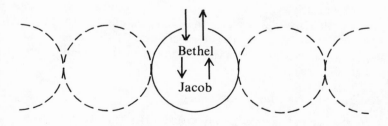

Figure C   Jacob Story of E

In each system certain linguistic features invite consideration. Ricoeur (1971: 308–9) notes that a word is what it is in a given period "paradigmatically"; that is, a word selected to be part of a given text was chosen from a group of possible words that might have served that function. This selection is comparable to our selection of a fitting word from those listed in an entry of Roget's *Thesaurus* or from among the stock of words stored in our personal vocabulary. Normally there exists only *one* word that will express precisely our intention. Thus in P's Jacob story the syntactical subject is principally the deity, in E's account it is the human being involved, while in J both subjects are dialectically related to each other. Similarly, the key verbs are profiled paradigmatically: P selects "to bless" and "to appear" from their closer or more remote synonyms, E chooses the verb "to fear," while J has a wider range.

Another feature of structural analysis must be mentioned. Linguistic structures correspond to other structures, those observed in nature (animals, plants) or those of social organization. Ricoeur points out that "linguistic structures stand in a certain relationship of homology with all the other structures and it is in this play of structures that language can operate" (309). In the Jacob stories the relatively self-sufficient and literarily closed structures of E and P suggest homology between them and the circles who shaped, received, and transmitted them. These may well have been marked by well-ordered social structure, a systematically reasoned theology and relatively closed, if not narrow, horizons. J contrasts with this in more than one way. On the other hand the homology is not iron-clad; Ricoeur's use of the word "play" to characterize this relationship is noteworthy. After all, a text can come into being either as a reinforcement of or as a challenge to its group.

Each narrative is comparable to a photograph fixing on film an image both in its totality and with its interrelating constituents. So it now "is"; as such it meets the observer's eye. On this level it is a little linguistic universe in its own right; in this sense the narrative as text is "frozen language."

The Text as Interplay of Language

In the second section of his article (310–15), Ricoeur seeks to develop a "phenomenology of speaking." Here he is concerned with the relation between language form (French: *langue*, a mute system of signs) and speech (French: *parole*, language-becoming-event). The word "happens" in a fleeting, yet decisive moment. It is expression, communication, and signification; somebody says something about something to somebody else. Ricoeur gives primacy to reference or signification, that is, to the ability "to represent reality through signs and to understand signs as representing reality" (311). Through the speaker-initiated combination of signs into discourse the speaker directs himself toward an aspect of reality, addresses himself to somebody, and manifests his intention.

A phenomenology of speaking is thus a description of the transition of a system of signs into the event of speech. Each transition enriches the word used, returns it to the language from which it was taken, and so gives it a temporal dimension. Here appears the problem which linguistic structuralism has not solved—the relation of the synchronically perceived system to the diachronically analyzed history of systems. We shall return to Ricoeur's phenomenology of speaking after a discussion of the contextualizations of the Jacob tradition and their relation to each other.

The text of the Jacob tradition as it now stands comprises Gen 25:19-Exod 1:7 (cf. Weimar's analysis of P, reviewed above). Literary criticism suggests that the complexity of the text is due to the merging of three originally separate Jacob stories. The circles who were responsible for the Priestly Cult History (P) were probably also those who gave final form to the Pentateuch (Tetrateuch); in other words, P =R ^{PJED} . The nature of the relation of the Elohistic and the Yahwistic Jacob stories to each other and, possibly, to a common source (Noth's G) is a matter of debate. Other contextualizations of the Jacob tradition are not our concern here (cf. Hos 12:3-7, Sir 44:23, Wis 10:9-12, *Jub.* 19:22-45, also Deut 26:5b and 1 Chron 2:1-2).

It is often assumed that these contextualizations succeeded each other and that the second one (E) is a reinterpretation of the first (J), just as the third (P) reinterprets both its predecessors. The internal coherence of each (allowance being made for redactors' exclusions, especially in the case of E) argues against the thesis that they are primarily reinterpretations of earlier contextualizations.

It is likely that the Jacob tradition was transmitted in different, to a certain extent contemporaneous, groups within ancient Israel. *How* the tradition of one group became part of the tradition of another group was determined by upheavals in Israel's history and their effects on the various groups. For instance, certain priestly circles survived the exile as an institutionally based group because they became the priesthood of the Second Temple. As such they were the guardians of sacred traditions. They became the final shapers of the Pentateuch (Tetrateuch) because they were the ones who placed the Elohistic-Deuteronomic tradition (E, D) and the more court-oriented Jerusalem tradition (J) within their comprehensive "priestly" perspective.

It is telling that the priestly circles received and incorporated the Jacob tradition at all. (For the Chronicler, by way of contrast, this tradition has become nothing more than an element in a genealogical list.) For P the earlier Jacob traditions became "word" (*parole*). According to Ricoeur, theology is more interested in speech (*parole*) than in a language system (*langue*), for in the former the existence of the interpreters is expressed. This is a shared interpretation, so that the church becomes a "community of interpretation" (313).

How does the Priestly contextualization relate to the inherited Jacob tradition? Two overriding concerns are evident: (1) the focusing of the decisive happenings—the name change of Jacob to Israel and the renewal of the promise by El Shaddai—into a narrative minimum and a theological maximum (Gen 35:9–13). As a narrative minimum a framework is maintained, almost bare with reference to human action and describing divine action abstractly and summarily. For a theological maximum P employs the notion of blessing (root: *brk*) to bracket and theologize the tradition. P concretizes this notion in a reformulation of Gen 32:29a (J) and of 28:13–14 (J) as nondialogical divine announcements. (2) The schematization of the people's continuity in its formative period through sequences of binary histories: Ishmael's is contrasted with the following story of the younger line which was to continue into blessing, that of Isaac (Gen 25:19, etc., P). Similarly Esau's and Jacob's "toledot" are set side by side in Part III in P's Jacob story (portions of Gen 36:1–Exod 1:7).

The inherited Jacob tradition was passed on by the priestly editors within the context of their own Jacob interpretation, relatively intact—at least as far as J is concerned. What the redactor presents is a dialectic of the two Jacob contextualizations, each with its internal coherence. To be sure, the two traditions have to be seen diachronically in relation to each other, as predecessor and successor, as tradition and interpretation, as text and sermon, if you will. Yet no inherited text is exhausted by any or all of its expositions, no tradition is once for all unfolded by its exegeses.

The Priestly Jacob interpretaton is only one of the ways in which the Jacob tradition became actualized. It is different, for instance, from 1 Chron 2:1–2. The juxtaposition of two contextualizations creates a dialogical relation between them. They are related to each other yet also stand in their own right. They surface the Jacob tradition in different perspectives and so create new features of that tradition. They may diverge from each other and move on different planes. They may relate to each other by having in common merely the name of central figures, places or seasons. Their relationships mirror the range of relationships of the groups which stand behind the stories; these are indirect relationships, to be sure, when the communities are not contemporary or not in historical continuity with each other.

The harmonization of diverging features of the three Jacob stories into a composite picture does as little justice to them as do Gospel harmonies to the Gospels—an issue which the early church faced (cf. Tatian's *Diatessaron*). The catholicity of the forces that moved toward canonization of the OT did not allow the elimination of earlier or minority contextualizations. It favored their inclusion into the merging body of normative scripture, without sectarian claims.

To illustrate: The Priestly Jacob who is the silent and passive recipient of divine decrees stands in tension with the Yahwistic Jacob who is the verbal and active shaper of his life. The Elohistic Jacob who anxiously tests God's presence at Bethel through a vow based on a condition to be met by God, is not the Yahwistic Jacob for whom the LORD's revelatory words are but confirmation of the divine presence with him in spite of (or because of?) his own highly goal-oriented actions. The Priestly Jacob is put into the legitimizing continuity of a comprehensive divinely-ordained history, while the Elohistic Jacob seems to be centered in Jacob's personal responses.

The temporal-spatial-psychological horizons of the three Jacob stories call for discussion. P's Jacob story is set within a temporal-linear, consecutive-concentric framework while J's Jacob story moves in the spatial-extensive, simultaneous-dialectic plane. P's Jacob is part of a temporal chain, J's patriarch the organizing element of a cluster of traditions. The Elohistic Jacob, on the other hand, is highly focused on the person of the patriarch; he constitutes himself through his response to the divine—a one-dimensional response at that! P is a time-table compiler, J an architect, and E a case history writer.

The dialectic of tradition and interpretation as well as the dialogic relationship between various contextualizations make the Genesis text of the Jacob tradition an interplay of languages. They relate diachronically and synchronically. Diachronically, a later or otherwise dependent contextualization is what it is both through its affirmation of, and its differentiation from, the earlier tradition. It seeks to bracket, expound, or absorb it, yet at the same time derives its claim to be heard from it. It attests that the past is alive in the present. Each contextualization also stands synchronically as a part of its own contemporary scene, forming one story among the many others which in fact or potentially exist. Its paradigm is defined in relation to other actual or possible stories. It employs words which are in themselves polysemic (capable of several meanings), but which in this linguistic structure are strongly restricted in their range of meaning.

It is at the intersection of the diachrony of tradition and interpretation with the synchrony of the actual contextualizations that meaning occurs. The words and phrases of earlier Jacob stories and contemporary linguistic usages supply the polysemic font on which the new contextualization draws. In Ricoeur's words: "If all our words are . . . polysemic, all our discourses are not" (1971: 314). He observes that a contextualization excludes all but one range of the meaning of words used and thus serves as a reinforcement of the intended sense. He points out that poetic language is organized in such a fashion that all the sense possibilities are consolidated, maintained, and preserved "in a sort of festival of sense." Only the contextual structure makes polysemy an ordered polysemy (*une polysémie reglée*). Ricoeur concludes with the observation that biblical theology rests "on word keys which incessantly are interpreted or reinterpreted with the resources of the cultural intelligence of the period," to form "the comprehension of existence in a particular community of interpretation" (314).

What is significant and constructive in this approach is the interaction of diachrony and synchrony. It frees the interpreter both from the compulsion of having to come up with *the* meaning of the text and from the paralyzing discovery that words by themselves may say anything and everything. It introduces the notion of an ordered polysemy and, with reference to poetic texts, of a "feast of sense." In this celebration of sense the present text of the Jacob stories in Genesis is an interplay of languages.

The Text as Invitation

Ricoeur is persuaded that neither the linguistic-structural nor the phenomenological-historical discussion is sufficient to exhaust language as the medium of a given text. Language has ontological roots in being itself. He probes this issue in the context of the third interpretive level of his essay (315–19).

Ricoeur moves into Heidegger's horizons by characterizing linguisticality as one of the fundamental characteristics of human "existence" (*Dasein*). The human being, who speaks, is the guardian of self-disclosing "being." Speaking occurs after the person has stood silently before the sense that manifests itself in language. To be silent (but not mute!) in the presence of sense signifies that "our primary relation to language is listening rather than speaking" (316).

While on the linguistic-structural interpretive level the word functions as a contrasting item within a system and on the phenomenological-historical level as a meaning-giving constituent of a larger unit, on the philosophical-ontological level the word reflects "the passing of speech which addresses us into speech which we express; it is the transition from saying to speaking" (316). That which manifests itself moves through the narrow, strangling passage of the human word which Ricoeur can strikingly describe as the "violent act of poet or thinker" (316).

Following Heidegger, he characterizes the happening of the word both as the human being's submission to the opening of being that occurs there and then and as the responsibility of the speaking person to "preserve," through the word, being in its openness. The word is not only the place where system and event encounter each other, where structure and genesis meet, but also and basically the place where self-disclosure of being is fixed into the enclosure of the word responding to it. Ricoeur concludes by observing that the human mastery of the word—this being laid hold of and laying hold of—brings us to the point where jointly are born the things that come into being and the speaking person who is ready for them. "When the word is born, things come into being as that which they are, and the human being stands erect" (317).

The word of Jacob was born several times in the communities of ancient Israel and early Judaism: apart from the three contextualizations in Genesis, the Deuteronomic preachers tersely point to it (Deut 26:5), Hosea unfolds it in an uncomfortable manner (Hos 12:3–7, 13–14), the Chronicler includes it in his genealogy with a minimum of words (1 Chron 2:1–2), as does Jesus ben Sira in his review of famous men (Sir 44:23). The Wisdom of Solomon and Jubilees, two intertestamental contextualizations, formulate the word of Jacob in the wide horizons of their perspectives (Wis 10:9–12; *Jub* 19: 22–45).

In varying degrees, each Jacob text was born in a "violent act of poet or thinker." Each had an impact positively or negatively, being accepted or rejected. The violent act of its creation gave it shape, applying force both to the generally accepted Jacob tradition and to the horizons of those addressed. The more jarring and shaking the clash of horizons, the more likely a negative response; the reception of many a prophetic word illustrates this. The bolder and more open-ended the juxtaposition of horizons, the more intriguing and freeing the impact; the feeling of overwhelming suspense called forth by the poetic word attests that. The more illuminating the interaction of horizons, the more is set in motion a quest for finding a stand and for understanding; the work of probing thinkers illustrates it. On the other hand, the more congruous the horizons, the less impact their meeting makes; the more conventional and expected the content, the more it is "the same old stuff."

It is the degree of that violent creativity which makes and marks poet, thinker, and theologian. Interpreters of texts find themselves invited by them to those acts of creative violence which brought those very texts into being, or rather, brought "being" into text. No texts— however old, hallowed or despised, no configuration or harmony of texts—can by themselves bring forth the text to be born. Furthermore, it is only after the lapse of time that the birth of a new text becomes evident to more than a few. It is authenticated when people under its impact constitute themselves through their response as a group for whom clarity of recognition has been attained for that time and in that place.

The Jacob traditions also are invitations to such actualizations here and now. Following Ricoeur, one may say that such contextualizations will mark the unveiledness of being (Greek: *aletheia*) as centered in steadfastness/truth (Hebrew: ʾ*emeth*; 1971: 318). The contextualizations of "Jacob" explore the temporal, spatial, communal, and individual horizons within which the human being finds itself held by a courage not its own. Usually the horizons of contextualizations are congruous with those of the hearer's expectations. Yet there are times and places where the creative violence of poet, thinker, or theologian "not only preserves real experiences but also anticipates unrealized possibilities, widens the limited range of social behavior by new wishes, demands, and goals, and thereby opens avenues for future experiences" (Jauss: 33).

Chapter 7

Theological Interpretation By Way of Literary and Tradition Analysis: Genesis 25–36

John G. Gammie
The University of Tulsa

It is the intent of the present essay to reflect on the theological significance both for the ancient writers and for contemporary persons of some of the central concerns and features of Genesis 25–36. By theological significance I mean (i) what these traditions say to both earlier and contemporary audiences of the way the divine is operative in human affairs and (ii) what overall philosophy (i.e., theology) they espouse or presuppose as worthy of adoption in theory and practice.

Responsible theological interpretation will, in my view, attempt to be sensitive to recent developments in the study of the patriarchs and in hermeneutics, to form criticism, to stylistics and, in so far as possible, to the sociological setting of the sacred traditions under scrutiny. Three approaches to literary analysis will be utilized in order to determine the main concerns and features of Genesis 25–36. They are motif analysis, analysis of structure or pattern of arrangement, and stylistic analysis. These all deal with the text as it stands in its present context in the Hebrew Bible and treat it synchronically. Some attention to the secular or theological import of the traditions in earlier stages of transmission is, further, requisite to appreciate fully the distinctive viewpoint of the ultimate authors of the text. As difficult and inevitably tentative as it is, diachronic analysis may furnish insight into the concerns and theology of successive transmitters. The present essay, accordingly, will pay

117

attention to tradition history before attempting to make some final theological observations in the light of the literary analyses.

Genesis 25–36 forms a complex lying between the Abraham traditions and the Joseph cycle. It focuses especially on Esau and Jacob and may with some justification be labeled the Esau-Jacob Cycle. This designation is not altogether satisfactory, however, for these chapters include the final portions of the Abraham cycle as well as traditions in which Isaac and Jacob's sons (other than Joseph) are the protagonists. The material, according to most modern critics, is comprised of the so-called Yahwistic and Elohistic strands, with only a modicum of material coming from the Priestly school. In the main, source criticism will not command attention in this essay.

A.   Motif Analysis: The Predominance of Strife

A number of commentators have observed the predominance of the motif of strife in the chapters under consideration. J. P. Fokkelman shows, for example, how the rivalry in Gen 25:27–34 deals with the *běkōrâ* ("birthright") and in Gen 27:1–46 with the *běrākâ* ("blessing") (Fokkelman: 86–112). Two further instances of strife develop before the Esau-Jacob strife is resolved: (i) The relationship between Jacob and his uncle (and father-in-law) at Haran becomes increasingly strained so that Jacob finally takes his leave without so much as a farewell (Gen 31:17–31). This contention ends in a pact or covenant between Laban and Jacob in Gilead (Gen 31:43–54). (ii) The relationship between Jacob's wives becomes increasingly strained as Leah is fruitful and Rachel barren. The tension between the two sisters is a clear variation on the rivalry between Esau and Jacob. The first-born (Leah/Esau) are not favored; the younger (Rachel/Jacob), though favored, must wait for the coming of the fruits (children/flocks) which the preferred status implies. The strife between the two sisters is nowhere explicitly resolved, but finds surcease in their joint agreement to leave their father (Gen 31:14–16).

Strife also finds expression in two passages (chaps. 26 and 34) which immediately precede and follow the Esau-Jacob rivalry. In chapter 26, Isaac and the Philistines contend over material resources (notably water, but presumably also pastures for grazing); friction develops, further, over Isaac's wife. In chapter 34, the contention is between Shechemites and the sons of Jacob; the chief source of inimical relations is the rape of Dinah. In the latter instance, Jacob becomes apprehensive about how his sons' reprisal against the Shechemites will have affected his social relations with the inhabitants of the land by making him odious among them (Gen 34:30). In chapter 26 a covenant (*běrît*) brings the contention to a conclusion (vv 26–30); in chapter 34 a covenant is deceitfully promised and not honored by the sons of Jacob (vv 8–25).

In sum, there can be little question that the dominant motif in Genesis 25–36 is the motif of strife.

Two fairly prominent sub-motifs which constitute an integral part of the strife motif are deceit and retribution. Instances of deception are these: Isaac of the Philistines (Gen 26:7); Rebekah / 1/ and Jacob of Isaac (Gen 27:5–45); Laban of Jacob (Gen 29:18–25; cf. also 31:41); Rachel of Laban (Gen 31:19–35); and the sons of Jacob of the Shechemites (chap. 34). The motif of retribution is implicit throughout the cycle. Some form of punishment falls upon the deceitful: Isaac, who deceives the Philistines, is in turn deceived (chap. 27); Rebekah, who is the chief instigator of the deception of Isaac, is deprived of her son's presence (Gen 27:43–45); Laban, who deceives Jacob in his promise of Rachel and in his agreement to terms of wages, is in turn deceived by his daughter and is the poorer for his deception of Jacob (Gen 31:9, 19–35); Rachel, who deceives her father as to her possession of his household gods—or because of her possession of them! —suffers an early death (Gen 35:16–20). (On the latter view, see especially Plaut: 312.) Jacob, after the deceit of his father, must undergo an exile of arduous labor (chaps. 29–31), is plagued with a limp (Gen 32:32 [Engl. 32:31]), and—to cite evidence from outside the cycle proper—is forced through famine to leave the promised land for Egypt (cf. Gen 43:1; 45:6; 46:26). Finally, the two chief instigators of the deception of the Shechemites, Simeon and Levi, are cursed to be scattered (Gen 49:5–7).

Other motifs related to the strife motif are a decline in status of the first-born (chaps. 27, 29–31); the giving of wages (*maśkōret*, *śākār*) (Gen 29:15; 30:28; 31:7; etc.); God's being moved to favor the one oppressed (29:31; 31:12, 42); and the bestowal of gifts (Gen 25:5–6; 32:4–22 [Engl. 3–21]; Gen 33:10–11) /2/.

Two motifs in chapters 25–36 indirectly related to that of strife are the motifs of theophany and the founding of shrines. Shrines include

Beersheba (26:23-25), Bethel (28:10-22), Penuel (32:23-33[Engl. 32:22-32]), Shechem (35:1-5), Bethel (35:6-7, 9-15: P). Theophanies without the erection of a shrine object also occur to Isaac (Gen 26:1-5) and to Jacob (Gen 32:2-3[Engl. 32:1-2.). How these motifs should be interpreted in relation to the strife motif will be considered in the next section.

Another fairly prominent motif is that of journeying, travel, or movement. Jacob finds it necessary to leave his parental home either in flight for fear of his brother (Gen 27:43-45: J) or in order to procure in Haran a wife (Gen 28:1-7: P). His stopping places, going and coming, are duly recorded; so are the length of his stay in Paddan-Aram (P's terminology) and his return as a man of wealth to Isaac at Mamre (Gen 35:27: P). Travels of Esau are also noted: his movement up from "the land of Seir, the country of Edom" to encounter Jacob in Transjordania (Gen 32:4-7[Engl. 3-6]) and his return to Seir (Gen 33:12-16) and migration to Edom when his possessions and cattle in the land of Canaan become too great to support both him and his brother Jacob. This motif alerts us to the presence here of a theology of the successful migrant as well as of one concerning the displaced migrant. The motif contributes also to the dynamism of the stories and plays an important role in the organizational arrangement of the entire cycle.

B. Analysis of Composition: Concentric Arrangement and Ironic Reversals

Westermann has noted that chapters 25-28 and 32-33 deal with the relation between the two brothers and that intermediary between these chapters has been placed the Jacob-Laban episode (1964:75). In his study on the Jacob cycle, J. P. Fokkelman observes that the genealogies form an outer frame to the cycle. Fokkelman goes on to note that the placement of chapters 26 and 34 within the cycle constitute a "second frame of reference" (239-240). M. Fishbane observed, even more extensively, a mirror-like arrangement throughout the Jacob cycle (Gen 25:19-35:22). Independently of the above-mentioned authors, I reached a similar conclusion, *viz.*, that the material in Genesis 25-36 has been consciously arranged in a concentric or chiastic pattern. The increasing awareness of such a pattern of arrangement by a number of persons laboring relatively independently strongly suggests that the pattern was consciously chosen by one of the biblical compilers-editors and therefore is of significance for interpreting the texts.

The pattern may be expressed topically as follows:

A. Genealogy of Abraham-Keturah (peoples of "land of the East") (Gen 25:1–11), with mention of Abraham's sending sons of concubines eastward, away from Isaac (Gen 25:5–6)

B. Death of Abraham / Burial by two sons (Isaac & Ishmael) / Genealogy and death of Ishmael / Birth and youth of Esau & Jacob (Gen 25:12–34)

C. Regional strife (in southern Israel): Isaac vs. the Philistines / Honorable covenant (Chap. 26)

D. Beginnings of fraternal strife in Cis-Jordan (Jacob vs. Esau: settler-farmer vs. hunter) / Isaac blesses Jacob not Esau (Chap. 27)

E. Departure of Jacob alone to northeast with theophany enroute at Bethel (Chap. 28)

F. Arrival alone at the northeast (Haran in Upper Mesopotamia) / Marriage to Leah & Rachel / Acquisition and naming of sons by Leah / Commencement of strife with Laban (Chap. 29)

G. Acquisition and naming of sons by handmaidens and of first son (Joseph) by Rachel (Gen 30:1–24)

G' Preparation to leave the northeast / Acquisition of herds (Gen 30:25–43)

F' Departure from the northeast with flocks, progeny, and two wives / Conclusion of strife with Laban in a covenant in Gilead (Gen 31:1–32:3[Engl. 32:2])

E' Return from the northeast with theophany enroute at Penuel / Change of name to Israel (Gen 32:4–33[Engl. 3–32])

     D'   Conclusion of fraternal strife in Transjordania
          (Jacob vs. Esau: herder vs. herder) / Jacob blesses
          Esau (Gen 33:1–17)
     C'   Regional strife (in northern Israel): Jacob's sons vs.
          Shechemites / Deceitful covenant / Putting away of
          foreign gods (Gen 33:18–35:5)
     —   Theophany at Bethel / Change of name to Israel (Gen
          35:6–7, 9–15)—combines parts of E and E'
   B' Birth of second son by Rachel (Benjamin) / Death of
      Rachel / Genealogy of Israel / Death of Isaac/Burial by
      two sons (Esau & Jacob) (Gen 35:8, 16–29)
A' Genealogy of Esau and Seir the Horite / Rulers in the "Land of
    Edom" (Chap. 36)—includes mention of Esau's movement from
    Canaan to Seir (Gen 36:6–9)

The following observations may be made on this pattern of arrangement.

1. The material in Genesis 25–36 is so arranged that seven major segments of material from Gen 25:1–30:24 have counterparts in Gen 30:25–36:43 in reverse order. The chiasm is not perfect, however; in the second half, Gen 35:6–7, 9–15 (P) stands without a structural parallel in the first part. As noted above, the full chiastic pattern includes the final portions (Gen 25:1–18) commonly assigned to the Abraham cycle.

2. Where the *dramatis personae*, or human subjects, differ in the corresponding segments in the second half, similarity is to be found in the genre and in the kinds of data recorded (A–A': both segments contain genealogies and reports of migrations of peoples whose ancestry is traced in the same section; B–B': both contain genealogies and reports of births, deaths, and burials; C–C': both record conflict with neighbors involving a real or putative sister, a covenant, and the strained reception of Israelites in the land).

3. Where the *dramatis personae* include the same two main characters in corresponding segments of both halves, the action in the corresponding segment of the second half usually brings to a clear resolution a strife or tension which commenced in the first (D–D': between Esau and Jacob; F–F': between Jacob and Laban; less clearly, G–G': between Leah and Rachel).

4. Where the segments in the first half of the pattern record a

movement of the leading character of the cycle away from the home of his parents, the corresponding segments in the second half record his movements back toward that home (E, F: going; F', E': returning).

5. The central four segments deal with the main character's acquisitions during his period of sojourn: of progeny (F–G), and of herds (G'–F'). The turning point in the cycle is reached when the main character has borne, by his most highly favored wife, a son (Gen 30:24: Joseph is born of Rachel). Immediately upon the birth of this son, the main character requests permission to return to his homeland (Gen 30:25).

6. What transpires in the central four segments allows a contrast to be drawn between the status of the main character who in the first half, at his departure, is alone and without wealth or progeny (E), but in the second half, at his return, is possessed with an abundance of both (E').

7. Theophanies, for the main character, Jacob, occur at critical moments in corresponding segments of both halves. (E: prior to the opportune sojourn; E': prior to meeting with his estranged brother).

The various segments in the cycle have been assembled with such a demonstrable artistry that sound interpretation not only permits but requires viewing the segments as integrally related parts of a continuous whole. As the parts are viewed in the context of the whole, meanings emerge which would not have inhered in them separately. A few examples will suffice to show this.

That the theophanies occur when the protagonist is enroute suggests that the compiler adheres not to a theology of place but rather to a theology of divine manifestation at the place of his choosing. (For the former, a theology of place, see the separate segment, Gen 35:6–7, 9–15: P) /3/.

Fokkelman has convincingly shown how the divine sending of messengers at "Two camps" (Mahanaim) (Gen 32:2–3 [Engl. 1–2]) may be taken as prompting Jacob with the idea of sending messengers on ahead to Esau and of dividing his party (for protection) into two camps (199–202). A similar kind of meaning emerges in the theophany at Penuel (Gen 32:23–33[Engl. 32:22–32]). The man (ʾîš) with whom Jacob wrestles (Gen 32:25 [Engl. 32:24]) may at an earlier stage have been a river (or a nocturnal) demon, but the man uppermost in Jacob's mind, when one looks at the continuous narrative, is clearly Esau. In its context the man with whom Jacob wrestles, whatever his identity, furnishes Jacob with an idea which he puts into practice when daybreak comes, *viz.*, that just as he refused to let the man go until he blessed him, so does he come to realize that Esau will not let him go until he blesses him. Note the change in Jacob's attitude. Plenteous gifts were already sent on to Esau before Penuel; the motivation appears to be fear (Gen 32:8, 14–22 [Engl. 7, 13–21]). After Penuel, Jacob presses Esau to accept them not as a sign of his anxiety but of his gratitude and blessing: "Take, I pray thee, my blessing (*birkātî*) which has been brought to you, for God has had favor on me and because I have plenty. And he urged him; and he (Esau) accepted" (Gen 33:11).

The afore-mentioned passage, as several commentators have observed, contains an element of ironic reversal. Jacob, who is told when blessed by Isaac that his mother's sons will bow down to him (D: Gen 27:29), ends up bowing down to his brother and giving him a blessing (D': Gen 33:3, 11). Less well noted is the ironic reversal which takes place in connection with Isaac's blessing of Esau: Esau is told that he will live by the sword (D: Gen 27:40), yet in the course of the narrative it is not Esau but Jacob's sons who employ the sword (E': Gen 34:26). The occurrence of a second ironic reversal of Isaac's blessing along with the concentric arrangement of traditions enables the interpreter to conclude with some certitude that the arranger of these texts viewed the slaughter of the Shechemites by the sons of Jacob/Israel (Genesis 34) as a culpable act. The violence of Jacob's sons (C') is contrasted with the less devious and more irenic response of the Philistines to the Israelite presence (C). The arranger of these texts thus urges Israel to reflect at once on the virtues of her antagonists and on her own offenses. As we shall see in the concluding section, this feature of the Esau-Jacob cycle has important implications for a theology of strife.

C. Stylistic Analysis: Plays Upon Proper Names

One of the prominent literary features of Genesis 25–36 is the frequency with which a play is made upon proper names. Thus, each of the twelve sons born to Jacob is associated with an incident in the personal experience of the mothers (Gen 29:31–30:24; 35:16–18). Other proper names explained by the narratives are place names. Some of these are the names of holy places wherein an altar or pillar is erected (Gen 28:19: Bethel; Gen 32:31[Engl. 32:30]: Penuel); some of them are well sites which were places of contention (Gen 26:20–22, 33: ^cēśeq "Contention," śiṭnâ "Quarrel," rĕḥōbôt "Wide Places." bĕ^ɔēr šeba^c "Oath-well"); some of them, including the last one listed, mark places where disagreements were settled (Gen 31:48–49: gal^cēd "Heap of Witness"; miṣpâ "Watch Tower"). The protagonists of the cycle come in for multiple plays on words in relation to their names: Esau/Edom (^cēśāw/^ɔĕdôm), who at birth is red/ruddy (^ɔadmônî) and hairy/rough (śē^cār), sells his birthright for a red dish (^ɔādom) (Gen 25:30), and dwells in the hill country of Seir (cf. Gen 36:9). Similarly, Jacob (ya^căqōb) at birth grabs the heel (^cāqēb) of Esau and supplants him (^cqb) (Gen 25:26; 27:36). And his name change to Israel (Gen 32:29 [Engl. 32:28]: yiśra^ɔēl) is explained on the grounds that he has striven (śrh) with God (^ɔĕlohîm) and with man and has prevailed. Other instances of a play on words in the cycle occur in connection with the personal name of Isaac (Gen 26:8) and with the place name Jabbok (32:25[Engl. 32:24]). Mahanaim (32:2–3[Engl. 32:1–2], Succoth (Gen 33:17), and Oak of Weeping (Gen 35:8) are so named to commemorate events which transpired in these places.

James Barr has pointed to the tendency of the Biblical Theology Movement to make unwarranted claims on the inherent power of word and name in the Hebrew language (1969/70). Barr's objections, however, do not focus on the expressive power of language to touch the human emotions and to evoke intimations of a metaphysical realm beyond the phenomenal world. For inquiries of the latter sort one must consult writers such as Ernst Cassirer, Philip Wheelwright, Nathan A. Scott, Paul Ricoeur, and Luis Alonso Schökel. Even though the etymological explanations of some of the personal and place names mentioned above may be inaccurate from the perspective of contemporary philological and linguistic analysis /4/, this datum is of decidedly secondary importance alongside the power of some of the passages in which the questionable etymologies occur to evoke a sense of wonder, awe, and intimation of the presence of the divine. The theophanies at Bethel (Gen 28:10–22) and Penuel (Gen 32:23–33[Engl. 22–32]), in particular, belong to such a category. It would be a mistake to think that etymological accuracy and evocative power are necessarily correlative. A literarily sensitive theology will attempt to concern itself with the evocative power of language and paronomasia.

D. Analysis of the History of Traditions

Four different views of the patriarchs have enjoyed widespread favor among scholars in the present century: (1) they are historical individuals, clan leaders, each originally independent, worshipping deities with different names; (2) they are to be viewed as founders (either legendary or historical) of tribes and nations; they are thus more than historic individuals, being representatives of larger groups; (3) they are poetic types: Abraham of the faithful and obedient worshipper; Jacob of the settler; Esau of the hunter; Joseph of the ideal wiseman; (4) they are founders (whether legendary or historical) of originally Canaanite sanctuaries: Abraham of Mamre; Abraham and Jacob of Shechem; Isaac of Beersheba; Jacob of Bethel. In the Esau-Jacob cycle each of the above characterizations of the patriarchs can be applied with some justification. For in the Book of Genesis, as we have it, traditions from different times and places have been joined, fused, and confused. Two examples from Genesis 25–36 may be cited to underline the importance of distinguishing, where possible, layers of tradition /5/.

1. *Jacob and Esau as ecological types, brothers, and fathers of nations.* In the oldest layer of tradition Esau is a hunter; Jacob a settler. In Gen 25:32 Esau returns home famished and says to Jacob, "I am about to die; of what use is my birthright to me?" In the present merged state of the text the significance of this question is difficult to understand. Why would a brother, coming home from the field, from a hunt, utter such a cry? Surely he would have had a portion at his father's or brother's hearth, and thus would not really be in any danger of perishing through want of food. Only when separation and distinction is made, does the above cry of Esau begin to make sense and fall into place. If the present text joins a tradition concerning the contrast between hunter and farmer with a tradition about the rivalry of two brothers, then the cry of Esau makes sense. As Gunkel showed with great clarity (1910:297), the hunter must live from hunt to hunt, from hand to mouth; a failure to make a kill could mean starvation. The agriculturist, on the other hand, has the animals and the crops he needs at hand. In chapter 27 a similar point is made, that the agriculturist is able to prepare his meat more quickly.

The second layer of tradition pertains to two brothers who are fraternal twins and rivals. This layer deals with references to their presence together in the womb (Gen 25:22) and to their being blessed by their aged father (chap. 27). This second layer has not only been joined to the first but also to a third, wherein the brothers are viewed not simply as individuals, but as prototypes of the nations: Edom and Israel. Thus two nations (goyîm) are said to be struggling in Rebekah's womb (Gen 25:23). If the attempt is not made to disentangle these three layers of tradition, clarity of interpretation can hardly be expected.

One can discern at least two factors which permitted and facilitated this fusion of the originally separate traditions: (i) each tradition dealt with a rivalry, and (ii) the social circumstances changed for the group preserving the oldest (hunter vs. settler) tradition. The change occurred in that (a) the group's most pressing rival turned from a band of hunters into pastoralists (like itself) who were driven out (Gen 33:12-14; 36:6-8), and in that (b) its rival eventually became Edom while the group developed an increasing awareness of its own identity as a nation, Israel.

In the present state of conjoined traditions, it is difficult to assess with certainty how old is the conviction of divine providence. The oldest hunter-settler tradition does not seem to focus on it at all, but simply describes the superior circumstances of the settler-agriculturalist in a time of over-population of the forest area or of sparse game. Recent studies have shown that as far back as the end of the Epi-Paleolithic Era, a hunter culture (Kebaran) persisted in the Palestinian hill country even after their off-shoots (the Natufians) practiced intensive plant collection and animal domestication in the plains and valleys /6/. It is unlikely, of course, that the tradition of hunter-settler rivalry recorded in Genesis goes back so many thousands of years, i.e., to ca. 8000 B.C.E.; it does seem safe to say, however, that the roots of the hunter-agriculturalist rivalry recorded in Genesis may go back to the third millenium. A sense of divine providence does not clearly appear to be a part of this older tradition. Rather, an originally secular tradition, i.e., one with no divine reference, has been merged with two later traditions which, at least in their present state, do have a divine reference.

2. *Theologization and the fate of humor in later traditions.* A similar process of theologizing originally quite secular traditions may be observed elsewhere in Genesis 25–36. In chapter 27 a not-too-kindly humor is displayed in which the persons held up for a source of

amusement are a blind and aging father who has almost, but not quite, lost his wits, and an almost monstrously hairy people whose arms and necks were as thick with hair as goats (Gen 27:15–27). Other comic elements are mistaken identity (v 23), and the utterance of a true statement, the full significance of which the speaker is only partially aware (v 22) /7/.

The comic in Genesis 27, however, has become obscured through the merging of the undoubtedly popular, but originally largely secular, tradition with the later tradition of a patriarch's conveying a divine and irrevocable blessing on the trickster. Theological tradition has thus incorporated an unkindly joke and fraud. It was able to do so because of a dual conviction about (i) divine providence (the superiority of the trickster had already been established by God from the womb [Gen 25:23]) and (ii) the morality of the deceit (the birthright had already been purchased [Gen 25:29–34]). Thus the original humor has been obscured by a traditionist who incorporated into the story the account of a deceived old man, with an eye not so much to humor as to the incident's illustration of the inexorable workings of a divine providence.

This incorporation leaves the contemporary interpreter with a problem: do the texts in their present state teach a suspension of the ethical? That is, are we really justified in concluding that the elect may, with divine approval, use deceit and fraud? The motif of retribution, mentioned above, argues against such a view. It seems more probable that the final traditionist intended for his readers to conclude (i) that the Almighty may continue to be present with the elect despite his, and his mother's, stooping to deceit and (ii) that the harsh realities of old age may be handled more satisfactorily if the aged themselves may be led to see that which is laughable in their own frailty.

Thus we have seen that, as important as is the interpretation of the text as a whole, attention to layers of tradition helps to clarify parts of the text which remain obscure or perplexing without it.

E. The Theological Import of Genesis 25–36

1. *Towards a Theology of Paronomasia.* The use of paronomasia serves to reassure the user that he is correct in perceiving relationships and in grasping divine and human realities. Meaning for the Israelite,

as for contemporary man, was a part of sound. If the sound was ambisignificant, it pointed the hearer to a deeper level of reality, to the divine plan underlying all human events, and to God himself. To take notice of Israel's paronomasia is not simply to engage in a textbook exercise in rhetoric; it is to become attuned to the way the Israelite resonated with the divine reality whose mysterious presence was encountered.

Some of the instances of paronomasia listed above hardly seem "religious." That Esau was "hairy" and "ruddy" in appearance seems to belong to the category of the incidental rather than to the vital, to ethnic trivia rather than to divine ultimacy. Nonetheless, a number of such plays on words may be viewed as attempts to establish one's own and others' identities and to form relationships with other persons and places and, in the end, with God. Past strife was not buried but itself given some room for contemporary and future consciousness. Thus the personal name Naphtali (lit., "contest of God": Gen 30:8) gives expression to the conflict between Leah and Rachel, and the place names "Contention" (Gen 26:20), "Quarrel" (Gen 26:21), "Heap of Witness" (Gen 31:48) commemorate conflicts resolved.

It is well known that the name Jacob originally was theophorous, i.e., it bore a meaning pertaining to God. Thus the name Jacob in all probability meant "May (God) protect." (See Noth, 1928: 177–78, 197). The Bible records a secularized, detheologized and "folk" meaning of this name. A similar (but not identical) situation occurs in regard to the name Israel. Originally it too was probably theophorous and meant "Let God strive (or contend)." In the Penuel pericope (Gen 32:23–33[Engl. 22–32]), Jacob is told his name shall be Israel, "for you have striven with God and with men and have prevailed" (v 29[Engl. 28]). It is thus not only Ishmael's lot to be at odds with his fellow man (Gen 16:12), but Jacob's / Israel's as well. Genesis 25–36 stresses, however, another dimension of the strife for Israel: it shall include down through history a wrestling with God. The very name Israel would henceforth serve as a reminder of the destiny of the people of God to contend with the divine.

The import of the above thoughts is clearly this: contemporary biblical theology cannot rest satisfied with mere description and literal translation of the biblical record. It must also assist in the recovery of a more sensitive awareness of the social and religious function which the biblical traditions served and of the ways in which the very sounds of the words of the biblical tradition provided deeper links with social and divine realities.

2. *Towards a Theology of Strife.* The Greek sage Hesiod observed that there are two kinds of strife: one leads to a healthy competition, as among craftsmen; the other is harmful, leading to the evils of war and bitter quarrels in the courts (*Works and Days*, 11–32). The philosopher Heraclitus similarly distinguished between the two, but instead of viewing them in sharp contrast saw them as but two sides of the same coin: without strife nothing would come into being; war is the common condition; strife leads to an eventual justice, and contention to harmony (Wheelwright, 1959: fragments 25–27, 98). No such philosophic meditation on the ubiquity and creative function of strife is found in the Hebrew Bible although something approaching it is found in Sirach 33:14–15. The traditions of Genesis 25–36 seem, rather, to provide a blueprint for the handling of the familial, ethnic, and socioeconomic strife it describes so fully /8/. The outlines of the practical theology of strife in the Esau-Jacob cycle can be sketched here.

a. The traditions of Genesis 25–36 reveal an astounding degree of empathy with Israel's antagonists. One would suspect that in a survey of various contentions there would be a portrayal of one's foes in bold strokes, depicting their culpability more than their humanity and their peculiar concerns. Such, however, is not the case. The Philistines may contend for water holes and wells but are highly moral in their dealing with Isaac's deception that Rebekah was his sister (Gen 26:8–11). Esau is named first, ahead of Jacob, when the burial of Isaac by his sons is recorded (Gen 35:29). Esau is portrayed as gracious in accepting Jacob's overtures for reconciliation (Genesis 33). Whether Esau's sale of his birthright is viewed as a defect in character is difficult to say with certainty, for the account seems primarily aimed at providing legitimation for Jacob's usurpation of the blessing for the first-born. Surprisingly, Esau's subservience to Jacob is not the last word. In his blessing of Esau, Isaac says: "And you shall serve your brother; but when you break loose, you shall break his yoke from your neck" (Gen 27:40). Here is a clear theology of liberation—for Esau/Edom! Genesis 27 helps Esau/Edom to understand why he is in the present fix (providence ordained it; my rival used deceit). The chapter does not solve the predicament of subservience, but it does make it more bearable because it has been

placed in a divine perspective; it also holds out for Esau / Edom some
hope. Such empathy with the predicament of one's foes and
perception of the divine will for self-determination is suggestive of the
kind of attitude which antagonists today, desirous of alleviating
tension and conflict, may well seek to foster.

   b. The traditions of Genesis 25–36 lay stress on the noble and
common heritage of Israel's antagonists. The genealogies list the
"princes" of Ishmael in their settlements and encampments (Gen
25:15), the "tribal chieftains" (ʾallûpîm) of the sons of Esau (Gen
36:15–19, 40–42), the "tribal chieftains" of Seir the Horite (Gen
36:29–30), and the "kings" who reigned in the land of Edom (Gen
36:31–39). All of these betray, not simply an antiquarian interest in,
but an acknowledgment of the noble and common heritage of Israel's
near (the sons of Esau and of Seir) and more distant (the sons of
Keturah and of Ishmael) social contacts or neighbors. It is
remarkable that an entire chapter (Genesis 36) should be devoted to
data on non-Israelites and that the compilers of the traditions in these
chapters chose to open them with similar genealogical data on the
sons of Keturah and of Ishmael. Practically speaking, these data
underline Israel's interrelationship with her rivals (their common
father was Abraham [A, B] or Isaac [B'A']) /9/. The fact that the
data pertain to the illustrious leaders of Israel's rivals rather than to
their villains also furnishes a provocative clue for resolving even the
severest of contemporary antagonisms. Stress is placed on common
heritage; interest is taken in the illustrious leaders of one's rivals.

   c. The traditions of Genesis 25–36 portray group strife in personal
or personalistic terms. Tales of brothers have been utilized to express
and explain friction between Edom and Israel. The friction between
Israelites and the Philistines, Aramaeans, and Canaanites is similarly
expressed in personal terms: Isaac and Abimelech, Jacob and Laban,
the sons of Jacob and the sons of Hamor. There is to be found in this
aspect of the biblical tradition as well a relevant model for giving
expression to and thus providing a handle for, bringing under control
intergroup antagonisms /10/.

   d. The traditions of Genesis 25–36 provide a worthy model of
theonomous self-criticism. In the motif analysis given above it was
noted how often these chapters acknowledge the use of deception by
Israel's own: Isaac of the Philistines, Jacob and Rebekah of Isaac, the
sons of Jacob of the sons of Hamor. If Laban the Aramaean's

treatment of Jacob seems shoddy with respect to altering the terms of Jacob's contract for a wife or for wages, the reader is reminded that the mother (Rebekah) and spouse (Rachel) of Jacob/Israel are cut from the same cloth. For Rebekah, the sister of Laban, is the chief promoter of the deception of Isaac, and Rachel, his daughter, prevaricates in the incident of the teraphim. Although Jacob's appropriation of the blessing intended for Esau is clearly legitimate for the biblical authors, it is nonetheless culpable—otherwise Esau's wrath and Jacob's flight would not seem at all justified or explainable. Similarly, the sons of Jacob, as we have shown above, are seen as having committed a culpable—though perhaps understandable—act in their treacherous wielding of the sword against the sons of Hamor. Such almost ruthless self-criticism is borne of a faith that nothing may be hidden from Yahweh; that in the end he is the one with whom Israel and all humankind have to do. This aspect of the traditions in Genesis 25–36 is particularly relevant in furnishing a clue for the resolving of potentially destructive contemporary antagonisms: in the absence of the frankest of self-criticism, reconciliation can hardly be expected. Israel's dual conviction of the providential sovereignty of Yahweh (Gen 25:23; 26:12–14, 17–24; 31:7; 33:11) and of the inexorable working of his retributive justice appears to be the chief source of its rigorous self-criticism.

Attention to the literary and stylistic features of the biblical text has thus led us to a renewed awareness of its practical theology in that it furnishes a relevant and still timely blueprint for the resolution of the ubiquitous problem of human strife.

Notes

/1/ For a provocative discussion of Rebekah as a worthy spiritual model, see the essay by Allen in this volume. The correctness of Allen's interpretation that Rebekah is not only justified in her deceit but directed of God to practice it, hinges upon whether or not the oracle in Gen 25:23 contains an implicit imperative. The absence of any explicit evidence and the prevalence of the motif of retribution (see below) speak against Allen's evaluation of Rebekah's and Jacob's deceit as pleasing to God. See also Gen 31:7; 50:20.

/2/ A devastatingly realistic appraisal of some of the psychological motivations for the bestowal of gifts is found in Gen 32:4-22 (Engl. 3-21). These include fear, excessive anxiety, and the desire to feel out the possibility of a reconciliation with the offended. In Gen 33:10-11, gifts are shown to emanate from a profound theological motivation: gratitude to the Almighty for material abundance and the desire for human reconciliation. For a classic study of the complex economic, social, and psychological ways the gift was viewed in antiquity, see M. Mauss.

/3/ In his impressive study of the motifs of divine promise and of cultic legends in the cycle of Jacob, Albert de Pury comes to the conclusion that interest in the place of Bethel belongs not only to Gen 35:1-15 (primarily P) but also to the older written and oral stages in J and E traditions (Gen 28:10-22); see especially part IV (389ff.). The prominence of the travel motif in chapters 25-36 suggests a necessary modification of De Pury's emphasis on place, for in the present arrangement of the texts the loci of Bethel, Mahanaim, and Penuel are decidedly secondary in importance to that of the autonomy of divine manifestation.

/4/ See Barr, 1969/70. Already in the last century I. Casanowicz demonstrated how some etymological explanations of names are philologically impossible (Casanowicz: 36-38). Casanowicz offers a still-valuable survey of different kinds of paronomasia and a list of over 500 examples of it in the OT. Of recent commentators with a keen eye to the employment of paronomasia, including some which Casanowicz missed, see B. Vawter. Important form-critical studies on the so-called etymological etiologies of personal names have been conducted by J. Fichtner and B. Long (1968).

/5/ J. Van Seters is rightly skeptical as to how full a recovery of the circumstances of successive layers of tradition is possible (263). Particularly provocative and convincing are Van Seter's analyses of the defects in Gunkel's methodology in the determination of oral tradition (135-66). With the publication also of Thomas L. Thompson's study (1974) and William G. Dever's and W. Malcolm Clark's contributions to the volume edited by John Hayes and J. Maxwell Miller, the study of the patriarchal traditions and their date has moved into the forefront of contested issues in OT scholarship. In the fascicles of his Genesis commentary which have appeared at the time of this writing, C. Westermann (1977) has taken note of the newer developments.

/6/ See Ofer Bar-Yosef: 187-201. Recent sociological studies show that in the ancient Near East two off-shoots from hunting-gathering economies were forest agriculture and pastoral nomadism (Sahlins: 28-33). Thus the shift of Esau as a hunter (Genesis 27) to a herder, i.e., pastoral nomad (Genesis 33), replicates known sociological practice. In Genesis 26 the economy of Isaac appears to be close to pastoral nomadism, whereas in Genesis 27 the economy of Isaac, Rebekah, and Jacob appears to be close to forest agriculturalism where some reliance on domestic animals was practiced along with food raising and food collecting (Sahlins: 29). In the present essay the terms farmer, settler, and agriculturalist are used more or less synonymously. For further discussion on the sociological background of the patriarchs, see the essay by Gottwald in this volume.

/7/ For a classic analysis of the components of the "comic," see H. Bergson.

/8/ War may be absent from Genesis, but certainly not strife. The observation is made fairly often that the book of Genesis is, relatively speaking, a peaceful book. Apart from the military campaign of Abraham (Genesis 14), the book contains no accounts of great battles such as are found in Joshua, Judges, Samuel, and Kings. For a provocative recent article on the deliberate demilitarization in the patriarchal traditions of Genesis, see Rose, who interprets the demilitarization as a clear sign that the Yahwist can no longer be dated in the Solomonic era but must come rather from a period of national crisis when the family became increasingly valued. He suggests the 7th and 6th centuries B.C.E. as the likely period of composition.

/9/ For the ontological necessity of the individual to know his/her "place" and to have a sense of orientation and belonging, see P. Tillich, I: 194–95. For recent studies on biblical and ancient Near Eastern genealogies, see J. M. Miller (1974) and R. Wilson.

/10/ Alan Paton's depiction of inter-group conflict in the novel *Cry, the Beloved Country* is a noteworthy example of how artistic expressions may foster reconciliation.

Part IV

Dynamic Form: Human Issues

Introduction

Martin J. Buss

For certain purposes it is appropriate to give primary attention to structure or form. (These two words can be used synonymously; they differ, however, in emphasis, in that "structure" points to the relation between the parts within the whole, while "form" designates especially the emergent qualities of the whole.) Forms or structures as such are nontemporal or transtemporal, but their concrete manifestations occur in time. These manifestations are constituted by processes involving movement; in fact, it is questionable whether within existence any static conditions occur at all. Forms, however, can describe the shape of movement, and their transtemporal character allows them to be relevant to more than one occasion so that they are not tied to a dead past.

The discussions by Dale Patrick, Stephen Reid, Christine Allen, and Ann Vater focus on patterns of human existence, while recognizing the importance of historical study. It may be noted that on the whole these authors are fairly young, at least in terms of their place in the discipline. Do they express a relatively new mood?

Patrick offers guidelines for political exegesis, which seeks direction for the organization of society. He illustrates the guidelines with reference to two models, one based largely on Genesis stories, the other drawn from Exodus. In his view, biblical scholarship can and should examine texts for their conceptions of political justice and right. Historical analysis is regarded as indispensible, along with

135

other elements of scholarship. Yet political exegesis, as described, is not concerned with the past for its own sake, but with the use of a text in regard to politics. This text gains authority from the fact that it stands within the canon of the community to which the interpreter belongs. Patrick urges the interpreter to consider the whole canon, so that its varied perspectives can condition each other.

Reid develops a black hermeneutic, one speaking out of black experience and facing its questions in regard to action toward others within society. On the basis of biblical tradition, he depicts three possible responses to an encounter with absurdity. They are suicide (Saul's), violence and vengeance (by Jacob's sons in relation to the Shechemites), and confrontive self-disclosure (in the image of the Suffering Servant). The story of Jacob's sons, as he points out, indicates that vengeance does not provide a solution. Reid's essay demonstrates that the human subtlety of a text yields to a sensitive opening of the reader to its function. He proposes a literary hermeneutic, which sees in literature "an expression of the encounter between persons and existence, something which points to the structure of existence" (p. 154). In such a role, the text can provide illumination for the decision of a hearer to whose existence it speaks.

Allen considers sex identity as a factor in the reader's perspective. She explains that a perspectival approach reflects an interaction between the interpreter and the text. Such a procedure is not arbitrary, but considers features related to certain questions and interests. Allen includes in her perspective a belief in God, with a desire to apprehend the divine plan. As she sees it, Rebekah plays the role of a saint in the story as it stands and in the history of faith. She has no difficulty showing that different, derogatory views of Rebekah have been influenced by value orientations for which deception and the challenging of a husband are major evils. Allen, by profession a philosopher, presents to students of the Bible a fresh point of view which offers "a model of profound significance for women and men of today" (p. 171).

Finally, Vater employs musical analogies in order to attend to forms of motion. She discusses tone, meter, and rhythm in music; these engage not only rational, but also affective and intuitive processes. In part following Martin Buber, she notes that biblical words resonate in sound and in meaning, intimating reality. Their resonance on different levels is compared to the discovery of new dynamic potentials in tones. In stories of Jacob and of Tamar, she finds varied patterns of narration for the conveying of a message, with different emphases on sender, messenger, and message. These patterns provide rhythms of communication. She then shows how a word enters existence by describing the way in which rhythms reach women in consciousness-raising groups, creating harmony and an opening to the present and the new. Vater concludes that interpretation lies in recognizing a congruence between the movement of words and of life.

Chapter 8

Political Exegesis

Dale Patrick
Missouri School of Religion

"Political exegesis" is concerned with the application of biblical texts to political issues. It has been a part of synagogue and church life since their beginning. Paul has been enlisted to encourage obedience to government, the classical prophets and Jesus have been harnessed to the causes of democracy and socialism, and apocalyptic writings have inspired utopian revolutions /1/. Such practices will occupy our attention in the paragraphs that follow.

The essay will provide the rationale for political exegesis, describe models and formulate criteria for the legitimate application of Hebrew Scripture to political issues, and offer an example of the practice. The objective is not to offer a specific theory of biblical political thinking, but to justify the practice of application and to enunciate the criteria which any political exegesis must meet to achieve legitimacy.

A. The Justification for Political Exegesis

Political exegesis is a common phenomenon in popular culture. Sermons, tracts for the times, presidential addresses, oral discussions, church pronouncements, and lay Bible classes enlist biblical texts in support of political perceptions, sentiments and policies. This sort of "exegesis" does not aspire to formal, precise, and sound argumentation. Texts are applied to political issues on an *ad hoc* basis. They may be used to express a "noble sentiment" or to support a position in a political controversy. Whatever the context and purpose, the operating procedure is far removed from formal exegesis.

A casual observer of cynical disposition may conclude that political exegesis as actually carried out is more a process of confirming the prejudices of Bible users than of conforming thought and practice to biblical norms. Whether this observation is just or not, it does not constitute a relevant objection to the practice as such.

The most serious questions that must be answered with respect to political exegesis are these: Does the political thought of this ancient document have any relevance to modern political life and thought? Could one not hold the OT to be relevant to one's theological formation and personal piety but not to penultimate matters like politics? The answer to these questions can be expressed through a counter-question: Can a theology and piety informed by biblical thought be separated from politics? The biblical tradition itself witnesses to God's action in events on the plane of political history as well as within the walls of the sanctuary. The classical prophets made no distinction between religious, political, economic, and social norms in judging the faithfulness of Israel to its divine vocation. The God of Israel, to whom Jews and Christians witness in theology and piety, made a claim on all of life.

One might hold the view that Christianity secularized and relativized political life. This is the position taken by James Barr (1966: 166, 200). He argues that once the people of God ceased to be a nation with both political and religious functions and once they became a missionary movement within states which did not operate under the same concepts of truth and right, the basing of political judgments upon biblical texts became illegitimate.

Against Barr's objection to political exegesis stands the fact that church members are citizens of nations and that their perceptions and attitudes shape political life. Is it not the responsibility of the church to teach its members to apply faithful concepts of truth and right to their performance as citizens? If it does not, the members will by default adopt the perceptions and attitudes of the society in which they live and the social strata to which they belong.

Not only do church members readily adopt the politics of their social milieu, they often identify these with the will of God. According to the sociologist P. Berger, religion functions in society to legitimize the social order and cultural system (1967:29–39, 53–55, 90–99). When Christianity is the religion of a society or a subgroup within society, it invariably takes on this legitimizing function. The church's faith becomes fused with the cultural and political faith and hope of the host community. This fusion has certainly taken place in America, where the church ethos is well-nigh identical with the national ethos (documented by Hadden; Berger, 1961; Herberg, 1955). To avoid a false sanctification of the political order, the church must be engaged in a continuing scrutiny and qualification of the attitudes of its members in the light of its concepts of truth and right.

Inasmuch as the Bible is the religious document around which the church forms and according to which it seeks to shape its concepts of truth and right, it is only natural that biblical literature will be used by church members for a fusion of faith and life. Political exegesis is a spontaneous activity of Jewish and Christian citizens. Hence, the scrutiny of the attitudes of members will involve judging the legitimacy of popular political exegesis.

Informal popular political exegesis should not be repudiated or disdained, for it properly seeks to apply faith to life. What the biblical scholar and theologian can and should do is to evaluate the application of Scripture, encouraging it where it is defensible and criticizing it where it is not. Formal exegesis can relate to informal appeals to Scripture as formal logic does to everyday reasoning.

The scholarly exegete has methods and theories for evaluating the faithfulness of popular applications of Scripture to the biblical text. In evaluating, criticizing, and deepening popular political exegesis, the scholar exercises the authority of the church to subject the perceptions and attitudes of members to the test of the concepts of truth and right communicated in Scripture. In turn, his or her performance is scrutinized by the church community and by other scholars.

If it is granted that political exegesis is legitimate, it could still be asked: Why should a Christian seek political guidance from the OT? The answer is: The OT is the "political" Testament. The NT is dominated by an eschatological perspective which ignores the "more and less" of political existence. The OT, on the other hand, tells the story of a nation living out the vocation of being God's people. The political concepts and experiences of this people provide a perspective for interpreting the dynamics of political process, for discriminating between more and less adequate policy, and for sanctioning political commitment.

B. Guidelines for Political Exegesis

James Gustafson offers a typology of the ways Scripture is used by Jewish and Christian ethics (439–47). His typology constitutes a good entry point into the question of legitimacy in political exegesis.

Gustafson finds four ways of using Scripture in ethics: I. The Scripture is taken to contain revealed moral laws and principles that can be applied to contemporary situations by the interpreter. II. The Scripture is understood as enunciating moral ideals for the aspiration of the believer. These ideals are often associated with the promised fulfillment of history, i.e., the "kingdom of God" or an equivalent. III. The Scripture is read as a record of right and wrong actions which can be applied to contemporary issues by analogy /2/. Divine actions and promises may also be adapted to political situations by analogy. IV. The Scripture is regarded as containing a variety of moral values, norms and perspectives that form an intellectual context for making ethical and political decisions. The aim in this case is to formulate a biblically based theological anthropology and theology of history that informs political judgment.

Gustafson himself prefers the last of these approaches. It has a number of advantages: (1) It avoids "literalism," i.e., the belief that the linguistic symbols of the text are unconditionally true and authoritative; (2) it appropriates the diversity of Scripture exposed by modern critical scholarship; and (3) it frees the ethicist to exercise responsibility and judgment. The political exegete is well-advised, for these reasons, to follow Gustafson's lead. However, the fourth approach does not itself present an exegetical procedure. There is no explanation of how the interpreter collects, organizes and weights the texts that exemplify the "variety of moral values, norms and perspectives" to construct "an intellectual context" for decision-making. That is, an anthropology claiming a biblical basis must be built up from the interpretation of texts, but Gustafson's fourth approach does not contain a procedure for doing so.

When the ethicist takes up the task of political exegesis, actual texts must be interpreted and applied to contemporary issues according to some systematic and compelling procedure /3/. First, the political import of a text must be identified and explicated according to the norms of sound scholarly exegesis. Second, the text must be related to other scriptural teaching. Third, some theory and procedure must be provided for applying specific texts to contemporary political issues. The following paragraphs will expand upon these steps.

1. Since political exegesis seeks the concepts of truth and right as these are applicable to politics, the exegete must be able to identify the political meaning of texts. Politics is the organization of groups of people into societies with institutions governing the social, economic, cultural, and religious interaction of members and interchange with other societies. Most biblical texts touch in some way on political arrangements or hopes for future arrangements. The implied or explicit norms for, and understanding of, the political process can be recognized and described by the exegete who is sensitive to law and politics.

The exposition of the political meaning of a text must proceed on a sound scholarly basis. The exegete must utilize the methods and theories used generally in scholarly exegesis. Modern critical scholarship is oriented toward the historical meaning of the text, i.e., what the author meant and the audience understood. Formal political exegesis within this intellectual context is obligated to seek the historical meaning and adopt it as the communication of the text to the reader today /4/.

Some of the more common types of misinterpretation can be avoided by sound exegetical method. Perhaps the best-known type of mistake is that of taking a statement out of context. Bible readers throughout the centuries have desired to find the most general and plastic meaning in a given text, and removing it from its context has provided that freedom. Modern critical scholarship is committed to finding the determinate, historical meaning of the text; the literary context works in tandem with the verbal form of the text to limit the meaning.

Another prevalent kind of error is what might be called a "genre mistake." For example, a descriptive statement may be taken as a commandment. In the history of the church the OT descriptions of the role of women were taken as prescriptions and transformed into a legitimation of subordination. Careful attention to style, form, thought, and social setting facilitates the identification of the kind of utterance found in a text.

2. As a normative procedure related to theology, political exegesis cannot move directly from specific texts to application. Some account must be given of the relation of the text expounded to the teaching of the rest of Scripture. It is the OT, not this or that text within it, that is accepted by the synagogue and the church as authoritative. Since the appeal to a text in support of some political recommendation depends upon the authoritativeness of the text, which in turn depends upon its being a part of the Bible, the political exegete is claiming that Scripture itself supports the recommendation. The claim is valid only if the text is indeed representative of the fundamental lines of scriptural thought on the subject and consonant with other important teachings. It is this need to relate each text to the broader thought of Scripture that leads the exegete initially to construct a system along Gustafson's lines.

Arbitrary selectivity has plagued popular political exegesis. The nonscholarly reader of the Bible is often ignorant of the diversity of Scripture or dogmatically committed to its noncontradictoriness, so that it seems natural to take the communication of a given text as "the" teaching of Scripture. Critical scholarship has undermined the idea that all texts teach the same thing, and formal political exegesis must take this diversity into account and attain a level of generalization that comprehends it. Another kind of arbitrary selectivity is involved when an exegete appeals to Scripture on some subjects but refuses to do so on others /5/. If one is willing to appeal to Scripture to support political recommendations, consistency demands that the same sort of appeal be allowed for all subjects. The exegete who believes that scriptural teaching is relevant on some subjects but not on others must justify the principle of selectivity carefully.

3. The political exegete must give a reasonable account of the "transferability" of a given biblical perspective or preachment to the contemporary political context. Such an account would explain why and how the OT is relevant to the political views and policies of Jews and Christians, e.g., why a theological anthropology should be "biblically based" and how biblical texts are to be employed in its construction. It would also provide criteria for adopting and applying specific texts.

An account of the "transferability" of scriptural teaching might go as follows /6/: Scripture establishes the identity of the God in whom we believe. The stream of tradition in which Jews and Christians live is marked off and united by the recognition of the biblical God as God indeed. Essential elements of the biblical depiction of God are divine challenges, commands, calls, and judgments regarding political life. For the community that believes in the biblical God, the political will of this God remains the norm of political thought and action /7/. That is, the political judgments of believers must be consistent wth the identity of the biblical God.

Political analysis and action consistent with the biblical God need not mean consistency with every political teaching derivable from Scripture. While Scripture establishes the identity of God for Jewish and Christian tradition, this identity is not so static and fixed as to be identified for all time with a specific set of rules and principles. The Christian, for instance, is commanded to test the OT law against the law of love (Gal 5:1–14). Hence, for the Christian no OT political teaching is automatically valid, but must be shown to meet this criterion.

The contemporary exegete has precedent in exegetical tradition for exercising judgment as to what in the text continues to identify the biblical God. Jews and Christians have consistently made distinctions between weightier and lesser matters of the Law, e.g., between "moral" and "ritual" law. Moreover, even in premodern times there was a recognition of a degree of historical relativity: laws relevant to one set of social conditions were reinterpreted to fit new circumstances.

Most interpreters today would also allow that the authors of Scripture were occasionally mistaken. They may have misunderstood the processes of nature, psychology, society, and politics. The current dispute among church people over homosexuality centers on whether homosexuality is a natural psychological condition or a freely chosen moral stance. The biblical prohibitions—if that is the correct interpretation of Lev 18:22 and 20:13—may be based on mistaken premises regarding psychology.

It is also necessary to acknowledge the possibility of sinful self-assertion and compromises with evil within Scripture. Both Jeremiah (Jer 8:8) and Jesus (Matt 5:21–48) charge as much. Scripture itself thus requires the exegete to ferret out sinful and compromising depictions of God's will and purpose. Being in Scripture is not sufficient warrant for accepting a teaching as the will of the biblical God.

There is an aspect of political exegesis that is outside of the scope of exegesis in a strict sense: the application of a scriptural passage to a particular political issue. Such appliction requires an understanding of the contemporary situation in its social, political, and legal dimensions. A degree of finesse in this regard is required that surpasses the ability of a biblical exegete qua scholar. The political exegete is advised, therefore, to take a seat alongside colleagues in other disciplines, especially those in theological social ethics.

C.   Political Exegesis in Practice

To furnish an example of political exegesis of the OT, the Jacob and exodus narratives will now be examined for their models of the origin and character of the Israelite political order. These models of political order can be used in the construction of a theological anthropology. The argument will proceed according to the rules enunciated for formal political exegesis. It is divided into two parts: an identification of the models of political order depicted in the Jacob and exodus accounts and an analysis of the theological basis of each model.

Models of Political Order in the Jacob and Exodus Narratives

The OT narrative offers two models of the origin of the body politic: (1) Israel derives from the family of the patriarchs; (2) Israel was forged into a community in the struggle for liberation from Egyptian slavery. These two models are juxtaposed in the biblical text in such a way as to condition and qualify each other.

When I first began thinking about the political implications of the Jacob tradition, I could give only a negative assessment: it does not offer a natural example for political exegesis because it reflects a social structure of a prepolitical era. The Jacob stories are family stories (Westermann, 1964:58–91). The family is the only cohesive social grouping, and the family is not strictly speaking a political entity. To be sure, it has a structure of domination, an economy, a law, a religious self-understanding, etc. However, the dynamics of family life are sufficiently different from cities, nations, and empires to exclude family stories from "political" exegesis / 8 /. The God of the patriarchs acts within the destiny of the family; social grouping is based upon blood ties and servanthood; living space is not political territory, but open range; law and cult are under the direct supervision of the patriarch.

I recognized, of course, that the persons in the family stories were associated with nations and tribes, but I perceived this association as artificial (cf. von Rad, 1961:270–71). My chief concern was, frankly, to apologize for Israel's dangerous procedure of using such stories to make political judgments.

I have since come to realize that the patriarchal traditions must be taken seriously as a model of the origin and character of the people of Israel. They represent the body politic as, to put it naïvely, "one big family." Family images are persistent and pervasive in biblical literature, ranging from genealogies to corporate personality. Being an Israelite meant belonging to a community forged together by family links (for analogies to this type of thinking, cf. de Vaux: 4–6).

The exodus tradition presents a different picture of the origin and character of political life in Israel. Here the people are a "many," a group encompassing many families and disparate groups, united by the common condition of being enslaved and by common loyalty to a deity and human agents, possessing at least the rudiments of public institutions, and sharing a common destiny. This picture corresponds more to political society as modern thought has come to envisage it.

These two models of the origin of Israel stand in juxtaposition. Traditio-historically they probably represent distinct cycles of tradition. However, they have been set side by side and intertwined so that each conditions the other. The participants in the exodus are traced to a common ancestor (Exod 1:1–7, etc.; but note 12:38), somewhat eclipsing the role of the exodus in national formation. However, the patriarchal origin of Israel is qualified significantly by the events of the Mosaic era, so much so that biblical literature refers back more frequently to the exodus than it does to the patriarchal stories.

The Theological Bases of the Two Models

Each model of the origin and character of the body politic depicts God's relation to the community according to a logic intrinsic to the model. It is through its God-language that each model becomes relevant to contemporary politics. (1) The status of the family before God is a free gift, and the status is passed on by inheritance. (2) The status of the people suffering under Egyptian slavery is based upon God's concern for the oppressed and downtrodden. These two themes constitute dialectical poles in the politics of the biblical God.

1. The patriarchal stories assume Israel to be the inheritor of the divine promises to the patriarchs. The Deuteronomic preacher expresses this idea succinctly in the confession: "Yahweh set his heart upon your fathers and chose their descendants after them, you above all peoples, as at this day" (Deut 10:15). Nothing that Israel was (Deut 7:7-8) or did (Deut 9:4-5) accounts for God's choice: The great boon was the free gift of the God who has the rights of disposal over all creatures (Deut 10:14).

To the free gift of election corresponds its inheritability. Abraham has received the promise to the family, and it passes from generation to generation until it reaches the nation (Gen 12:2-3, 7, 13:14-16, etc.; 26:2-4, 24, etc.). Inheritance is a family institution. Law circumscribes who the heir is to be. Much of the patriarchal narrative is devoted to the issue of inheritance. Isaac is finally born in Sarah's old age to become Abraham's heir, and the struggle between Esau and Jacob concerns inheritance.

In the Jacob narrative, two fateful events interrupt the normal course of inheritance. First, Rebekah gives birth to twins, a fact which renders primogeniture problematic. Second, when the time comes for Isaac to pass on the family blessing to the "first" twin (Esau), Rebekah and Jacob successfully conspire to gain it for the "second." Rather than rectifying the injustice, God ratifies the outcome of the human conflict by passing the promise to Jacob (Gen 28:10-22) and declaring him father of the nation to come (Gen 32:23-33). The status of election is a family possession which is subject to seizure!

The political import of the story reaches beyond the shocking hint that Israel has prevailed over God to attain election. It involves international politics, for the election was taken away from Edom, Israel's neighbor to the southeast. Such a claim courts the danger of chauvinism. However, the Yahwist at least avoids claiming moral superiority for Jacob and his successors. Esau's willingness to be reconciled with Jacob while the latter continues to dissemble (Genesis

33) suggests Esau's moral superiority. In any case, J protects the status of election from becoming a source of self-righteousness or a reason for imperialism.

However, J does include an oracle that may have been used by the Davidic royal house to justify later imperialism and mass murder (cf. 2 Sam 8:13-14):

Two nations are in your womb,
 and two peoples, born of you, shall be divided;
the one shall be stronger than the other,
 the elder shall serve the younger (Gen 25:23).

This oracle does not fit the story, but assumes a period when Israel claimed a divine right to rule Edom. It is the sort of arbitrary justification of Israelite imperialism that calls for a model of election based upon justice /9/.

2. In the exodus account the people are the object of the concern of a God who identifies with and empowers the victims of oppression and injustice. This proposition has become a principle in liberation theology, particularly in James Cone's black theology of liberation (1969:43-45; 1970:94 *et passim*). Cone has surely identified an authentic biblical theme and has made it a powerful theological instrument (for a fuller discussion, see Patrick, 1976).

Statements in the text of Exodus 1-15 can be enlisted in support of Cone's contention. When Yahweh inaugurates the course of events leading to liberation, the fact of the people's suffering under the Egyptians is singled out as the reason for action (Exod 3:7-10, JE; 2:23b-24, 6:5-6, P). The story that follows is the account of Yahweh's liberation of this people from slavery. It pits God as the advocate of the slaves against the Egyptian pharaoh (Exodus 7-13); God intervenes to deliver the slaves and overthrow their masters at the Sea of Reeds (Exodus 14).

Several other themes of the exodus account back up the liberationist thrust: (a) The demonstration of divine power prominent in the plague narratives makes Yahweh a God whom the people of Israel can count on in the face of insuperable odds. (b) The portrait of the enslaving power is a realistic depiction of the stubbornness and irrationality of oppressors. (c) The slaves are freed from servitude in order to enter the service of God (Exod 3:12, E; cf. Lev 25:42) /10/. (d) The "despoiling" of the Egyptians is symbolic restitution for Israelite suffering (Exod 3:21-22; 11:1-3). (e) God demands that the people leave the security of slavery and accept the uncertainty of freedom, a move that they were loath to make (cf. Exod 14:11–12, etc.).

There is one aspect of the exodus story that qualifies the liberation theme. Exodus 1–15 assumes that "Israel" already exists and is Yahweh's charge. God "owes" the people protection because of this link (above all, Exod 6:4–5). This assumption is due to conditioning by the patriarchal tradition. The two models of the origin of Israelite peoplehood are bonded together in such a way that the liberationist theme belongs to a delicately balanced dialectic.

One might argue that the biblical God does not identify with victims of oppression qua victims, but only with God's victimized people. Against this, however, is the fact that biblical literature reiterates the theme of God's identification with the powerless and oppressed (e.g., Exod 22:20–27, 1 Sam 2:1–8, Psalm 113; in the NT, 1 Cor 1:18–21). It would not therefore be true to the spirit of the Bible to deny the liberationist theme in the exodus tradition. God's identification with Israel is unique and once-for-all, but it manifests a pattern of identifying with the oppressed and downtrodden.

D. Concluding Reflection

The analysis of the Jacob and exodus narratives meets the criteria of political exegesis proposed in section B. The focus of attention was on the models of political order. They can provide constituents of a biblically based theological anthropology and theology of history. The models were reached by a process of inference from individual texts and from the general structure, form, and impression of the larger narrative complexes. Scholarly methods and theories were assumed throughout and employed explicitly to interpret the literature. Moreover, each model was related to other scriptural passages and themes to substantiate their conformity with the thought of the Scripture as a whole.

The theological correlates of the two models were treated separately. It is through the identification of God in each narrative complex that the models of political order become relevant to the synagogue's and church's political thinking. In fact, theologies of hope and liberation have built a theo-political program on the exodus narrative and the stream of tradition affirming Yahweh's identification with the oppressed. The exegetical basis of this program was reviewed in the course of the discussion. In the Jacob narrative, the theological theme of "free grace" was discovered to be related to the family model of political order.

No attempt has been made in this discussion to determine in detail the application of the two models of political order to contemporary political life. Theologies of hope and liberation have made a strong case for the exodus theme: the biblical God shows grace by rectifying the injustices of human society. This theme can be and has been applied to countless examples of political, legal, economic, and social injustice. The fittingness of these applications is beyond the purview of this essay. The question that arises out of this study is whether liberation theology is not too univocal and onesided. Probably it should be juxtaposed to the "family" theology of the patriarchal tradition. Politically speaking, the familial model of political order would accentuate kinship, personal loyalty, and traditional order / 11 /. Such an emphasis would be an antidote to the overemphasis on rational justice in modern society and political thought.

Dale Patrick

Notes

/1/ Much of the history of political applications in the church is covered in Ernst Troeltsch (1931); see Rosemary Ruether (1970) on the modern history of radical political exegesis.

/2/ E. Levi: 1–2 describes legal reasoning as a three step process: a proposition covering the precedent case is formulated into a rule of law, which in turn is applied to a similar situation. This description makes Gustafson's I and III methods rather similar.

/3/ Although Gustafson's fourth approach eschews direct application of texts to political issues, the citing of texts in support of anthropological theses is application, not too different from treating texts as containing revealed moral principles. Moreover, one would expect a "biblically based" anthropology to justify the bulk of specific utterances and the general trend of biblical thought. Consequently, citation of texts in connection with contemporary situations would be justified.

/4/ The formal political exegete would be expected to employ current philology, linguistics, text criticism, source criticism, form criticism, traditio-historical criticism, and critical history. Of course, an exegete can reject the regnant methods and theories, but not without careful justification.

/5/ This is not a merely "academic" problem: there is a division within the American church between those who quote Scripture on subjects of public morality and patriotism and those who appeal to it on subjects of economic and racial justice and international order.

/6/ The account offered is a sketch of my OT theology. I am in the process of composing a MS developing the ideas much more thoroughly.

/7/ For a contemporary defense and explication of a "divine command theory of ethical wrongness," see Robert M. Adams' essay in Outka-Reeder: 318–47.

/8/ A major contribution of Reinhold Niebuhr was to insist that the morality applicable to face-to-face community is not applicable to large collectives: 1932:xiff, 1ff.

/9/ There are several other Jacob narratives with political import, *viz.*, Jacob-Laban (Genesis 29–31) and Shechem-Jacob and children (Genesis 34), but there is not space here to expound them.

/10/ The covenant at Sinai provides very important images of the origin and nature of the body politic and its theological foundation, but space limitations prohibit examining it. It does fit the model of political order and theological basis of the exodus (cf. Patrick, 1976).

/11/ Perhaps Reinhold Niebuhr's renewed appreciation of the "organic" factor in community formation (1955:163–82) could be developed as a political concept bearing the values suggested by the "family" model.

Chapter 9

Violence & Vengeance: Ingredients for Tragedy

Stephen Breck Reid
Emory University

In his first major work, *Black Theology and Black Power*, James H. Cone devoted a section to the issue of violence (1969:138–43). From that time, this question has been an unanswered one in black theology. Even though the question has been addressed, there has not been significant biblical reflection on the issue. It is the goal of this essay to wrestle with the issue of violence.

In the process of this wrestling, a hermeneutic will become apparent. There are three aspects of this hermeneutic. First, the hermeneutic presupposes a functional view of biblical scholarship, especially biblical theology. As Brevard Childs points out, the role of biblical theology is to help in the articulation of theology on behalf of the church (92–95). Second, a black hermeneutic, in order to be black, must not be a blind repetition of white movements toward a hermeneutic. Finally, a black hermeneutic must be literary. A black hermeneutic upholds the historical-critical method, for to the degree that it represents acculturated black society as a product of the Enlightenment this hermeneutic must think in historical categories. At the same time, the Bible and especially the OT material is, in the life of the black church, the story of one oppressed people told to another oppressed people. This means that for a black hermeneutic the irony of the story is as important as the historical situation which can be deduced from the story.

Before venturing further into the issue of violence, one might consider what makes it an issue for black theology. Violence is often a byproduct of the confrontation of black existence with absurdity.

This category of French existentialism has been used in black theology since Cone's first work (1969:8). No other word better conveys the paradox of black existence. Absurdity, according to Cone, is the encounter of the black person, who has an image of redeemed creation which is intrinsic to the black experience, with the demonic world in which the black person exists. Black people have always known that they were more than the white world defined them as being, yet the black community has never had a false perception of what the white world considered to be the worth of black existence. Hence we see the absurdity involved in black existence.

Absurdity is the intuitive feeling of self-worth amidst the cultural and historical milieu which is effacing of the black self. There are basically three ways to come to grips with this absurdity. The first alternative is suicide, either physical or psychological. The second alternative is that of violence and revenge. The third option is one of confrontive self-disclosure.

As is to be expected in an essay on biblical hermeneutics, there is the implicit assumption that these existential alternatives have literary expressions in the biblical text. These literary expressions can be seen only if one utilizes a literary hermeneutic which values the story as story. For a story is a social construct acting reciprocally with the society which created it or adapted it. A story is not merely a historical datum to reconstruct a history, even if it is a salvation history /1/. A literary understanding of the material proposes that it is an expression of the encounter between persons and existence, something which points to the structure of existence.

The first alternative as reaction to absurdity is suicide. Traditionally this alternative has not been accepted by the black community; for that reason, black theology is a survival theology (Cone, 1970:34). Nevertheless, one might commit suicide. The story of the downfall of Saul becomes a helpful lens through which to perceive this alternative (1 Sam 28:6–31:13). After losing his sons and his country—his only bids for immortality—Saul commits suicide. In Camus' play *Caligula*, the emperor Caligula realizes that there is no existence apart from guilt. At that point, his existence like that of Saul experiences a loss of meaning. He is overcome by the sense of nonbeing, nothingness. Given this knowledge, proceeding in quite logical manner, Caligula too is driven to suicide.

To understand the structure of existence to which the Saul story points, one should remember that it is a tragedy. There are similarities between this story and Shakespeare's play *Macbeth*. In both stories a witch/seer facilitates the occasion for the main figure to behold his destiny. In both cases the protagonist attempts to control his own destiny inauthentically: Macbeth through his misunderstanding of the oracle of the witches, Saul by breaking the law (1 Sam 15:9, 20). In both cases it was sheer folly to attempt to control destiny.

This folly, in the contexts of their respective stories, makes both men counterexamples. Their action is not perceived as an authentic living-out of existence. Therefore it becomes clear to the OT community and later to the black community that while suicide is a possibility it is not an option for authentic existence.

The second alternative is that of revenge and violence. This alternative is represented in the story of the rape of Dinah (Gen 34:1–31). Dinah, who was presumably attractive, had committed no impropriety; there was no hint of seduction /2/. Shechem, son of Hamor, raped Dinah and then fell in love with her. He asked for permission to marry her. The sons of Jacob told Shechem that the men of the town should be circumcised before the wedding. Then the sons of Jacob attacked the city, while the men were recuperating from their surgery, killing all the men, plundering the city, and taking the women and children.

In Genesis Jacob is clearly a trickster figure. He is able to reap rich gains from little effort; he is a cunning person in the cycle of stories. Now in the story of Dinah, it is the sons of Jacob who act as tricksters (cf. Speiser: 268). Noth intimates that the original story had nothing to do with Jacob (1972: 86). The redactor of the story who inserted Jacob into the story thereby inserted a note of irony. The trickery and cunning of the traditional Jacobite style was effective in attaining revenge, but here such activity is viewed as ambiguous (Gen 34:30). After all the loss of life, there is still no meaning; the sons of Jacob asserted themselves, but attained no new self-understanding.

Speiser points out that the story of Dinah is a reflection of corporate personalities, representing ethnic concerns (266). It is paradigmatic for what could happen in the black community. Franz Fanon, in his book *The Wretched of the Earth*, proposes that to find real self-affirmation the black man and woman would have to experience revenge. "The first shall be last" is the heart of Fanon's concepts of revolution and self-affirmation. According to Fanon, only as they are able to kill that which symbolizes their oppression, namely the white colonizers, can the colonized affirm themselves (1968:635–37). However, one of the problems with revenge in black theology, as in the story of Dinah, is that it is not useful. It does not reduce fear and anxiety; rather, it creates more. If black theology is to be a survival theology in the midst of the American social scene, then to kill the source of black dehumanization is not an option.

The black community, like Dinah, has been raped in innocence, due to its attractiveness. This rape has been experienced both individually and corporately in the black community, physically as well as psychologically. To kill the rapist, however, only serves to destroy the husk of the symbol of destruction. It does not destroy the symbol itself. As Paul Tillich has pointed out, symbols are neither created at will nor are they destroyed at our discretion (I: 240). The community cannot now, nor will it ever be able to, forget its rape. No matter how many whites die or confess their corporate sins, the rape cannot be forgotten. Jacob gains no meaning from his sons' revenge. The black community gains no meaning by killing the whole white community, whether physically or psychologically through induced debilitating guilt. The revenge does not minimize the loss.

Black theology must acknowledge that there is no way to ignore the rape. This is what Fanon makes clear in his book *Black Skins and White Masks*. The black community experiences language constriction because of its denial of the rape and of its attempt not to verbalize it. According to Fanon, as a black person becomes more educated the language constriction becomes worse. Vulgarity, as it reflects a segment of the black experience's encounter with absurdity, is something that the university-trained mouth cannot shape itself to articulate (1967:17–40).

The third alternative, presented in the suffering servant poems (Isa 42:1–4; 49:1–6; 50:4–9; 52:13–53:12), is confrontive self-disclosure. Warlike (Isa 49:2) and legal (Isa 50:8) terminology indicate a confrontive side of the suffering servant corpus. There is, nevertheless, a strong theme that the servant does not make reprisals against the smiters. It is important not to gloss over the confrontive elements of the material in order to have a certain amount of homogeneity.

The black community, like the servant (Isa 49:2), is called to be incisive toward the white community. As Rollo May has indicated, to the extent that the community has language which is expressive and expansive there is less need to kill the symbol of oppression (1972:246). This means a movement away from euphemisms. Euphemism is common in the OT; likewise a euphemistic tone permeates the speech of the black middle class. The mouth of the suffering servant was as sharp as a dagger (Isa 49:2) in confronting the smiters who have done violence to him. For alcoholics, drug addicts, and those who have been sexually abused, it is likewise important to be able to articulate what happened.

The ability to say that one has been violated is not unlike the power of naming. It is important for the black community to name the crime of the white community. The white community cannot say that it has raped the black community because it has not worked through the demonic in its own existence. By being able to name the demon, the black community does not have to become demonic, aping the demonic in the white community /3/. To use the demon's gun on one who is possessed by the demon is to be possessed by the same demon. According to the definition of "black" articulated by Cone and established in the black community, blackness has a value system different from its white counterpart. Attempting to actualize freedom in white terms using white means is to become white.

The suffering servant embodies a different actualization of freedom in confrontive self-disclosure. Part of the process is self-affirmation, defined by May as an internal stating of where one is (1972:132). Self-affirmation is a process of saying "I am" with meaning and authenticity. By so doing the person says to him/herself that he/she is not nothing. It is in affirmation that to some degree the person can say "no" to the powers of non-being, which induce the inability to say "I am."

May distinguishes self-assertion from self-affirmation; the former is the setting of the limits of the infringement upon one's space (134). Whereas self-affirmation says "I am here," self-assertion says "you will not go beyond such a point." Without the step of self-assertion, self-affirmation cannot long survive, for the boundary between oneself and others becomes diffuse.

If one uses a literary hermeneutic for the Bible, the issue of violence is as ambiguous as existence itself. If anything is perfectly clear, it is that violence will not save the black community or any other community, as the black community has known for some time. The literature discussed forms something that points to the structure of existence, in this case black existence. The structure of literature and black existence cannot be reduced to anything as simplistic as a philosophical-political hermeneutical principle, even one such as liberation. Nor can it be reduced to a historical datum, for that would put the reader one step further removed from the structure of existence to which the literature points. Given the literary approach, biblical literature is paradigmatic for the black church and black existence. The black community will not commit suicide, as did the tragic figure Saul. Nor will the remorse of Jacob be the remorse of the black community. For the biblical material speaks a note of warning: vengeance and violence are ingredients for tragedy.

Notes

/1/   Cone's hermeneutic places more emphasis on the history of the exodus event than on the story itself (Bennett). The story itself is as important as the history it provides, even if that is the history of salvation. An emphasis on the historical leads invariably to a search for the historical event, for instance, the exodus. This search for the historical event may or may not be successful; however, the success of such a search can never be the ground of faith.

/2/   Seduction is a key theme elsewhere in J, most notably in Gen 6:1–4. This theme becomes very important in apocalyptic material; it is especially prominent in the *Testaments of the Twelve Patriarchs*. It is clear here, however, that Dinah is not a seductress; the theme appears in terms of a distinction between Dinah and a seductress-prostitute (Gen 34:31).

/3/   Terminology that names evil as articulately as does apocalyptic literature remains as yet an untapped resource for the black church and black theology.

Chapter 10

"On Me Be the Curse, My Son!"

Christine Garside Allen
Simone de Beauvoir Institute of Concordia University

Comments on Methodology

In seeking to uncover the spiritual dynamics of Rebekah in Genesis 23–29, this paper draws upon traditional Hebrew, Protestant, and Catholic interpretations as well as contemporary feminist considerations. Hermeneutics of the OT has passed through different stages. Some interpreters have concentrated on the question: Who are the writers of the texts? With the help of careful examination of writing style, it has been possible to delineate four different groups of writers of Genesis. This means that if one is attempting to uncover the original meaning of the text which records the story of Rebekah, extensive historical data must be brought to bear upon the interpretation. For each line of the text one examines, a judgment must be made as to its source, context, and purpose. In this process some startling results occur. For example, the claim is made that the links between Abraham, Isaac, and Jacob, namely the wooing of Rebekah and the stolen blessing, represent a later stage of the text. The purpose of this addition was to develop firmly a patriarchal history. "For here the figures of the patriarchs, at first quite independent of one another, are being put into family relationships" (Eissfeldt: 41).

In contrast to such an historical thesis I want to discuss the role of Rebekah in reference to the function she plays as mediator between Abraham and Jacob. It is my thesis that on the level of spiritual call she can be viewed as handmaiden, vessel, prophet, sacrificial victim, suffering servant—in short, as the point where God's will became known on earth at a certain crucial time in salvation history.

Does the acceptance of one of these points of view necessarily exclude the other? The answer to this question entails a brief look at what criteria one can use to determine the *truth* of the conflicting theses. The most obvious way would be to attempt to discover the facts. However, we are not able to seek out Rebekah and ask her: "Are you the sister of Laban? Did you deceive Isaac? Why? Etc." These facts are not within our grasp. There is, however, a book.

One might ask how this book, the nature of which is in question, can be itself the *criterion* for affirming or denying an interpretation. It is tempting to shift to a very loose theory of *coherence* to account for the apparent conflicts in the two proposed theories of interpretation. Then any theory which holds together is as true as any other. Needless to say, there is a certain relativism in this approach which is repugnant to the scholar.

A solution to this problem is to adopt a *perspectival* approach in which the text serves as a point where the interpretation begins and ends. One is not free simply to develop just any theory at all without regard to the words and phrases of the text, as one could if coherence were the only criterion. Yet there are many possible perspectives from which a single text can be examined. A statement which is true within one perspective might be considered false or irrelevant within another. For example, it may very well be that Rebekah was not the mother of the man who married someone called Rachel and who fathered Joseph and that historically the account is an addition to the text. Yet we may think about the role of God in creating salvation history, remembering that we are not examining an ordinary book, but rather a sacred one. Here we might allow ourselves to question why it seemed important at a particular time in history to link Abraham, Isaac, and Jacob together. Why does God *want* us to think of them as joined?

In view of the fact that one always interprets a text from a particular perspective, it should be made manifestly clear what exactly this perspective is. When I mentioned God, it was implicit in my interpretation that a religious perspective was being employed. I could have given a political-historical answer as well, by stating that the Israelites wanted to recreate their roots in a national identity, and probably there is some truth in this. What interests me in the story of Rebekah, however, is not primarily the question of the authenticity of her material link between the patriarchs, or her role in the social history of the Israelites. Rather, I am concerned to extract from her life a religious model which might play a role in contemporary woman's spiritual quest. In doing this I follow the suggestion of Professor Martin Buss: "One can argue that socio-psychological analysis—whether formal or informal—is needed or at least helpful to form a bridge from the text to the hearer and that it is a major task of the scholar to provide one. The aim of such a study would not be primarily to establish the original sense in a positivistic manner. . . , but to open the human meaning of the text" (1973/74:137) This means that the insights of technical research in archaeology, philology, textual, literary and form criticism which have dominated hermeneutics in this century must be placed in a certain human and religious context.

In addition to a variety of perspectives found in the original writers and the subsequent interpreters, we are also faced with a multiplicity of perspectives in different readers. Attempts to classify readers have used the division: Hebrew, Protestant, and Catholic. Location in history, age, national identity, cultural heritage, vocations, and sex also contribute to the perspective from which the reader comes to the text. In this paper, I want to consider sex identity as a determining factor in the perspective of the reader and interpreter.

During the medieval period, women entered the world of hermeneutics. St. Francis de Sales expresses this fact in the following way: "That we may realize that such writing issues with better results from the devotion of lovers than from the learning of scholars, the Holy Spirit has willed that many women should work wonders in it. Who has ever expressed the heavenly affections of sacred love better than St. Catherine of Genoa, St. Angela of Foligno, St. Catherine of Siena, or St. Mechtilde?" (38–39). He mentions also the "most learned ignorance" of the Blessed Teresa of Jesus who later was proclaimed Doctor of the Church (40). The technique of interpretation of these women consisted in meditation on the gospel and silent prayer. In each case they attempted to uncover the meaning of the passage in terms of the nature of God and of their own vocation to sanctity.

In the modern period, women have begun to receive the same formal education as men. It is not surprising, then, that they are entering the field of hermeneutics using the same tools of interpretation as their male colleagues. The question remains as to whether threads of sexual identity will show in the pattern they weave. One rather marvelous example of vivid female thread is found in Elizabeth Cady Stanton's words in *The Woman's Bible* (46):

> It was certainly a good test of her patience and humility to draw water for an hour, with a dozen men looking on at their ease, and none offering help. The Rebekahs of 1895 would have promptly summoned the spectators to share their labors, even at the risk of sacrificing a desirable matrimonial alliance. The virtue of self-sacrifice has its wise limitations. Though it is most commendable to serve our fellow beings, yet woman's first duty is to herself, to develop all her own powers and possibilities that she may better guide and serve the next generation.

Mrs. Stanton wrote, first of all, to win women to the cause of suffrage; as will be seen later on, this political thread is interwoven with other threads of Protestant ethical values and white racial values. She turned to the Bible not to bring women closer to God, but to break the power of the Bible on their consciousness.

Another woman, Sister Emma Thérèse Healy, seeking to explain and draw readers to the state of perpetual virginity, focuses primarily on Rebekah before the marriage: "And in truth, Mary was, like Rebekah, an exceeding comely maid, and a most beautiful virgin, and not known to man" (21). In the classic, *All the Women of the Bible*, we find a very sympathetic interpretation of Rebekah: "No young woman in the Bible is so appealing" (21). While the author, Edith Deen, considers the religious dimension of Rebekah's personality, her main tendency is to classify the women in terms of the men who are closest to them. She divides the women of the Bible into daughters, wives, mothers, widows, and other unnamed women. Of Rebekah herself she states: "Does she not typify the mother down the ages who, weak in faith, imagines herself to be carrying out the will of God?" (26).

In contemporary women's writing we can discern several general trends. The first is that of Mary Daly which calls for a leap out of tradition and into a new form of religion. Unlike Lot's wife, she does not look back. For her, there may well be nothing to be gained by reexamining Rebekah. Another approach is seen in Rosemary Ruether's collection of essays entitled *Religion and Sexism*, which combines careful scholarship with a feminist consciousness; she writes: "By looking back at these images, by establishing an autonomous subjectivity and standpoint from which to study, evaluate and judge these images, women today also shatter this mirror and, with it, shatter their own false mirror role. They establish the basis for a new humanity beyond patriarchy which must be based on dialogue and reciprocal consciousness" (1974:12–13). Like Stanton, she is interested in studying tradition in order to break out of it.

It seems to me that there is another approach one may take which does not replace either of the other two as worthy and valid experiments in research, but which stands beside them as an authentic alternative. This approach calls one back into the Bible as a sacred book; it demands a re-interpretation and re-evaluation in depth of the mysteries contained there.

Some Traditional Interpretations of Rebekah

There is a great variety among traditional interpretations of Rebekah. One of the most positive is found in the Midrash Rabbah, the compilation of commentations by early Hebrew teachers. Here Rebekah is recognized as a matriarch (*Num. Rab.* 12.17, etc.), a prophet (on Gen 27:42, *Gen. Rab.* 67.9), a "lily among thorns" (*Lev. Rab.* 23.1), blameless (*Num. Rab.* 14.11), and led by an angel of God (on Gen 24:7, *Gen. Rab.* 67.9). The matriarchs are given the utmost respect and viewed as working hand in hand with the patriarchs in response to divine commands.

This role is not recognized by many Christian interpreters, as the following passage by A. S. Herbert (76–77) will demonstrate:

> Jacob's fraudulent acquisition of the blessing . . . is one of the most unpleasant stories of the book of Genesis. . . . Again, the conduct of Rebekah was such as to arouse the most vigorous condemnation in ancient Israel. For not only did she instigate this deception; she was, by her conduct, acting against her husband and so destroying the unity of the family.

The view that Rebekah, through the act of deception, was doing something wrong persists in many Christian commentaries. For instance, S. R. Driver (255) says:

> The narrative tells how, instigated by his ambitious and designing mother, Jacob deceives his aged father, and wrests from his brother his father's blessing. That the action of Rebekah and Jacob was utterly discreditable and indefensible, is of course obvious.

According to Walter Bowie (668):

> Rebekah's love for Jacob was so fiercely jealous that it broke loose from any larger loyalty. As between her twin sons, she wanted Jacob to have the best of everything, no matter how he got it; and to that end she would not scruple at trickery and unfairness both towards her husband and her son, Esau. There was something of the tigress in Rebekah, instinctively protecting the cub that by physical comparison was inferior. . . . The story is a study of the way in which an emotion essentially beautiful may become perverted. It is instinctive and right that a woman should love passionately. But the greatest love must always be subject to a greater loyalty: loyalty to truth, to honour, to the relationship of life to God.

He compares Rebekah to Jezebel and Lady Macbeth, although he also acknowledges her sensitivity to hidden value. The pervasiveness of this view is reinforced by J. P. Fokkelman (119–20), who says:

> Finally we see scheming behind the scenes the originator of all misery and the one who is responsible in the first place, Rebekah. She denies her husband and her marriage, she contrives to deprive Esau of his being for her darling's benefit, she urges Jacob to his vile deceit. She is the only one guilty with respect to all the others.

One cannot help but be struck by the intensity of condemnation of Rebekah by commentators of the last two centuries. In searching for a reason why the earlier views of Hebrew and Christian commentators had been overturned, it is tempting to place the blame on a sexist reaction to the emerging feminism of the nineteenth century. However, the evidence disallows this interpretaton in that early feminist Christian writers also condemned Rebekah. Clara Colby, co-author of *The Woman's Bible,* claimed that Rebekah's "great error was deceiving her husband to carry her point" (Stanton *et al.*:54). Most surprising perhaps is the view of Elizabeth Cady Stanton, one of the founders of the women's suffrage movement in the United States. She decries the "supreme wickedness of Rebekah in deceiving Isaac, defrauding Esau, and undermining the moral sense of the son she loved" (52). She states further: "it is a pitiful tale of greed and deception. Alas! where can a child look for lessons in truth, honor, and generosity, when the mother they naturally trust, sets at defiance every principle of justice and mercy to secure some worldly advantage" (53).

One must then ask why the positive valuation of the Hebrew commentators was lost and why so much importance was given to deceit. To answer this question it would be necessary to delve into the complex history of the relations between Christianity and Judaism, involving in some Christians the need to devalue the writings of the OT. One also would need to consider the predominance of ethics in Protestant Christianity, the kind of absolutism of ethics which Kierkegaard criticized in *Fear and Trembling*.

Within such a framework, telling a lie would always be considered a sin regardless of the context. When the further factor of a woman deceiving her husband was added, the ethical context would necessitate condemnation. In general it appears that Catholic commentators have not been as concerned with the deception as were Protestants. In *The City of God*, St. Augustine refers to the act as not a lie but a mystery (357). Similarly St. Thomas Aquinas in the *Summa Theologica*, in referring to Jacob's part in the deception, claims that Jacob spoke in a mystical way when he said he was Esau, Isaac's firstborn son (1947:1667). In these Catholic interpretations, however, the commentator seems more concerned with what Jacob and Isaac are doing than with what Rebekah is doing.

Feminist scholars are currently concerned with the question of how women's history has been devalued and neglected. Rebekah is an obvious case in point. In recent centuries she appears to be either invisible in commentaries which prefer to concentrate on Isaac and Jacob, or else she becomes condemned when brought into the light. Why is it, one might ask, that Abraham is not condemned for being willing to kill his son while Rebekah is condemned for being willing to deceive her husband? This question is particularly important in view of the belief that God from the beginning seems to want to test the strength of the faith of the chosen people and that the divine will often seems to want to overturn natural relationships between father and son, elder and younger siblings, and perhaps even wife and husband in order to manifest the absolute demands of the transcendent.

A further proof of the devaluation of the feminine is given when we study commentaries written closer in time to the original text. As has been previously mentioned, the Midrash Rabbah takes a positive approach to all the matriarchs. Another example chosen from the early church father St. John Chrysostom is even more striking. In a discussion of the life of Rebekah in his 53rd homily on Genesis, he enters into her spirituality and recognizes the extraordinary qualities manifested in her willingness to risk everything for God (195–96):

> Behold the great love of the mother, or rather the management of God. For it was he himself who gave to her this stratagem, and took care that all things should turn out well. . . . What, therefore, of Rebekah . . . for she acted not only according to her own intention, but she serves the divine oracle and sought with all eagerness to free the boy from fears and strengthen his soul that he might accomplish the stratagem; nor did she promise him that he could mislead the father and hide it. But what of this 'Upon me be your curse, my son, only obey my word, and go get them for me'.

It cannot be claimed then that all Christian commentators condemned Rebekah. In fact, St. John's interpretation not only praises Rebekah, as do the Rabbinic scholars, it also enters into the spiritual dynamics of her life. He recognizes that in the act of taking the curse upon herself, Rebekah gave evidence of spiritual maturity. This paper will follow that example by bringing Rebekah back into the light, not for her condemnation, but for her praise.

Rebekah as Saint

Rebekah should be of particular interest to contemporary women and men. She is the first woman in the Bible to be described in sufficient detail to serve as an example of sanctity. She is also the first person in the Bible to offer herself in reparation for someone else. In her immortal words, "On me be the curse, my son," she took upon herself the consequences of her spiritual direction to Jacob. While this may be seen as the ultimate act of her life, Rebekah also gave evidence of sanctity in other ways. The remainder of this paper will be devoted to the examination of the specific examples.

The first words we have of Rebekah are "Drink, my Lord" (Gen 24:18). The servant of Abraham has reached the end of his search for a bride for Isaac. He had been bound by oath to find someone to be a mother to the chosen people. The servant had asked her for a "little water" from her pitcher and she had responded immediately and generously. Not only did she offer water to Abraham's servant but she added: "I will draw water for your camels, too, until they have had enough" (Gen 24:19). She who is destined to bear the seed of Israel in her womb offers water from her pitcher to servants and animals. Her work is to continue to offer this source of life not until *she* is tired but until "*they* have had enough." Her will is to be of service to the creatures of God.

The next words she speaks are to identify herself and to offer the hospitality of her home to the strangers: "I am the daughter of Bethuel, the son whom Milcah bore to Nahor. . . . We have plenty of straw and fodder, and room to lodge" (Gen 24:25). The true purpose of this meeting is soon revealed, and Rebekah is seen to be the woman God has chosen for Isaac. The fact that she was chosen by divine guidance is emphasized several times in the text. Abraham says: "He will now send his angel ahead of you, so that you may choose a wife for my son there" (Gen 24:7). The servant prays to God for a sign so that "she (will) be the one you have chosen for your servant Isaac" (Gen 24:14). The sign, the generous offering of water, was given. While Rebekah's response is usually attributed to her natural qualities of spontaneity and generosity, it could easily have been the result of a private inspiration in prayer. God might have revealed to her sometime before that she would be asked to leave. He could easily have indicated to her the way to recognize the servant who would lead her to the fulfillment of her vocation. He would be the one, a stranger, who asked her for a "little water." If God had asked her whether she would accept His call at that earlier time, then He could as easily have indicated to her the sign she was to give to the servant. It is important to consider the possibility of Rebekah's own inner sense of the religious significance of the event, particularly because some commentators seem to be convinced that this response is not in any way a sign of her sanctity. Driver states that Rebekah "quickly, though unconsciously, announces herself as his master's niece" (230).

A. S. Herbert confirms the same interpretation: "The truth of the story lies in the fact that God guides even when men are *quite unaware* of his guidance" (59–60).

We are told in the Bible that Rebekah's sufferings began once she conceived. "The children struggled with one another inside her, and she said, 'If this is the way of it, why go on living?'" (Gen 25:22). The suffering was so acute that (according to one version of the text, at least) she felt the temptation to suicide. Instead of giving in to this temptation, however, she went to consult Yahweh at a holy place, to discover what meaning this could have in the plan of God. She was told: "There are two nations in your womb, your issue will be two rival peoples. One nation shall have the mastery of the other, and the elder shall serve the younger" (Gen 25:23). The conflict between Jacob and Esau has been interpreted in many different ways. The obvious first way is to see the struggle as one between two brothers for priority. In Mal 1:2–5 it is interpreted as a struggle between the Israelites and the Edomites. St. Paul (Rom 9:7–13) considers it as a struggle between the children of nature and those of God. St. Augustine (257) and St. Thomas Aquinas (1947:1667) both claim that it is a sign that the younger, the Gentiles, will take the place of the elder, the Jews. Again it is interesting to see how different interpreters chose threads of interpretation which reflect the perspective from which they are writing. In this paper I want to emphasize the role of Rebekah in the struggle. Her function is to make it possible for the divine blessing to be given to the one who was chosen by God.

In order to understand why Rebekah was needed to fill this function it is necessary to examine the character of Isaac. Isaac began his biblical life in the most extraordinary way through the recognition of his father's call to sacrifice him. In fact, the profound dynamics of his spirituality probably came through his transcendence of apparent betrayal in forgiving his father who was willing to murder him and in forgiving a wife who was willing to deceive him. What is noticeable, however, is that he does not in the biblical text receive a specific call, or pass a test of faith in the way that both Abraham and Jacob did. In fact, in the only two records we have of direct communication between God and Isaac, we are told that he will be blessed "in return for Abraham's obedience" (Gen 26: 2–6) and "on account of my servant Abraham" (Gen 26:24). It is tempting to bring Rebekah into relief by maintaining that Isaac was not a saint. In this way Rebekah would be the necessary link between Abraham and Jacob /1/. However, it is not necessary to do so to justify the claim that Rebekah herself gave evidence of extraordinary spiritual depth.

Before studying Rebekah's function, one possible alternative must be considered. God could have told Jacob directly to carry out the deception. He certainly had demonstrated his ingenuity in claiming the birthright. Jacob appeared to be afraid of such a move; in particular, he feared receiving a curse from Isaac instead of a blessing (Gen 27:12). He needed Rebekah's strength, and in particular her willingness to offer herself as victim, should Isaac give a curse. It was only after he was free from a potential curse that he was able to act.

Rebekah had been prepared for this ultimate act through offering her body to a stranger to save Isaac's life. She allowed herself to be passed off as Isaac's sister "in case they killed him" (Gen 26:8). As in many cases where a sacrifice is offered, but not carried out, Rebekah did not have to live the consequences of the sacrifice. This in no way detracts from the seriousness of the offer. She is seen to be willing to give her body to save a life. In the same way she says to Jacob: "On me be the curse, my son."

"Rebekah happened to be listening while Isaac was talking to his son Esau." And as promptly as she had said to Abraham's servant "Drink, my Lord," she calls Jacob to her side: "Now my son, listen to me and do as I tell you. Go to the flock, and bring me two good kids, so that I can make the kind of savory your father likes. Then you can take it to your father for him to eat so that he may bless you before he dies" (Gen 27:5–10). In this simple statement the stage for Rebekah's ultimate act is set. What are her alternatives?

First of all, Rebekah might have allowed her vocation to end with the material birth of Esau and Jacob and care of Isaac. This was the model Sarah had bequeathed her. Secondly, she might have recognized that Jacob was the chosen one but believed that she had no part in making this possible herself. In this case, she would merely wait for the prophecy she had received during pregnancy to work itself out. Still a third alternative would have been to recognize Jacob's call, to observe Isaac's blindness, and to decide to speak directly with her husband in the hope of dissuading him from blessing Esau. This course is later followed by Esther. If Isaac's blindness continued, she might have considered running away with Jacob to her brother Laban. However, she would have forfeited the patriarchal blessing of Jacob and in this way broken the spiritual link with Abraham. Because of the patriarchal structure of the society at the time, she could not as a mother pass the blessing on to Jacob. It is significant that Jacob received his first call from God *after* he had received the blessing from Isaac (Gen 28:14–15). Furthermore, Isaac was old and ill; it would not be a holy act to desert her husband in time of need.

Rebekah then chose a fourth alternative, which used deceit. Another holy woman, Judith, later on used deceit to murder an enemy. Rebekah's deceit was to fool Isaac into believing that Jacob was his elder son Esau. Can it be that God asked this particular deceit of her? In this case, Rebekah would not merely be acting on her own to fulfill the prophecy during the pregnancy, but she would be responding to a specific call to help the divine plan. Had not Abraham been asked to sacrifice Isaac? Could she not be asked to sacrifice her marriage trust? Had not Isaac been given back? Could not the marriage be reunited? Would not God suspend the ethical for teleological reasons (Kierkegaard)?

One can imagine the "fear and trembling" that this possibility must have aroused in Rebekah. Had she not left her family to serve God? If the act was unsuccessful, or the suggestion of an evil force, what would be the consequences? Had she not been told that woman from Eve on was prone to be deceived by the devil, and that God had placed woman under the subjection of her husband as punishment for the transgression? And yet it appeared to her that she was asked to go against her husband. How could she be certain? The only certainty would be the success of the act itself and of Jacob's vocation. This she could not know before the act was committed. It would have to be an act in the dark. If Isaac decided to send her into the desert to die as Abraham had done to Hagar, she would accept the consequences. She would offer her life so that the divine will might be done. She would risk humiliation, ill repute, and death so that the grace of God might descend on Jacob.

Furthermore, she would protect Jacob from harm by taking upon herself the full responsibility of the deceit. When Jacob was afraid that he would receive his father's curse instead of his blessing, Rebekah answered simply: "On me be the curse, my son!" (Gen 27:13). In these words we have evidence that the decision to deceive Isaac was a courageous and holy act /2/. Rebekah offered herself as a victim. Jacob was freed to receive the benefits of the blessing but not the punishment of the curse. As Abraham had to carry the weight of the knife he raised above Isaac, Rebekah had to carry the weight of the words which would come from her husband. Abraham was willing to sacrifice his beloved son, and Rebekah was willing to sacrifice her life. Even with a profound certainty that the deceit was divinely called for, she must have felt some fear before the act was completed.

One can say, then, that God needed Rebekah in order to complete the divine work and that she freely accepted a call to service. More than that, she offered herself as victim if the plan should fail. To be cursed would mean to be cut off from God and from his blessings for the rest of her life. In this way, the divine call cooperated with a human response; Rebekah met the test. In the case of Abraham, the sacrifice was transformed and Isaac was given back. In the present case, the feared curse was not uttered and Jacob became the son consecrated to carry out the ancestry of the chosen people. Rebekah was not sent out into the desert to die, but remained with Isaac until the end.

Finally, Rebekah was used for another purpose when she arranged for Jacob to receive Isaac's blessing before departing to her brother's home. She said to Isaac: "I am tired to death because of the daughters of Heth. If Jacob marries . . . one of the women of the country, what meaning is there left in life for me?" (Gen 27:46). It is interesting to note that even at this point Isaac did not suggest that Jacob leave to marry a woman of the chosen people, as Abraham had done before. It is through Rebekah that the divine will manifested itself. Instead of sending Jacob away secretly, however, she leads Isaac to give Jacob another blessing and an order to marry a woman from Paddam-aram. And as Esau noted, Jacob left "in obedience to his father and mother" (Gen 28:7).

Therefore, if we view the complete circumstances of Rebekah's life, her sanctity can stand as a model of profound significance for women and men of today. She serves as a model of courage, immediate acceptance of grace, long-suffering, and willingness to die for God. In her own response to God, she is a mother of the faith. More concretely, she is the mother of Jacob, i.e., of Israel /3/.

Christine Garside Allen

Notes

/1/ It is precisely this temptation that I gave way to in the published first draft of this essay (in Gross).

/2/ It is interesting to note that the Midrash Rabbah which had been so positive about Rebekah in general does not praise her in connection with this passage. Instead it offers two different suggestions. The first is that when a man sins his mother is cursed, since the ground is one's mother (cf. Gen 3:17, R. Abba b. Kahana), and the second is that Rebekah will "undertake to go in and tell thy father: Jacob is righteous and Esau is wicked" (R. Isaac) (on Gen 27:13, *Gen. Rab.* 65.15).

/3/ With agreement by the task group on method, an early form of this essay was used in Gross; the revised version is presented here with the permission of the American Academy of Religion, which holds the copyright for that work. The earlier version included a description of Isaac's blindness here omitted (see n. 1).

Chapter 11

The Rhythm of Communication in the Hermeneutical Process: Musical Analogies for the Impact of Biblical Prose Rhythms

Ann M. Vater
Western Illinois University

Musicologists have written of music's basic realities—tone, meter and rhythm—in ways that can illuminate the function of biblical prose in the hermeneutical process. For the purpose of this discussion, biblical prose is understood as composed of 1) resonating words, 2) genre meters, and 3) the rhythms of the narration patterns. Biblical poetry, or even the biblical text as set to music, is not considered in what follows. A study of the poetry or text set to music could be based upon this discussion, but I have chosen to begin with the less obvious case. Of immediate concern is how the *prose* text is like music, how its rhythms cause the listener to *hear* the words.

After demonstrating the appropriateness of the analogy and summarizing recent theories concerning musical tone, meter, and rhythm, elements of biblical prose will be defined on the basis of certain passages from the family stories of Genesis by attending carefully to the narration process. Then through a discussion of women's consciousness-raising, I will suggest that the rhythms of biblical narration cause words to be received and to incite us, just as music's rhythms cause the flow of time to be perceived and to transport an audience. Real hearing is moving and being moved to act, as the šᵉ*ma'*, "listen!," of Deut 6:4 tells us. Thus I am attempting to approach the hermeneutical question through the imagery of hearing rather than of seeing, of feeling the flow of energy rather than of understanding the meaning of symbols.

Paul Ricoeur's discussions of the hermeneutical problem seem at first sight to have opened the understanding of hermeneutics to the auditory realm. He places feeling, that reality which is communicated more rapidly by hearing than by seeing, in a prominent place in his theory of how symbols call forth reflection. He defines the hermeneutical problem as the articulation "in a systematic way of the inventory of symbols—[though they be] scattered in contingent cultures, opaque and ambiguous, submitted to questionable exegesis—with a rational process of reflection" (1961:1). Symbols lie between the *telos* of rationality and the *Ursprung* of experience (the realm of the "practical and affective," "the level of the origin and source of levels of meaning"; Bourgeois: 233–34). The hermeneutics of symbols—the attempt to interpret the double sense of the symbol's intentional structure—is an indirect way of turning from language to experience (the affective realm) and then back to language.

Access to this same realm, "the affective-instinctual side of meaning," is also claimed by Wilson Coker in his "semiotic-gestural theory of music."

> The primary function of any object as a sign is emotional, and all other significatory effects of a sign are dependent upon this prior affectivity. So we must find that the meaning of anything acting as a sign includes along with its semantical, syntactical, and pragmatic dimensions an affective or emotional component ("charge") as well (3).

Both Ricoeur and Coker open the discussion of the meaning of signs to the more than rational—the affective realm, the realm often considered as music's primary site in the human being, a realm which is heard before it is seen. Yet neither of these approaches has adequately described the hermeneutical process, for both refrain from a discussion of the dynamic, the movement of symbols or signs /1/. How does the audience hearing a sacred story perceive motion and move?

The basic presupposition which underlies this exploration is that biblical literature is very much like music, particularly in regard to the phenomenon of rhythm. "Rhythm is not a specifically musical phenomenon. It is the one element which music has in common with other phenomena and processes" (Zuckerkandl:69). Certain passages in Isaiah could even be said to exhibit ecstatic rhythm, as G. F. Händel realized ("and his name shall be called Wonderful, Counsellor, The mighty God, The everlasting Father, The Prince of Peace," Isa 9:6). The repetition so frequent in music, and so characteristic, each in its own way, of biblical poetry, the prose stories of the Pentateuch, and the phenomenon of paronomasia, also suggests the appropriateness of the analogy.

It is primarily because of the creative quality of biblical language, however, that the analogy is most apt. Because scriptural words and meaning have the creative potential to "sound" together simultaneously in a new way, biblical language, even prose, is like music.

> The acoustical event and its musical meaning are in no sense two independent phenomena, existing by themselves. They cannot be imagined separate. Except in the case of creative language (in the biblical sense of Adam's "naming" things) and of poetic language, where other, more "musical" relations come into play, language always has a finished world of things before it, to which it assigns words; whereas tones must themselves create what they mean (Zuckerkandl: 67).

Because scriptural words are creative, and ever newly creative, they are like musical tones, creating what they mean /2/.

Each tone is a dynamic symbol: "We can speak of the tones of music as dynamic symbols. We hear forces in them as the believer sees the divine being in symbols" (Zuckerkandl: 69). Biblical words, however, are not simply symbols in which the believer may see the divine. They are more like resonating tones, dynamic symbols. It is more appropriate to say that it is possible to hear forces there. "The ear is the organ particularly capable of perceiving the dynamic component of external events" /3/.

Musical Tone, Meter, and Rhythm

Most musicians do not concern themselves with the task of defining music in words. Instead, they ensure music's reality by making it. Whether due to this instinctual avoidance or to the difficulty inherent in the task, there is only a rough consensus on the part of musical theorists, aestheticians, and psychologists of music in the definition of music's basic realities, which we call tone, meter, and rhythm.

Tones, the sounds of music, "sounds of distinct pitch, quality and duration" (W. Morris: 1352), are the first reality to strike the ear. There would be no music without tone, without sound. To say "tone," however, is already to imply not only sound, but also time and motion. Tone involves the selection of certain sounds (or silences) in a particular sequence, with particular duration, conveying a particular sense of motion. That is, "tone" already implies time (sequence, duration) and motion, as Victor Zuckerkandl in particular has stated /4/.

Time and motion exist together also in music's other basic realities, meter and rhythm. Ordinarily we might think that meter and rhythm denote, respectively, the elements of time and motion in music. By meter is meant "the patterned grouping of beats recurring within a composition" (Christ and DeLone: 32), and by rhythm is meant "motion in the dynamic field of meter" (Zuckerkandl: 174). We began with the designation of music's basic realities as tone, meter, and rhythm as a way of suggesting that music is a complex of sound, time, and motion. Now it is apparent that time is important to tones (their sequence, their duration), as well as to meter (more stable time organization) and to rhythm (moveable time organization in a flow of energy). Motion is characteristic of tones (each tone has its own force and sense of direction /5/), meter (regularly measured heavy stresses), and especially of rhythm (points of stress and non-stress).

> Musical rhythm, particularly, is perceived as the very graph of motion—of a universally known, extramusical experience—and our actual awareness of rhythm, accordingly, is usually a considerably concrete presentation of motion imagery (Ferguson: 19).

When meter and rhythm coalesce, in a rhythm "designed to bring out the ceaselessly repeated beating of the metric wave" (Zuckerkandl: 174), it is called "ecstatic."

> What almost physically overwhelms the listener in certain compositions by Bach and Beethoven—the opening chorus of the St. Matthew Passion, for example, or the Gloria fugue in the *Missa Solemnis*—is the effect of the metric waves, which roll down upon

us, broad and powerful, with ever-increasing impact, each new wave driven on by the concentrated force of all those which have preceded it, and in turn driving another before it, irresistibly and inexhaustibly, until finally it becomes impossible to conceive how this surging flood could ever be stilled, and we feel that we are seized and borne along by eternal motion itself (Zuckerkandl: 174–75/6/).

Susanne Langer, Zuckerkandl, and others /7/ state that music is the art of time in a special sense.

What, then, is the essence of *all* music? The creation of virtual time, and its complete determination by the movement of audible forms (Langer: 125).

Music is a temporal art because, shaping the stuff of time, it creates an image of time (Zuckerkandl: 259).

Music creates a sense of time for the audience, a sense molded against the time-fed urge for repetition, yet satisfying that urge. "Thanks to music, we are able to *behold* time" (Zuckerkandl: 260).

Most interesting, however, is the element of force in time, an element imaged by the waves of the sea.

Temporal succession is never given as simple sequence, as simple flux, but as a combination of flux and cycle, as wave. . . . What is it that beats here as wave, what moves here? . . . The forces of the wave are forces of time—or better, are time as force. . . . Music is temporal art in the more exact sense that, for its ends, it enlists time as force (Zuckerkandl: 199–200).

Knowing the forces of time as beats, as meter, is a conscious process. But perceiving the forces of time as movement, as rhythm, is a more intuitive process.

Time pertains to self-conscious constructs, whereas rhythm is a matter of the immediate feeling of phases of tension, stress, relaxation, and repose. Hence, we equate time with cerebral and symbolic meaning and rhythm with an intuition and feeling of the flow of energy. Knowledge of time [wave-force as beats] is discursive, and knowledge of rhythm [wave-force as movement] is by acquaintance (Coker: 42).

It is easy enough to draw a picture of the notes on their pitchlines, with their duration markings: ovals, flags, dots, and rests, in their little measured boxes. But to make music, or to enjoy it, requires the feeling, the ear for motion in tones, meter, and rhythm.

Biblical Prose and Musical Motion

In a culture saturated with chant, with a sung biblical text, or sacred dance, the analogy suggested here would probably make immediate and obvious sense. In our culture, instead of moving with and hearing the sacred, we increasingly take on the TV and film watchers' stance of fixed observers, "waiting for the word." At the most, we investigate "deep structures." In the following section, with the help of Martin Buber's insights concerning "motif-word style," we will attempt to recover terms like "dynamic" and "flux," images of motion, when speaking of the biblical text, particularly Genesis 32–33, Jacob and Esau's reunion; and Genesis 38, Tamar's escape from the power of Judah, *pater familias*.

We will suggest a method for uncovering a sense of movement: resonating words which sound through various levels of a text, realistic story patterns which set up the various beats of a story, and in particular, narration patterns which provide the rhythms to play upon the beats and silences of the realistic story patterns /8/. Thereby we hope to awaken the ears of critics to the creative possibilities inherent in the narration dimension of the biblical text.

The Reunion of Jacob and Esau

The exciting and magnificent scene of Jacob and Esau's reunion opens with a message from Jacob, who is at Mahanaim, to Esau, who is in the land of Seir. These verses (32:4–6) are the first example of a message being sent in the book of Genesis. The message communication introduces the story of the reunion, Genesis 32–33, as well as the narrative of the embassy to Esau, Gen 32:2–22.

In Genesis 32 Jacob prepares assiduously for the moment of encounter with Esau, hoping by all his efforts to placate what he surmises is Esau's evil purpose. Many delicious ironies and wordplays in these chapters of the encounter make this basically J narrative a fine literary piece. Martin Buber has noted several examples of what he calls "motif-word style" in the Jacob cycle

(1964). Four motif words *šēm, bᵉrākāh, bᵉkōrāh,* and *mirmāh* are used in differing patterns to paint an honest portrait of the wily Jacob. The one who has taken away his brother's *bᵉkōrāh,* and his *bᵉrākāh* by guile (*mirmāh*), is deceived (*rimmîtānî*) by Laban. Laban says he cannot marry off the younger daughter Rachel before the firstborn (*habbᵉkîrāh*) Leah. The words *bᵉrākāh* and *šēm* are repeated again and again in 32:27–31—seven times. Jacob is no longer the supplanter, but by a new blessing the "one who strives with God." A final irony occurs in 33:11 in which Jacob pleads with Esau to accept *Jacob's* blessing (*birkātî*—often translated "gift").

In describing the over-all sense of movement that these motif-words produce, Buber writes:

> Through the respective differences, the total dynamic effect is carried quite often. "Dynamic" I call it, because between the characteristic sounds which play upon one another, at the same time, a movement realizes itself: whoever feels the presence of the whole feels the waves pounding here and there (Buber, 1964:1131).

There is a sense of wholeness, and yet a sense of waves. Therefore it is correct to speak of a "dynamic" in the text.

It is possible here to speak of resonating words or word stems, like *bᵉkōrāh* and *bᵉrākāh,* each a tone sounding with the help of the overtones nearby in the story. Each time one of these motif words sounds, one could speak of it as the sound of a beat. The beats occur in regular enough patterns in Genesis 32–33 to speak of a meter here. Beyond this, however, there is a sense of a dynamic in the story, according to Buber. There is movement in a greater field; Buber calls this an indication of "the inner rhythm of the text" (1964:1131).

When addressing the question of meaning, Buber says that the similarities of the sounds are the bearers of another level of meaning: "The higher meaning murmurs out of the unison for whomever listens attentively" (1133). When pressed to interpret this meaning in "Das ist das" language, he says it is not permissible. "The motif-style meaning can only be intimation, the presentation only pointing to something which is valid in its reality, but is not to be written down or thought again" (1134).

There is another way, we would propose, of uncovering a dynamic in the biblical story. More closely akin to the methods of historical-

critical exegesis, this method attempts to work within the broader
reality of narration itself. Let us return to Gen 32:4–6.

> Jacob sent messengers ahead to his brother Esau. . . . He
> commanded them saying, "Thus shall you say to my lord, to Esau:
> 'Thus says your servant Jacob: . . . I am sending to let my lord
> know, in order to find grace in your eyes.'"

Many form-critical conclusions have been drawn from the
language of these verses (Eissfeldt: 23). Both the Messenger Formula
and a commissioning formula are present here, as well as the verb *šlḥ*.
(Note that the verb is repeated in the message itself. It is possible to
construct an example of motif-word style from this observation /9/.)
There does not appear to be a written message; rather, messengers
seem to be sent to deliver an oral message. There is a clear formulaic
beginning for the message. That the ending is not a well-worn
formula can be seen from the subsequent reiteration of Jacob's desire
to "find grace" in Esau's eyes, Gen 33:8. These form-critical
comments say virtually nothing about the movement in the passage,
however.

The particular pattern for narrating this message communication
raises a very interesting question of movement in the story. By
examining the 230 occurrences of message or oracle communication
narrated in the prose of the OT, it is possible to speak of eight patterns
used to narrate this situation (Vater, 1976). The realistic pattern
(meter) for communicating a message or oracle is: 1) originator *sends*
a particular message by commissioning a messenger with oral (and
often also written) words; 2) messenger *delivers* message in presence
of receiver. The narration patterns (rhythm) provide the emphasis, or
points of stress and nonstress, for this communication and create
waves in a broader flow of energy. For example, in Gen 32:4–6 a
narration pattern is employed which emphasizes the sender, one
"wave" in the broader rhythm of sending and releasing characteristic
of the whole Jacob cycle. The nonstress element is the delivery of the
message by Jacob's messengers, which is indicated only indirectly.
Together with the enigmatic preparatory vv 2–3, the mysterious
delivery impels us into the next stress elements: the mysterious "man"
at the Jabbok, who raises the mystery of Jacob's own identity. Let us
elucidate these movements with detailed examples.

Gen 32:4–6 as a message communication is an example of the

narration pattern in which the message is narrated only in the situation of its being commissioned, and then a brief notice of its deliverance is added, one of thirty-six such occurrences in the OT. Although no delivery scene is narrated, the return of the messengers suggests they have been obedient in delivery of the message. Jacob's fearful response to his messengers' report that Esau is coming to meet him makes the reader doubtful as to whether Jacob's original message ever reached Esau. In Genesis 32 the narrator makes us wonder about Esau's attitude towards Jacob. On the level of the simple story the narration pattern (message narrated only in commissioning, brief notice of delivery) emphasizes the importance of the sender, in this case Jacob. So in Gen 32:4-6 we learn only the sender's attitude, his plight. We do not know Esau's attitude towards Jacob, nor does Jacob himself. He expects the worst.

On another resonating level, that of the faithful scribal traditor, the narration pattern employed in Gen 32:4-6 allows for a play upon the mysterious obedient messengers of v 4. Gen 32:2-3 confronts us before the story with God's own messengers (E stratum).

> Then God's messengers encountered Jacob. When he saw them he said, "This is God's encampment." So he named that place Mahanaim.

Thus we know that the image of the messenger is already in the foreground of the narrator's view. These two sets of messengers, God's and Jacob's, set up the rhythm of the following story: two sets of face-to-face encounters—Jacob and God (as wrestling angel) and Jacob and Esau. In each case there is an obedient figure, fulfilling a role, who is at the same time a figure of mystery: God's messengers, Jacob's messengers, "some man," Jacob himself. The mystery in the first two cases is, what did the messengers actually do? In the other two cases the mystery is, who is this figure? who is Jacob? (He receives a new name from God, v 29). Esau's own question about Jacob is, has he changed? shall I trust him? (33:8). As one moves then, from one segment of the story to another, we can see how the nonstress element of the narration pattern is employed by the narrator.

On the resonating level of a final narrator, this narration pattern can function actually to swallow up the obedient messenger in the sender's voice. Gen 32:4-6 is the fullest form of commissioning a message that occurs in the OT. The repetition of the verb *šlḥ* in Jacob's voice is particularly noteworthy. The elaborate sending of the message and messengers in vv 4–6 by Jacob himself (he who up to this time has been sent and released [*šllḥ*] by others) marks a shift in his fate, for now he has gained the power to release God from his hold (Gen 32:27) (cf. n. 9). He has truly come of age. Thus Gen 32:4–6, with the emphasis on Jacob's voice, is an accented moment in the broader rhythm of sending/releasing characteristic of the Jacob story. Uncovering the narration pattern allows us to feel that rhythm and realize its significance.

The Power Struggle Between Tamar and Judah

The dramatic confrontation of the righteous Tamar and the powerful but wicked father-in-law Judah takes place in the narration of Tamar's message to Judah, Gen 38:25–26. By it she wins her life, climaxing her pursuit of full Semitic womanhood—the conception of a legitimate (hopefully male) child, a pursuit controlled by the custom of levirite marriage (cf. Coats). Judah's cheeks burn with shame, while she escapes the flames of death.

The richness of the story cannot be reduced to the concern for the fulfillment of the levirite obligation. The confrontation of Judah and Tamar, with Tamar forcing Judah to *hakkēr* (verify, recognize) her as righteous is the main point, and vv 12–30 focus on this, the message and its response being the climax of the story. The two-part structure of the message itself, the second part beginning with "verify," tips us off to this main point.

The message of Gen 38:25–26 is told in the story according to a narration pattern different from the one for Gen 32:4–6. Tamar's words are told to us by a pattern in which a brief notice of a message being sent is followed by the message narrated in neither commissioning nor delivery scenes, but cited as a quotation. There are some sixty-two examples of this pattern in the OT, which usually reads, "He sent to N.N., saying. . . ." On the level of the simple story, this narration pattern focuses special attention on the message itself. From the level of the traditors, the pattern displays the message's immediate impact on events. On the resonating level of the final narrator, the pattern removes the messenger's voice from the scene, so as to unite in a dramatic way the two parties who are separated by a physical gulf.

The importance of the message itself and its immediate impact upon the events which follow, as well as the dramatic unification of two parties who are separated by an impassable gulf, are all dynamic resonances inherent in the narration pattern of Gen 38:25-26. They are also elements telling Tamar's story, apart from the content of her own words. In Genesis 38 a brief notice of a message being sent by Tamar is followed by the message, cited as a quotation.

> But as they were bringing her out, she sent word to her father-in-law, "It is by the man to whom these things belong that I am with child. Please verify," she added, "whose seal and cord and whose staff these are." Judah recognized them and said, "She is more in the right than I am, since I did not give her to my son Shelah."

We are to listen carefully to the words of the message. They are the turning point of the story, changing the course of events. The messenger's voice, the commissioning, and the delivery disappear so that two persons—the condemned and the judge—are dramatically united. As the story ends, they are united in life once more, "but he had no further relations with her." Her energy and "Klugheit" or prudence (Gunkel) are apparent in her words, which really "reach" Judah.

The meter of the pattern used to narrate the message of Gen 38:25-26 groups its beats so that the main impulse is the message. Tamar's own voice enters the message with a new energy in the last part of Gen 38:25, "and she said, 'Verify whose these are. . . .'" Her voice is right in Judah's ear. The two-part structure of the message itself is disclosed, with special emphasis on *hakkēr* and the immediacy of her voice to Judah. Unlike Jacob in Gen 37:32-33, who is told by his sons to *hakkēr-na'* the long bloody tunic and who sees it as a message of death, Judah verifies the items to save Tamar's life. Unlike the long devious avoidance by Judah and his sons from "fulfilling" Tamar, her own immediate words bring legitimate life. Various rhythms in the story are climaxed in these words.

The words of the text, then, are tones in the sense that they resonate through various levels of perception. Each generation of commentators discovers new levels and tries to persuade themselves and others of new meaning on the older levels. They are like composers discovering the new dynamic potential in tones.

The narration patterns for any given situation presuppose a "realistic" meter (in this case, the recital of the words of a message or oracle both in the commissioning and delivery scenes), which is played out in the story according to its own moveable time signature (the pattern of Gen 32:4–6 accentuates the commissioning scene, so that the beats are grouped into a type of 2/4 meter; the pattern of Gen 38:25–26 accentuates the message, so that the beats are grouped into a type of slow 3/4 meter). But the narrator sets up the rhythmic feeling in the story by providing his or her own broader context of stress and nonstress elements. In the immediate *communication* situation, for example, there is a presence and absence of voices in the story which set up their own rhythm. The movement inside of the listener is the question, who is speaking now?, whose voice is that?

Ultimately, the changing voices claim to speak one reality. The hermeneutical question becomes this, how do we recognize God's voice here? And then: how do we bring to consciousness, how do we enact the movement already generated in us through the hearing of the word of God?

Hermeneutics as Rhythmic Consciousness

> I've got the music in me,
> I've got the music in me,
> I've got the music in me. (Contemporary song.)

There is a discovery of harmony, of the promise of wholeness in real hearing, be it of music or of scriptural words. These words come inside of us. They move us into another world, whereby we accept the pain, the craziness of this world, and release into a new world of infinite tranformation. Against the ever-moving meaningless beats of our lives, these words transmit us into meaningful movement. Rhythms cause understanding.

The experience of women in consciousness-raising groups can provide us with an example of this process /10/. The speaking that women do with one another, and the way their words move others, is a good illustration of how interpretation takes place.

What happens when we hear sacred words in the stories of our sisters? The meters trip off one by one—the realistic meters of ordinary woman-life situations, the meters of a narration pattern which group the other beats into recognizable time signatures. The meters, then, are based on logic, based on life, or based on like to like—the repetition of favorite words.

Then the words begin to enter rational consciousness. The message constitutes what *is* now, with a recognizable beginning, middle, and end. The masks of deceit are torn away, one by one. But the rhythm keeps us moving, going on, carrying us through the edge where the words' body and our bodies meet. When we return to self-consciousness, when we get back home, the music is already playing. The fire of change is already glowing.

The change begins in the recognition that we are closely related to one another: the sisterhood. Or, as in the oracles of the ancient Near Eastern goddesses Ishtar and Isis /11/, "Look! I am here with you" (Exod 3:14–22). We realize we are a people. "You shall no longer be spoken of as Jacob, but as Israel, because you have contended with divine and human beings and have prevailed" (Gen 32:29). We want life here and now. "She is more in the right than I am, since I did not give her to my son Shelah" (Gen 38:26). Next we can courageously face the pain of present life, because we share it together. Then one can want a new life. The feeling of harmony transmitted in the rhythm tells us it has already begun. We can let the words come to our consciousness—the words that tell us of what that present but new life is. Then comes the sense of resolution, of the individual in the group, of the words in a harmony which pounds on through every successive beat.

The process of interpretation, then, is the recognition of the congruence between the feeling of movement in sacred words (dynamic words, more like music than signs or symbols) and the movement in one's life. With the movement of the biblical words moving us, the quest for meaning can end and, paradoxically, we are there.

Notes

/1/   Coker speaks of "the rhythmic shapes of sonorous motion." Yet his basic terminology here of the "iconic function of rhythm," its function of *imaging* life in art because of its organic connections, and "gesture," sonorously moving structures which "put significant events before us," which are "right before us bearing attitudes and stimulating us" (18–19)—all this terminology presupposes the eyes, not the ears.

/2/   In this exploration I am further developing the insight that biblical literature discloses God to us as literary language discloses reality, in a much fuller fashion than ordinary language or its abstract neighbor, technical language (Luis Alonso Schökel, 1965).

/3/   Zuckerkandl: 63; he is summarizing the experiments of Gustav von Allesch, *Die aesthetische Erscheinungsweise der Farben.*

/4/   "It is not *two* components [physical . . . and psychic or emotional], then, which make up musical tone, but *three*. The words we use to describe this third component—words such as force, equilibrium, tension, direction—are significantly such as neither of the two sides claims for itself alone and, consequently, may well refer to a separate realm between the two, a realm of pure dynamics" (Zuckerkandl: 60–61, italics his). Note that he is using "dynamics" in a sense closer to the Greek *dynamis*, power, rather than the technical musician's meaning of the word as the variation of intensity, that is, the loudness and softness of a tone.

/5/   In the most recent era, tones have a basic dynamic of suspense, because of frequent key changes within a piece. But ordinarily, moving music from one key to another simply changes the dynamic possibilities of the tones themselves. It is even possible for composers to find new meaning in tones. But, strangely enough, music of one culture cannot be translated into music of another. These facts could perhaps lead to some striking analogies with biblical translation, as well as the boundaries of religions themselves.

/6/   When the churches stopped chanting, other religious chants filled the vacuum—American Indian, Hindu, and Buddhist examples come readily to mind. The vacuum was a loss of the sense of eternal motion.

/7/   Ferguson defines the two basic elements of music as tension, or "tone-stress," and "ideal-motion," with little discussion of time, and virtually none of meter!

/8/   This method may be called narration criticism, and can be seen in Vater, 1976.

/9/   The words *šlḥ* and *šllḥ* (used eleven times) in the Jacob cycle are beats connecting and commenting upon Jacob's journeys. Rebekah sends for Jacob (27:42) that he might be sent to Laban (27:45). Isaac capitulates to his wife's desire and sends Jacob off (28:5). Esau, however, notes that Jacob was "released" (*šllḥ*) from his power, in being sent off to get a proper wife. Jacob desires to be released from Laban after Rachel has borne Joseph (30:25). No release takes place, but an escape. Once Laban catches up, Jacob justifies his action by saying that if God had not been on his side, even now Laban would have released him empty-handed (31:42). Gen 32:4–6 reinstates Jacob as the sender. To Esau he sends a message and a present (32:19), whereas it is God himself whom he releases from his hold (32:27, 30). Finally, 33:1–27 provides a conclusion. Jacob gets Esau to accept his blessing, and successfully refuses Esau's pace and pacers, journeying instead to Succoth "by easy stages" with the $m^e l\bar{a}$ '$k\bar{a}h$ (another motif-word of the two chapters). The one who sends and releases is finally free.

/10/   Hear Judith Plaskow, "The Coming of Lilith: Toward a Feminist Theology" (mimeo.), particularly the "Yeah Yeah Experience" (3–5).

/11/   See, e.g., the oracles of Ishtar to Esarhaddon, "I, Ishtar of Arbela, will go before you and behind you"; and, "Because I have spoken to you, I will not abandon you" (Oracles concerning Esarhaddon," i 23–24; iii 39–40, Pritchard: 605–6). See also an oracle of Isis, "Behold I am come to take pity of thy fortune and tribulation; behold I am present to favour and aid thee. . ." (Apuleius, *Metamorphoses*, in Kee: 80–81).

BIBLIOGRAPHY

Albright, William Foxwell
    1942   *Archaeology and the Religion of Israel*. Baltimore: Johns Hopkins Press.

Alonso Schökel, Luis
    1963   *Estudios de Poética Hebrea*. Barcelona: Juan Flors.
    1965   *The Inspired Word: Scripture in the Light of Language and Literature*. New York: Herder.

Alt, Albrecht
    1953   "Aegyptische Tempel in Palaestina und die Landnahme der Philister." Pp. 216–30 in *Kleine Schriften*, I. Munich: Beck. (Original, 1944.)
    1966   "The Settlement of the Israelites in Palestine." Pp. 133–69 in *Essays on Old Testament History and Religion*. Oxford: Blackwell. (Original, 1925.)

Altizer, Thomas J. J.
    1977   *The Self-Embodiment of God*. New York: Harper.

Anderson, Barry F.
    1975   *Cognitive Psychology*. New York: Academic.

Anscombe, G. E. M.
    1957   *Intention*. Oxford: Blackwell.

Apel, Karl-Otto
    1973   *Transformation der Philosophie*, 2 vols. Frankfurt: Suhrkamp.

Arnheim, Rudolf
    1974   *Art and Visual Perception*, 2nd ed. Berkeley: University of California Press.

Ashby, W. Ross
    1962   "Principles of the Self-Organizing System." Pp. 255–78 in *Principles of Self-Organization*. Eds. H. Von Foerster and G. Zopf. Oxford: Pergamon.

Augustinus, Aurelius, Saint, Bp. of Hippo
    1948   *The City of God*. Pp. 1–663 in *Basic Writings of Saint Augustine*, II. New York: Random House.

Austin, J. L.
    1975   *How to Do Things with Words*, 2nd ed. Cambridge, MA: Harvard University Press.

Babbitt, Irving
    1910   *The New Laokoon.* Boston: Houghton Mifflin.

Baird, J. Arthur
    1976   "Content-Analysis and the Computer." *JBL* 95: 255-76.

Barbour, Ian G.
    1966   *Issues in Science and Religion.* Englewood Cliffs, NJ: Prentice-Hall.

Bar-Hillel, Yehoshua
    1964   *Language and Information.* Reading, MA: Addison-Wesley.

Barr, James
    1966   *Old and New in Interpretation.* New York: Harper and Row.
    1969/70   "Symbolism of Names in the Old Testament." *BJRL* 52: 11-29.
    1973   *The Bible in the Modern World.* New York: Harper and Row.

Barth, Karl
    1936-58   *Church Dogmatics,* 4 vols. Edinburgh: T. & T. Clark.

Barthes, Roland
    1964   *Essais Critiques.* Paris: du Seuil. (Engl. trans.: *Critical Essays.*
                    Evanston: Northwestern University Press, 1972.)
    1966   "Introduction à l'analyse structurale des récits."
                    Communications 8:1-27.
    1967   *Elements of Semiology.* London: Jonathan Cape.
    1970   *Writing Degree Zero.* Boston: Beacon.
    1971   "La lutte avec l'ange." Pp. 27-40 in *Analyse Structurale et
                    Exégèse Biblique.* By R. Barthes, *et al.* Neuchâtel: Delachaux
                    Niestlé. (Engl. trans.: *Structural Analysis and Biblical Exegesis*
                    [Pittsburgh Theological Monograph Series, 3]. Pittsburgh:
                    Pickwick, 1974:21-33.)
    1974   *S/Z.* New York: Hill and Wang. (French original, 1970.)

Bartlett, J. R.
    1972   "The Rise and Fall of the Kingdom of Edom," *PEQ*:26-37.
    1973   "The Moabites and Edomites." Pp. 229-58 in *Peoples of Old
                    Testament Times.* Ed. D. J. Wiseman. Oxford: Clarendon.

Bar-Yosef, Ofer
    1970   "The Epi-Paleolithic Cultures of Palestine." Diss. Hebrew
                    University, Jerusalem.

Batson, C. Daniel; Beker, J. Christiaan; and Clark, Malcolm
    1973   *Commitment Without Ideology.* Philadelphia: United Church.

Beardslee, William
    1972   *A House for Hope.* Philadelphia: Westminster.

Beardsley, Monroe C.
    1966   *Aesthetics from Classical Greece to the Present Time.* New
                    York: Macmillan.

Beauchamp, Paul
1971   "L'analyse structurale et l'exégèse biblique." *VTSup* 22:113–28.

Bellah, Robert
1970   *Beyond Belief.* New York: Harper and Row.

Bennett, Robert A.
1976   "Biblical Theology and Black Theology." *Journal of the Interdenominational Theological Center* III, 2:1–14.

Bentzen, Aage
1949   *Introduction to the Old Testament,* II. Copenhagen: Gad.

Benveniste, Émile
1971   *Problems in General Linguistics* (Miami Linguistics Series). Coral Gables, FL: University of Miami Press.

Berger, Klaus
1977   *Exegese des Neuen Testaments.* Heidelberg: Quelle & Meyer.

Berger, Peter L.
1961   *The Noise of Solemn Assemblies.* Garden City, NY: Doubleday Anchor.
1967   *The Sacred Canopy: Elements of a Sociological Theory of Religion.* Garden City, NY: Doubleday.

Bergson, Henri
1917   *Laughter: An Essay on the Meaning of the Comic.* New York: Macmillan.

Berlo, David Kenneth
1960   *The Process of Communication.* New York: Holt, Rinehart and Winston.

Berlyne, D. E., ed.
1974   *Studies in the New Experimental Aesthetics.* Washington: Hemisphere.

Bernays, Paul
1958   *Axiomatic Set Theory.* Intro. by A. Fraenkel. Amsterdam: North-Holland.

Bernheim, Ernst
1908   *Lehrbuch der historischen Methode und der Geschichtsphilosophie,* 5th ed. Leipzig: Duncker and Humblot.

Betti, Emilio
1967   *Allgemeine Auslegungslehre als Methodik der Geisteswissenschaften.* Tübingen: Mohr.

Black, Max
1962   *Models and Metaphors.* Ithaca, NY: Cornell University Press.

Blau, Peter M.
1974   *On the Nature of Organizations.* New York: Wiley.

Bloch, Ernst
1959   *Das Prinzip Hoffnung.* Frankfurt/M: Suhrkamp.

Bohm, David
1957   *Causality and Chance in Modern Physics.* New York: Harper.

Boling, Robert G.
1975   *Judges (The Anchor Bible, 6A).* Garden City, NY: Doubleday.

Bonhoeffer, Dietrich
1967   *Letters and Papers from Prison,* rev. ed. New York: Macmillan.

Bosanquet, B.
1912   *The Principle of Individuality and Value.* London: Macmillan.

Bourgeois, Patrick
1971   "Hermeneutics of Symbols and Philosophical Reflection: Paul Ricoeur." *Philosophy Today* 15:232–35.

Bowie, Walter Russell
1952   "The Book of Genesis: Exposition." Pp. 458–829 in *The Interpreter's Bible,* I. New York: Abingdon.

Bradburn, Norman M.
1969   *The Structure of Psychological Well-Being.* Chicago: Aldine.

Brentano, Franz
1874   *Psychologie vom empirischen Standpunkt,* 2 vols. Leipzig: Duncker.

Brillouin, Léon
1964   *Scientific Uncertainty and Information.* New York: Academic.

Brooks, Cleanth
1947   *The Well Wrought Urn.* New York: Reynal & Hitchcock.

Brueggemann, Walter
1976   *Living Toward a Vision.* Philadelphia: United Church.

Brunner, Emil
1940   *The Christian Doctrine of God.* Philadelphia: Westminster.

Buber, Martin
1955   *I and Thou.* New York: Scribner. (Original, 1923.)
1964   "Leitwortstil in der Erzählung des Pentateuchs." Pp. 1131–49 in *Schriften zur Bibel (Werke,* II). Kösel: Kösel-Verlag.

Buccellati, Giorgio
1967   *Cities and Nations of Ancient Syria (Studi Semitici,* 26). Rome: Università di Roma.

Buckley, Walter, ed.
1968   *Modern Systems Research for the Behavioral Scientist.* Chicago: Aldine.

Budde, Karl
1921 "Eine folgenschwere Redaktion des Zwölfprophetenbuchs." *ZAW* 39:218–29.

Bühler, Karl
1934 *Sprachtheorie*. Stuttgart: G. Fischer.

Bultmann, Rudolf
1934 *Jesus and the Word*. New York: Scribner.
1955 *Essays: Philosophical and Theological*. London: SCM.

Burke, Kenneth
1959 *Attitudes Toward History*, rev. 2nd ed. Boston: Beacon.

Buss, Martin J.
1961 "The Language of the Divine 'I.'" *JBR* 29:102–7.
1963 "The Psalms of Asaph and Korah." *JBL* 82:382–92.
1965 "Self-Theory and Theology." *JR* 45:46–53.
1967 "The Meaning of History." Pp. 135–54 in *Theology as History*. Eds. James M. Robinson and J. Cobb. New York: Harper and Row.
1969 *The Prophetic Word of Hosea: A Morphological Study*. Berlin: Töpelmann.
1970 "Form Criticism: An Assessment." Discussion paper, distributed at the Form Criticism Seminar of the Society of Biblical Literature.
1973/74 Review of Walter Wink, *The Bible in Human Transformation*. *Union Seminary Quarterly Review* 29:135–38.
1974 "The Study of Forms." Pp. 1–56 in *Old Testament Form Criticism*. Ed. John Hayes. San Antonio: Trinity University Press.
1977 "The Distinction Between Civil and Criminal Law in Ancient Israel." Pp. 51–62 in *Proceedings of the Sixth World Congress of Jewish Studies*. Jerusalem: Academic.
1978 "The Idea of Sitz im Leben—History and Critique." *ZAW* 90:157–70.

Cantor, Georg
1895 "Beiträge zu Begründung der transfiniten Mengenlehre." *Mathematische Annalen* 46:481–512.

Carlyle, Thomas
1901 *Heroes, Hero-Worship and the Heroic in History (Works, V)*. New York: Scribner. (Original, 1841.)

Carney, Thomas F.
1972 *Content Analysis: A Technique for Systematic Inference from Communications*. Winnipeg: University of Manitoba Press.

Casalis, Matthieu
1976 "The Dry and the Wet: A Semiological Analysis of Creation and Flood Myths." *Semiotica* 17, 1:35–67.

Casanowicz, Immanuel M.
1892   "Paronomasia in the Old Testament." Ph.D. diss., Johns
               Hopkins University.

Cassirer, Ernst
1953   *Language and Myth*. New York: Dover. (Reprint of Harper,
               1946.)

Chabrol, Claude
1971   "Problèmes de la sémiotique narrative des récits bibliques."
               Langages 6, 22:3–12.

Chaney, Marvin
1976   "HDL-II and the 'Song of Deborah': Textual Philological and
               Sociological Studies in Judges 5, with Special Reference to the
               Verbal Occurrences of HDL in Biblical Hebrew." Ph.D. diss.,
               Harvard University.

Cherry, Colin
1957   *On Human Communication*. Cambridge, MA: M.I.T. Press.

Childs, Brevard S.
1970   *Biblical Theology in Crisis*. Philadelphia: Westminster.

Chomsky, Noam
1965   *Aspects of the Theory of Syntax*. Cambridge, MA: M.I.T.
               Press.

Christ, William, and De Lone, Richard
1975   *Introduction to Materials and Structure of Music*. Englewood
               Cliffs, NJ: Prentice-Hall.

Chrysostomus, Joannes, Saint, Patriarch of Constantinople
1834   *Collectio Selecta SS. Ecclesiae Patrum LXXI*. Paris: Parent-
               Desbarres.

Coats, George W.
1972   "Widow's Rights: A Crux in the Structure of Gen 38." *CBQ*
               34:461–66.

Coker, William
1972   *Music and Meaning: A Theoretical Introduction to Musical
               Aesthetics*. New York: Free.

Cole, Peter, and Morgan, Jerry L., eds.
1975   *Syntax and Semantics*, III. New York: Academic.

Collingwood, R. G.
1939   *An Autobiography*. London: Oxford.

Cone, James
1969   *Black Theology and Black Power*. New York: Seabury.
1970   *A Black Theology of Liberation*. Philadelphia: Lippincott.

Cooper, J. S.
1975 "Structure, Humor, and Satire in the Poor Man of Nippur." *JCS* 27:163–74.

Coseriu, Eugenio
1974 *Synchronie, Diachronie und Geschichte.* Munich: Fink.

Couffignal, Robert
1977 "Le songe de Jacob: Approches nouvelles de Genèse 28, 10–22." *Bib* 58:342–60.

Crane, R. S.
1953 *The Languages of Criticism and the Structure of Poetry.* Toronto: University of Toronto Press.

Crenshaw, J. L.
1969 "Method in Determining Wisdom Influence Upon 'Historical' Literature." *JBL* 83:129–42.

Cross, Frank M., Jr.
1973 *Canaanite Myth and Hebrew Epic.* Cambridge, MA: Harvard University Press.

Crystal, David
1971 *Linguistics.* Baltimore: Penguin.

Culley, Robert C.
1976 *Studies in the Structure of Hebrew Narrative.* Philadelphia: Fortress.

Daly, Mary
1973 *Beyond God the Father.* Boston: Beacon.

Daube, David
1963 *The Exodus Pattern in the Bible.* London: Faber.

Davitz, Joel E.
1969 *The Language of Emotion.* New York: Academic.

Deen, Edith
1955 *All the Women of the Bible.* New York: Harper and Row.

Derrida, Jacques
1973 *Speech and Phenomena.* Evanston: Northwestern University Press.

Detweiler, Robert
1978 *Story, Sign, and Self: Phenomenology and Structuralism as Literary Critical Methods.* Philadelphia: Fortress.

Dewey, John
1934 *Art as Experience.* New York: Minton, Balch.

Dijk, Teun A. van
1971 "Some Problems of Generative Poetics." *Poetics* 2:5–35.
1972 *Some Aspects of Text Grammars.* The Hague: Mouton.

1977 *Text and Context: Explorations in the semantics and pragmatics of discourse.* London: Longman.

Dilthey, Wilhelm
1921 *Gesammelte Schriften.* Göttingen: Vandenhoeck & Ruprecht.

Dockx, Stanislas I., and Bernays, Paul
1965 *Information and Prediction in Science.* New York: Academic.

Douglas, Mary
1975 *Implicit Meanings.* London: Routledge & Kegan Paul.

Driver, S. R.
1906 *The Book of Genesis.* London: Methuen.

Droysen, Johann Gustav
1943 *Historik*, 2nd ed. Ed. Rudolf Hübner. Munich: Oldenbourg.

Dus, Jan
1975 "Moses or Joshua? On the Problem of the Founder of the Israelite Religion." *Radical Religion* 2, 2–3:26–41. (Engl. trans. of *Archiv für Orientforschung* 39 [1971]:16–45.)

Ebeling, Gerhard
1963 *Word and Faith.* Philadelphia: Fortress.
1975 *Studium der Theologie.* Tübingen: Mohr.

Eichrodt, Walther
1961 *Theology of the Old Testament*, I. Philadelphia: Westminster.

Eissfeldt, Otto
1965 *The Old Testament.* Oxford: Blackwell.

Eister, Allan W., ed.
1974 *Changing Perspectives in the Scientific Study of Religion.* New York: Wiley.

Elhorst, H. J.
1891 *De Prophetie van Micha.* Arnhem: K. van der Zande.

Eliade, Mircea
1963 *Patterns in Comparative Religion.* New York: World (Meridian Books).

Eliot, T. S.
1957 *On Poetry and Poets.* London: Faber.

Engnell, Ivan
1949 *The Call of Isaiah.* Uppsala: Lundequistska Bokhandeln.

Erlich, Victor
1955 *Russian Formalism.* The Hague: Mouton.

Ernesti, J. A.
1822 *Elements of Interpretation.* Andover: Flagg and Gould.

Fanon, Franz
1967   *Black Skin, White Masks.* New York: Grove.
1968   *The Wretched of the Earth.* New York: Grove.

Faust, August
1931   *Der Möglichkeitsgedanke,* 2 vols. Heidelberg: Winter.

Ferguson, Donald N.
1960   *Music as Metaphor: The Elements of Expression.* Minneapolis: University of Minnesota Press.

Ferré, Nels
1951   *The Christian Understanding of God.* New York: Harper.

Feuer, Lewis S.
1974   *Einstein and the Generations of Science.* New York: Basic Books.

Fichtner, J.
1956   "Die etymologische Ätiologie in den Namengebungen der geschichtlichen Bücher des Alten Testaments." *VT* 6:372–96.

Fishbane, Michael
1975   "Composition and Structure in the Jacob Cycle (Gen 25:19–35:22)." *JJS* 26:15–38.

Fisher, R. A.
1935   "The Logic of Inductive Inference." *Journal of the Royal Statistical Society* 98:39–54.

Fiske, Donald W., and Maddi, Salvatore R.
1961   *Functions of Varied Experience.* Homewood, IL: Dorsey.

Fohrer, Georg
1972   *Theologische Grundstrukturen des Alten Testaments.* Berlin: de Gruyter.

Fohrer, Georg, *et al.*
1973   *Exegese des Alten Testaments.* Heidelberg: Quelle & Meyer.

Fokkelman, J. P.
1975   *Narrative Art in Genesis.* Amsterdam: Van Gorcum.

Foucault, Michel
1972   *The Archaeology of Knowledge.* New York: Random House.

François de Sales, Saint
1965   *On the Love of God,* I. Garden City, NY: Image Books.

Frege, Gottlob
1967   *Kleine Schriften.* Ed. I. Angelelli. Hildesheim: Olms.

Frei, Hans
1974   *The Eclipse of Biblical Narrative.* New Haven: Yale University Press.

Freud, Sigmund
1950   *Beyond the Pleasure Principle.* New York: Liveright.

Frick, Frank S., and Gottwald, N. K.
1975   "The Social World of Ancient Israel." *SBL 1975 Seminar Papers* 1:165–78.

Fried, M. H.
1967   *The Evolution of Political Society. An Essay in Political Anthropology.* New York: Random House.

Frye, Northrup
1976   *The Secular Scripture.* Cambridge, MA: Harvard University Press.

Fuchs, Ernst
1968   *Marburger Hermeneutik.* Tübingen: Mohr.

Gabor, D.
1946   "Theory of Communication." *Journal of the Institution of Electrical Engineers* 93:429–41.

Gadamer, Hans-Georg
1975   *Truth and Method.* New York: Seabury.

Galbiati, Enrico
1956   *La struttura letteraria dell' Esodo.* Alba: Paoline.

Garner, Wendell R.
1962   *Uncertainty and Structure as Psychological Concepts.* New York: Wiley.

Gaster, Theodor H.
1969   *Myth, Legend, and Custom in the Old Testament*, I. New York: Harper and Row.

Geertz, Clifford
1966   "Religion as a Cultural System." Pp. 1–46 in *Anthropological Approaches to the Study of Religion.* Ed. M. Banton. London: Tavistock.

Gilbert, Katherine, and Kuhn, H.
1939   *A History of Esthetics.* New York: Macmillan.

Goldmann, Lucien
1970   "Structure: Human Reality and Methodological Concept." Pp. 98–110 in *The Languages of Criticism and the Sciences of Man.* Eds. R. Macksey and E. Donato. Baltimore: Johns Hopkins Press.

Goldschmidt, Walter R.
1966   *Comparative Functionalism: An Essay in Anthropological Theory.* Berkeley: University of California Press.

Good, Edwin M.
1965   *Irony in the Old Testament*. Philadelphia: Westminster.

Goodman, Nelson
1973   *Fact, Fiction, and Forecast*, 3rd ed. Indianapolis: Bobbs-Merrill.

Gottwald, Norman K.
1974   "Were the Early Israelites Pastoral Nomads?" Pp. 223–55 in *Rhetorical Criticism: Essays in Honor of James Muilenburg*. Eds. Jared J. Jackson and Martin Kessler. Pittsburgh: Pickwick.
1976a   "Nomadism." *IDBSup*: 629–31.
1976b   "Early Israel and 'The Asiatic Mode of Production' in Canaan." *SBL 1976 Seminar Papers:* 145–54.
1978   "The Hypothesis of the Revolutionary Origins of Ancient Israel: A Response to Hauser and Thompson." *JSOT* 7 (May): 37–52.
in press   *The Tribes of Yahweh: a Sociology of the Religion of Liberated Israel, 1250–1000 B.C.* Maryknoll, NY: Orbis.

Grant, Fredrick C.
1968   "Psychological Study of the Bible." Pp. 107–24 in *Religions in Antiquity: Essays in Memory of Erwin Ramsdell Goodenough*. Leiden: Brill.

Grayson, A. K.
1975   *Babylonian Historical-Literary Texts*. Toronto: University of Toronto Press.

Greimas, A. J.
1966   *Sémantique Structurale*. Paris: Librarie Larousse.
1970   "Elements d'une grammaire narrative." Pp. 157–82 in *Du Sens*. Paris: du Seuil.
1971   "Narrative Grammar: Units and Levels." *MLN* 86:793–806.

Gros Louis, Kenneth R. R., *et al.*
1974   *Literary Interpretations of Biblical Narratives*. Nashville: Abingdon.

Grosch, Hermann, ed.
1971   *Religion in der Grundschule*. Frankfurt: Diesterweg.

Gross, Rita, ed.
1977   *Beyond Androcentrism*. Missoula, MT: Scholars Press.

Gülich, Elisabeth, and Raible, Wolfgang, eds.
1972   *Textsorten: Differenzierungskriterien in linguistischer Sicht.* Frankfurt/M: Athenäum.

Gunkel, Hermann
1901   *The Legends of Genesis*. Chicago: Open Court. (Reissued unchanged by Schocken, 1964.)

1910   *Genesis*, 3rd ed. (HKAT, 1/1). Göttingen: Vandenhoeck & Ruprecht. (Reissued unchanged in subsequent editions.)

1915   "Die Propheten als Schriftsteller und Dichter." Pp. XXXVI-LXXII in *Die Schriften des Alten Testaments in Auswahl*, II, 12. By Gunkel *et al.* Göttingen: Vandenhoeck & Ruprecht.

1933   *Einleitung in die Psalmen.* Completed by J. Begrich. Göttingen: Vandenhoeck & Ruprecht.

Gunneweg, A. H. J.

1977   *Vom Verstehen des Alten Testaments: Eine Hermeneutik.* Göttingen: Vandenhoeck & Ruprecht.

Gusdorf, Georges

1965   *Speaking (La Parole).* Evanston: Northwestern University Press.

Gustafson, James

1970   "The Place of Scripture in Christian Ethics: A Methodological Study." *Int* 24:430–55.

Güttgemanns, Erhardt

1971a   *Offene Fragen zur Formgeschichte des Evangeliums.* Munich: Kaiser.

1971b   *Studia linguistica neotestamentica.* Munich: Kaiser.

1978   *Einführung in die Linguistik für Textwissenschaftler*, I. *Kommunikations- und informationstheoretische Modelle.* Bonn: Linguistica Biblica.

Habermas, Jürgen

1971   *Knowledge and Human Interests.* Boston: Beacon.

Hadden, Jeffrey

1969   *The Gathering Storm in the Churches.* Garden City, NY: Doubleday.

Hardmeier, Christof

1978   *Texttheorie und biblische Exegese.* Munich: Kaiser.

Harrah, David

1963   *Communication: A Logical Model.* Cambridge, MA: M.I.T. Press.

Hartley, R. V. L.

1928   "Transmission of Information." *Bell System Technical Journal* 7:535–63.

Hartmann, Peter

1963   *Theorie der Grammatik.* The Hague: Mouton.

Hartshorne, Charles

1941   *Man's Vision of God.* New York: Harper.

Hasel, Gerhard

1972   *The Remnant.* Berrien Springs, MI: Andrews University Press.

Hauser, Alan Jon
1978 "Israel's Conquest of Palestine: A Peasants' Rebellion?" *JSOT* 7 (May): 2-19.

Hayes, John H., and Miller, J. Maxwell, eds.
1977 *Israelite and Judaean History.* Philadelphia: Westminster.

Healy, Emma Therese, Sr.
1955 *Woman According to Saint Bonaventure.* Erie, PA: The Congregation of the Sisters of St. Joseph.

Hegel, Georg W. H.
1832-87 *Werke,* 19 vols. Berlin: Duncker & Humblot.

Heidegger, Martin
1949 *Sein und Zeit,* 6th ed. Tübingen: Neomarius.

Heinrici, G.
1899 "Hermeneutik, biblische." *RE,* 3rd ed., VII:718-50.

Helck, W.
1962 *Die Beziehungen Ägyptens zu Vorderasien im 3. und 2. Jahrtausend v. Chr.* Wiesbaden: Harrassowitz.

Hempel, Carl
1965 *Aspects of Scientific Explanation and Other Essays in the Philosophy of Science.* New York: Free.

Hempfer, Klaus W.
1973 *Gattungstheorie.* Munich: Fink.

Herberg, Will
1955 *Protestant, Catholic, Jew: An Essay in American Religious Sociology.* New York: Doubleday Anchor.
1976 *Faith Enacted as History.* Ed. Bernhard W. Anderson. Philadelphia: Westminster.

Herbert, A. S.
1916 *Genesis.* London: Methuen.

Herdan, Gustav
1966 *The Advanced Theory of Language as Choice and Chance.* New York: Springer.

Hernadi, Paul
1972 *Beyond Genre.* Ithaca, NY: Cornell University Press.

Herrmann, Rudolf
1971 *Bibel und Hermeneutik.* Göttingen: Vandenhoeck & Ruprecht.

Heschel, Abraham
1973 *A Passion for Truth.* New York: Farrar, Straus and Giroux.

Hintikka, Jaakko, and Suppes, Patrick, eds.
1970 *Information and Inference.* Dordrecht: Reidel.

Hirsch, E. D., Jr.
1976   The Aims of Interpretation. Chicago: University of Chicago Press.

Holland, Norman N.
1968   The Dynamics of Literary Response. New York: Oxford University Press.

Holsti, Ole R.
1969   Content Analysis for the Social Sciences and Humanities. Reading, MA: Addison-Wesley.

Horkheimer, Max, and Adorno, Theodor W.
1972   Dialectic of Enlightenment. New York: Herder.

Horn, S. H.
1976   "Ammon, Ammonites." IDBSup:20.

Howe, Günter
1970   Die Christenheit im Atomzeitalter. Stuttgart: Klett.

Husserl, Edmund
1952   Husserliana, V. The Hague: Nijhoff.

Hutchison, John A.
1963   Language and Faith. Philadelphia: Westminster.

Ingarden, Roman
1960   Das literarische Kunstwerk, 2nd ed. Tübingen: Niemeyer.

Iser, Wolfgang
1974   The Implied Reader: Patterns of Communication in Prose Fiction from Bunyan to Beckett. Baltimore: Johns Hopkins Press.

Izard, Carroll E.
1977   Human Emotions. New York: Plenum.

Jacobson, Richard
1974   "The Structuralists and the Bible." Int 28:146–64.

Jakobson, Roman
1971   Selected Writings, 2 vols. The Hague: Mouton.

Jakobson, Roman, and Halle, Morris
1956   Fundamentals of Language. The Hague: Mouton.

Jaroš, Karl
1974   Die Stellung des Elohisten zur kanaanäischen Religion. Freiburg/Schweiz: Universitätsverlag.

Jason, Heda
1969   "A Multidimensional Approach to Oral Literature." Current Anthropology 10:413–26.

Jaspers, Karl
    1931   *Philosophie*. Berlin: Springer.
    1948   *Der philosophische Glaube*. Munich: Piper.

Jauss, Hans Robert
    1970   "Literary History as a Challenge to Literary Theory." *New Literary History* II, 1:7–37.

Johnson, Douglas L.
    1969   *The Nature of Nomadism*. Chicago: University of Chicago Press.

Jónsson, Jakob
    1965   *Humor and Irony in the New Testament: Illustrated by Parallels in Talmud and Midrash*. Reykjavik: Bókaútgáfa Menningarsjóds.

Jung, C. G.
    1954   *Answer to Job*. London: Routledge & Kegan Paul.

Kapelrud, Arvid S.
    1975   *The Message of the Prophet Zephaniah*. Oslo: Universitetsforlaget.

Kassis, Hanna E.
    1965   "Gath and the Structure of the 'Philistine' Society." *JBL* 84: 259–71.

Kaufmann, Yehezkel
    1960   *The Religion of Israel*. Chicago: University of Chicago Press.

Kee, Howard C.
    1973   *The Origins of Christianity: Sources and Documents*. New York: Harcourt Brace Jovanovich.

Keel, Othmar
    1969   *Feinde und Gottesleugner*. Stuttgart: Katholisches Bibelwerk.

Keenan, Edward L.
    1975   *Formal Semantics of Natural Language*. Cambridge: Cambridge University Press.

Kierkegaard, Søren
    1970   *Fear and Trembling*. Princeton: Princeton University Press.

King, Martin Luther, Jr.
    1963   *Strength to Love*. New York: Harper and Row.

Kirschenmann, Peter Paul
    1970   *Information and Reflection*. Dordrecht: Reidel.

Knierim, Rolf
    1973   "Old Testament Form Criticism Reconsidered." *Int* 27:435–68.

Knight, Douglas A.
    1974   "The Understanding of 'Sitz im Leben' in Form Criticism." *SBL 1974 Seminar Papers* I:105–25.

Koch, Klaus
1969   *The Growth of the Biblical Tradition.* New York: Scribner.

Kolakowski, Leszek
1968   *The Alienation of Reason.* New York: Doubleday.

Kolmogorov, A.
1967   "Logical Basis for Information Theory and Probability Theory." *IEEE Transactions on Information Theory,* IT–14:662–64.

Kosters, W. H.
1893   "De samenstelling van het Boek Micha." *TT* 27:249–74.

Kristeva, Julia
1969   *Semeiotike. Recherches pour une sémanalyse.* Paris: du Seuil.

Kubát, Libor, and Zeman, Jiří, eds.
1975   *Entropy and Information in Science and Philosophy.* New York: Elsevier.

Langer, Susanne K.
1953   *Feeling and Form: A Theory of Art.* New York: Scribner.

Lawall, Sarah N.
1968   *Critics of Consciousness: The Existential Structure of Literature.* Cambridge, MA: Harvard University Press.

Leach, Edmund
1969   *Genesis as Myth and Other Essays.* London: Jonathan Cape.

Leary, Timothy
1957   *Interpersonal Diagnosis of Personality.* New York: Ronald.

Le Guern, Michael
1973   *Sémantique de la métaphore et de la métonymie.* Paris: Larousse.

Leibniz, Gottfried Wilhelm
1969   *Philosophical Papers and Letters,* 2nd ed. Ed. Leroy E. Loemker. Dordrecht: Reidel.

Leont'ev, A. A.
1971   *Sprache-Sprechen-Sprechtätigkeit.* Tr. from Russian by C. Heeschen and W. Stölting. Stuttgart: Kohlhammer.

Lesser, Simon O.
1957   *Fiction and the Unconscious.* New York: Vintage.

Levi, Edward
1949   *An Introduction to Legal Reasoning.* Chicago: University of Chicago Press.

Lévi-Strauss, Claude
1963   *Structural Anthropology,* I. New York: Basic Books.

1966   *The Savage Mind.* Chicago: University of Chicago Press.
1976   *Structural Anthropology,* II. New York: Basic Books.

Lewis, David K.
1969   *Convention.* Cambridge, MA: Harvard University Press.

Lieberman, Josefa N.
1977   *Playfulness: Its Relationship to Imagination and Creativity.* New York: Academic.

Lindsay, Peter H., and Norman, Donald A.
1972   *Human Information Processing.* New York: Academic.

Lonergan, B.
1970   *Insight,* 3rd ed. New York: Philosophical Library.

Long, Burke O.
1968   *The Problem of Etiological Narrative in the Old Testament* (BZAW, 108). Berlin: de Gruyter.
1976   "Recent Field Studies in Oral Literature and the Question of *Sitz im Leben.*" *Semeia* 5:35–50.

Lotman, Jurij M.
1972   *Die Struktur literarischer Texte.* Tr. from Russian by R.-D. Keil. Munich: Fink.

Lowry, S.
1977   *The Principles of Samaritan Bible Exegesis.* Leiden: Brill.

Luhmann, Niklas
1975   *Macht.* Stuttgart: Enke.

Lukács, Georg
1954   *Die Zerstörung der Vernunft.* Berlin: Aufban-Verlag.

Lyons, John
1968   *Introduction to Theoretical Linguistics.* Cambridge: Cambridge University Press.

Mach, Ernst
1975   *Knowledge and Error.* Ed. Brian McGinness. Dordrecht: Reidel.

MacKay, Donald M.
1969   *Information, Mechanism, and Meaning.* Cambridge, MA: M.I.T. Press.

Malamat, Abraham
1973   "Tribal Societies: Biblical Genealogies and African Lineage Systems." *Archives Européennes de Sociologie* 14:126–36.

Mally, Ernst
1971   *Logische Schriften.* Dordrecht: Reidel.

Mandler, George
1975   *Mind and Emotion.* New York: Wiley.

Maritain, Jacques and Raissa
1955   *The Situation of Poetry*. New York: Philosophical Library.

Martin, Richard M.
1958   *Truth and Denotation*. Chicago: University of Chicago Press.

Martinet, André
1970   "Structure and Language." Pp. 1–9 in *Structuralism*. Ed. J. Ehrmann. Garden City, NY: Anchor Books.

Marx, Karl
1963   *Early Writings*. London: Watts.

Maslow, Abraham H.
1971   *The Farther Reaches of Human Nature*. New York: Viking.

Mathews, Shailer, *et al.*
1924   *Contributions of Science to Religion*. New York: Appleton.

Mauss, Marcel
1967   *The Gift: Forms and Functions of Exchange in Archaic Societies*. New York: Norton.

May, Rollo
1969   *Love and Will*. New York: Norton.
1972   *Power and Innocence: A Search for Sources of Violence*. New York: Norton.

McLuhan, M.
1962   *The Gutenberg Galaxy*. Toronto: University of Toronto Press.

Mead, George Herbert
1934   *Mind, Self, and Society from the Standpoint of a Social Behaviorist*. Chicago: University of Chicago Press.

Mehan, Hugh, and Wood, Huston
1975   *The Reality of Ethnomethodology*. New York: Wiley.

Mehrabian, Albert
1976   *Public Places and Private Spaces*. New York: Basic Books.

Mehta, Ved
1971   "Onward and Upward With the Arts (Linguistics)." *The New Yorker* 47 (May 8):44–87.

Melugin, Roy F.
1974   "The Conventional and the Creative in Isaiah's Judgment Oracles." *CBQ* 36:301–11.

Mencken, H. L.
1946   *Treatise on the Gods*, 2nd ed. New York: Knopf.

Mendenhall, George E.
1962   "The Hebrew Conquest of Palestine." *BA* 25:66–87.
1973   *The Tenth Generation. The Origins of the Biblical Tradition*. Baltimore: Johns Hopkins Press.

Menges, Günter, ed.
1974   *Information, Inference, and Decision.* Boston: Reidel.

Meyer, Leonard B.
1956   *Emotion and Meaning in Music.* Chicago: University of Chicago Press.
1973   *Explaining Music.* Berkeley: University of California Press.

Meyer zu Utrup, Klaus
1966   *Die Bedeutung des Alten Testaments für eine Transformation der Kirche heute.* Munich: Kaiser.

Miller, George A.
1956   "The Magical Number Seven, Plus or Minus Two: Some Limits on Our Capacity for Processing Information." *Psychological Review* 63:81–97.

Miller, J. Maxwell
1974   "The Descendents of Cain: Notes on Genesis 4." *ZAW* 86:164–74.
1976   *The Old Testament and the Historian.* Philadelphia: Fortress.

Mohammad, M. A. K.
1959   "The Administration of Syro-Palestine during the New Kingdom." *Annales du Service des Antiquités de l'Egypte* (Cairo) 56:105–37.

Moles, Abraham
1966   *Information Theory and Esthetic Perception.* Urbana: University of Illinois Press. (French original, 1958.)

Moltmann, Jürgen
1968   *Perspektiven der Theologie.* Munich: Kaiser.

Montague, Richard
1974   *Formal Philosophy.* Ed. R. Thomason. New Haven: Yale University Press.

Montgomery, James A., and Harris, Zellig S.
1935   *The Ras Shamra Mythological Texts.* Philadelphia: The American Philosophical Society.

Morris, Charles
1945   *Signs, Language and Behavior.* New York: Prentice-Hall.

Morris, William, ed.
1969   *The American Heritage Dictionary of the English Language.* Boston: American Heritage.

Mowinckel, Sigmund
1962   *The Psalms in Israelite Worship*, I. New York: Abingdon.

Mucchielli, Roger
1970   *Introduction to Structural Psychology.* New York: Funk and Wagnalls. (French original, 1966.)

Muilenburg, James
1956 "The Book of Isaiah, Chapters 40–66: Introduction and Exegesis." Pp. 381–773 in *The Interpreter's Bible*, V. New York: Abingdon.
1969 "Form Criticism and Beyond." *JBL* 88:1–18.

Mukařovský, Jan
1978 *Structure, Sign, and Function*. New Haven: Yale University Press.

Mumford, Lewis
1972 *The Transformation of Man*. New York: Harper and Row.

Nagel, Ernest
1961 *The Structure of Science*. New York: Harcourt, Brace, and World.

Nake, Frieder
1974 *Ästhetik als Informationsverarbeitung*. Vienna: Springer.

Narasimhan, Chakravarthi V.
1965 *The Mahābhārata*. New York: Columbia University Press.

Nauta, Doede
1972 *The Meaning of Information*. The Hague: Mouton.

Nida, Eugene A.
1960 *Message and Mission*. New York: Harper.

Niebuhr, Reinhold
1932 *Moral Man and Immoral Society*. New York: Scribner.
1955 *The Self and the Dramas of History*. New York: Scribner.

Nietzsche, Friedrich
1912 *Werke*, XVIII. Leipzig: Kröner.

North, Robert C., *et al.*
1963 *Content Analysis*. Evanston: Northwestern University Press.

Noth, Martin
1928 *Die israelitischen Personennamen*. Hildesheim: Olms.
1972 *A History of Pentateuchal Traditions*. Englewood Cliffs, NJ: Prentice-Hall.

Nowell-Smith, P. H.
1957 *Ethics*. Oxford: Blackwell.

Ogden, C. K., and Richards, I. A.
1946 *The Meaning of Meaning*, 8th ed. New York: Harcourt, Brace.

Olsson, Birger
1974 *Structure and Meaning in the Fourth Gospel: A Text-Linguistic-Analysis of John 2:1–11 and 4:1–42*. Lund: Gleerup.

Oomen, Ursula
    1971   "New Models and Methods in Text Analysis." *Georgetown Monograph Series on Language and Linguistics* 24:211-22.

Osgood, Charles, *et al.*
    1957   *The Measurement of Meaning.* Urbana: University of Illinois Press.

Otto, Rudolf
    1920   *Das Heilige.* Gotha: L. Klotz. (Engl. trans., 1923.)

Outka, Gene, and Reeder, John P., Jr., eds.
    1973   *Religion and Morality: A Collection of Essays.* Garden City, NY: Doubleday Anchor.

Palmer, Richard E.
    1975   "Toward a Postmodern Interpretive Self-Awareness." *JR* 55:313-26.

Pannenberg, Wolfhart
    1976   *Theology and the Philosophy of Science.* Philadelphia: Westminster.

Parsegian, V. L.
    1973   "Biological Trends Within Cosmic Processes." *Zygon* 1:221-43.

Parsons, I. R. M.
    1972   "Suffering in the Psalms." *AusBR* 20:49-53.

Parsons, Talcott
    1966   *Societies: Evolutionary and Comparative Perspectives.* Englewood Cliffs, NJ: Prentice-Hall.

Parsons, Talcott, and Shils, Edward A., eds.
    1952   *Toward a General Theory of Action.* Cambridge, MA: Harvard University Press.

Paton, Alan
    1948   *Cry, The Beloved Country.* New York: Scribner.

Patrick, Dale
    1976   "The Moral Logic of Election." *Encounter* 37: 198-210.

Peacocke, Arthur R.
    1971   *Science and the Christian Experiment.* London: Oxford.

Peirce, Charles S.
    1931-58   *Collected Papers*, 8 vols. Eds. C. Hartshorne, P. Weiss, and A. Burke. Cambridge, MA: Harvard University Press.

Pepper, Stephen C.
    1961   *World Hypotheses.* Berkeley: University of California Press.

Peterfreund, Emanuel
1971   *Information, Systems, and Psychoanalysis* (Psychological Issues VII, 1/2). New York: International Universities Press.

Peukert, Helmut
1976   *Wissenschaftstheorie—Handlungstheorie—Fundamentale Theologie.* Düsseldorf: Patmos.

Piaget, Jean
1977   *The Development of Thought.* New York: Viking.

Pierce, J. R.
1961   *Symbols, Signals and Noise: The Nature and Process of Communication.* New York: Harper.

Pike, Kenneth L.
1967   *Language in Relation to a Unified Theory of the Structure of Human Behavior,* 2nd ed. The Hague: Mouton.

Pitt-Rivers, Julian
1977   *The Fate of Shechem and the Politics of Sex.* Cambridge: Cambridge University Press.

Plaskow, Judith
1973   "The Coming of Lilith: Toward a Feminist Theology." Grailville. Mimeographed MS.

Platt, Michael
1975   "Interpretation." *Interpretation: A Journal for Political Philosophy* 5:109-30.

Plaut, W. Gunther
1974   *Genesis (The Torah: A Modern Commentary,* 1). New York: Union of American Hebrew Congregation.

Polanyi, Michael
1959   *The Study of Man.* London: Routledge & Kegan Paul.

Polzin, Robert
1977   *Biblical Structuralism: Method and Subjectivity in the Study of Ancient Texts.* Philadelphia: Fortress.

Pont, J. W.
1892   "Micha Studiën, III." *Theologische Studien* 10:329-60.

Pool, Ithiel de Sola, ed.
1959   *Trends in Content Analysis.* Urbana: University of Illinois Press.

Powers, William T.
1973   *Behavior: The Control of Perception.* Chicago: Aldine.

Pride, J. B., and Holmes, Janet, eds.
1972   *Sociolinguistics.* Baltimore: Penguin.

Prior, A. N.
1971   *Objects of Thought.* Oxford: Clarendon.

Pritchard, James B., ed.
1969   *Ancient Near Eastern Texts Relating to the Old Testament,*
                With Supplement, 3rd ed. Princeton: Princeton University
                Press.

Propp, Vladamir
1968   *Morphology of the Folk Tale,* 2nd ed. Austin: University of
                Texas Press. (Russian original, 1928.)

Pury, Albert de
1975   *Promesse divine et légende cultuelle dans le cycle de Jacob,* 2
                vols. Paris: Gabalda.

Quine, W. V.
1970   *Philosophy of Logic.* Englewood Cliffs, NJ: Prentice-Hall.

Rad, Gerhard von
1961   *Genesis: A Commentary.* Philadelphia: Westminster.
1962   *Old Testament Theology,* I. New York: Harper and Row.
1965   *Old Testament Theology,* II. New York: Harper and Row.
1970   *Das Buch der Bücher. Altes Testament.* Eds. Hans-Martin
                Lutz *et al.* Munich: Piper.
1974   *Gottes Wirken in Israel: Vorträge zum Alten Testament.*
                Neukirchen: Neukirchener Verlag.

Radcliffe-Brown, A. R.
1958   *Method in Social Anthropology.* Chicago: University of
                Chicago Press.

Radday, Yehuda
1973   *The Unity of Isaiah in the Light of Statistical Linguistics.*
                Hildesheim: Gerstenberg.

Radin, Paul
1956   *The Trickster.* New York: Philosophical Library.

Rapp, Hans
1967   *Gott, Mensch und Zahl.* Hamburg: Furche.

Rast, Walter E.
1972   *Tradition History of the Old Testament.* Philadelphia:
                Fortress.

Renger, J.
1973   "*mārat ilim:* Exogamie bei den semitischen Nomaden des 2.
                Jahrtausends." *Archiv für Orientforschung* 14:103-7.

Rescher, Nicholas
1975   *A Theory of Possibility.* Pittsburgh: University of Pittsburgh
                Press.

Richter, Wolfgang
1971   *Exegese als Literaturwissenschaft.* Göttingen: Vandenhoeck & Ruprecht.

Ricoeur, Paul
1961   "The Philosopher Before Symbols." First Terry Lecture, Yale. Mimeographed MS.
1967   *The Symbolism of Evil.* Boston: Beacon.
1971   "Contribution d'une réflexion sur le langage à une théologie de la parole." Pp. 301-19 in *Exégèse et Herméneutique.* By Roland Barthes *et al.* Ed. Xavier Léon-Dufour. Paris: du Seuil.

Ridderbos, Nic. H.
1972   *Die Psalmen: Stilistische Verfahren und Aufbau* (BZAW, 117). Berlin: de Gruyter.

Rilke, Rainer Maria
1942   *Sonnets to Orpheus.* New York: Norton.

Ringgren, Helmer
1950   "Oral and Written Transmission in the Old Testament." *ST* 3:34-59.

Robertson, David
1977   *The Old Testament and the Literary Critic.* Philadelphia: Fortress.

Rofé, Alexander
1970   "The Classification of the Prophetic Stories." *JBL* 89:427-40.

Rose, Martin
1976   "'Entmilitarisierung des Krieges'? (Erwägungen zu den Patriarchen-Erzählungen der Genesis)." *BZ* 20:197-211.

Rosenberg, Alfred
1937   *Der Mythus des 20. Jahrhunderts,* 105th ed. Munich: Hoheneichenverlag. (Copyright, 1930.)

Rosenzweig, Franz
1972   *The Star of Redemption.* Boston: Beacon. (Original, 1921.)

Rotter, Julian B.
1954   *Social Learning and Clinical Psychology.* New York: Prentice-Hall.

Rowton, M. B.
1973a   "Autonomy and Nomadism in Western Asia." *Orientalia* 42:247-58.
1973b   "Urban Autonomy in a Nomadic Environment." *JNES* 32:201-15.

Royce, Josiah
1968   *The Problem of Christianity.* Ed. John E. Smith. New York: Macmillan. (Original, 1918.)

Ruesch, Jurgen, and Bateson, Gregory
1951   *Communication: The Social Matrix of Psychiatry.* New York: Norton.

Ruether, Rosemary
1970   *The Radical Kingdom: The Western Experience of Messianic Hope.* New York: Paulist.
1974   Ed., *Religion and Sexism.* New York: Simon and Schuster.

Russell, Bertrand
1948   *Human Knowledge.* New York: Simon and Schuster.

Russell, Letty M.
1974   *Human Liberation in a Feminist Perspective—A Theology.* Philadelphia: Westminster.

Rust, Eric
1953   *Nature and Man in Biblical Thought.* London: Lutterworth.

Sahlins, Marshall
1968   *Tribesmen.* Englewood Cliffs, NJ: Prentice-Hall.

Sanders, J. A.
1976   "Hermeneutics." *IDBSup:*402–7.

Sandmel, Samuel
1972   *The Enjoyment of Scripture.* New York: Oxford University Press.

Saussure, Ferdinand de
1966   *Course in General Linguistics.* New York: McGraw Hill.
1967   *Cours de linguistique générale,* I. Ed. Rudolf Engler. Wiesbaden: Harrassowitz.

Savage, Leonard J.
1954   *The Foundation of Statistics.* New York: Wiley.

Sawyer, John F. A.
1972   *Semantics in Biblical Research.* Naperville, IL: Allenson.

Schelling, F. W. J. von
1927–59   *Werke.* Munich: Beck.

Schillebeeckx, Edward
1967   *Revelation and Theology,* I. New York: Sheed and Ward.

Schilling, Harold
1973   *The New Consciousness in Science and Religion.* Philadelphia: United Church.

Schleiermacher, Friedrich E. D.
1959   *Hermeneutik.* Ed. H. Kimmerle. Heidelberg: Winter.

Schmidt, Siegfried J.
1975   *Literaturwissenschaft als argumentierende Wissenschaft.* Munich: Fink.

Schutz, Alfred, and Luckmann, Thomas
1973   *The Structures of the Life-world.* Evanston: Northwestern University Press.

Scott, Nathan A.
1971   "Poetry and Prayer." Pp. 191–210 in *Literature and Religion.* Ed. Giles B. Gunn. New York: Harper and Row.

Searle, John R.
1969   *Speech Acts.* Cambridge: Cambridge University Press.

Sebeök, Thomas, ed.
1960   *Style in Language.* Cambridge, MA: M.I.T. Press.

Seebass, Horst
1974   *Biblische Hermeneutik.* Stuttgart: Kohlhammer.

Sewell, Elizabeth
1964   *The Human Metaphor.* Notre Dame: University of Notre Dame Press.

Shannon, Claude E.
1948   "The Mathematical Theory of Communication." *Bell System Technical Journal* 27:379–423, 623–656. (Reprinted in Shannon and Weaver.)

Shannon, Claude E., and Weaver, Warren
1949   *The Mathematical Theory of Communication.* Urbana: University of Illinois Press.

Silverstein, Albert, ed.
1974   *Human Communication: Theoretical Explorations.* Hillsdale, NJ: L. Erlbaum.

Slama-Cazacu, Tatiana
1961   *Langage et contexte.* The Hague: Mouton.

Smith, Alfred G.
1966   *Communication and Culture.* New York: Holt, Rinehart and Winston.

Speiser, E. A.
1964   *Genesis (The Anchor Bible,* 1). Garden City, NY: Doubleday.

Spencer, Herbert
1862   *First Principles.* London: Williams and Norgate.

Spiegel, Yorick
1972   *Psychoanalytische Interpretationen biblischer Texte.* Munich: Kaiser.

Stachiowiak, Herbert
1969   *Denken und Erkennen im kybernetischen Modell.* Vienna: Springer.

Staiger, Emil
1955   *Die Kunst der Interpretation.* Zurich: Atlantis.

Stanton, Elizabeth Cady, *et al.*
1895   *The Woman's Bible.* New York: European Publishing Co. (Reissued as *The Original Feminist Attack on the Bible.* New York: Arno Press, 1974, distributed by Harper and Row.)

Stein, Edith
1964   *On the Problem of Empathy.* The Hague: Nijhoff. (German original, 1917.)

Steinberg, Danny D., and Jakobovitz, Leon A., eds.
1971   *Semantics.* Cambridge: Cambridge University Press.

Stolz, Fritz
1970   *Strukturen und Figuren im Kult von Jerusalem* (BZAW, 118). Berlin: de Gruyter.

Strelka, Joseph P., ed.
1976   *Literary Criticism and Psychology.* University Park, PA: Pennsylvania State University Press.

Tart, Charles, ed.
1969   *Altered States of Consciousness.* New York: Wiley.

Taylor, Irving A., and Getzels, J. W.
1975   *Perspectives in Creativity.* Chicago: Aldine.

Teilhard de Chardin, Pierre
1959   *The Phenomenon of Man.* New York: Harper.

TeSelle, Eugene
1975   *Christ in Context.* Philadelphia: Fortress.

Thayer, H. S.
1968   *Meaning and Action. A Critical History of Pragmatism.* Indianapolis: Bobbs-Merrill.

Thomas Aquinas, Saint
1947   *Summa Theologica,* II. New York: Benziger.
1949   *On Being and Essence.* Toronto: Pontifical Institute of Mediaeval Studies.

Thompson, Thomas L.
1974   *The Historicity of the Patriarchal Narratives: The Quest for the Historical Abraham.* Berlin: de Gruyter.
1978   "Historical Notes on 'Israel's Conquest of Palestine: A Peasants' Rebellion?'" *JSOT* 7 (May): 20–27.

Tillich, Paul
1951–63   *Systematic Theology,* 3 vols. Chicago: University of Chicago Press.

Todorov, Tzvetan
1973   *The Fantastic: A Structural Approach to Literary Genre.* Cleveland: Case Western Reserve University Press.

Toulmin, Stephen
1972   *Human Understanding.* Princeton: Princeton University Press.

Troeltsch, Ernst
1924   *Der Historismus und seine Probleme* (*Gesammelte Schriften,* III). Tübingen: Mohr.
1931   *The Social Teachings of the Christian Churches,* 2 vols. New York: Harper.

Tucker, Gene M.
1971   *Form Criticism of the Old Testament.* Philadelphia: Fortress.

Turner, Victor
1974   *Dramas, Fields, and Metaphors.* Ithaca, NY: Cornell University Press.

Tylor, E. B.
1889   "On a Method of Investigating the Development of Institutions; Applied to Laws of Marriage and Descent." *Journal of the Royal Anthropological Institute* 18:267.

Ullmann, Stephen
1962   *Semantics.* Oxford: Blackwell.

Uttal, William R.
1975   *An Autocorrelation Theory of Form Detection.* Hillsdale, NJ: Erlbaum.

Van Seters, John
1975   *Abraham in History and Tradition.* New Haven: Yale University Press.

Vater, Ann M.
1976   *The Communication of Messages and Oracles as a Narration Medium in the Old Testament* (Ph.D. diss., Yale). Ann Arbor MI: University Microfilms.

Vaux, Roland de
1961   *Ancient Israel: Its Life and Institutions.* London: Darton, Longman and Todd.

Vawter, Bruce
1977   *On Genesis: A New Reading.* Garden City, NY: Doubleday.

Verner, David
1976   "Jacob and Esau: A Content-Analytic Approach to the Study of the Jacob Cycle." MS, used by permission.

Voss, Gerhard, and Harsch, Helmut
1972   *Versuche mehrdimensionaler Schriftauslegung: Bericht über ein Gespräch.* Stuttgart: KBW Verlag.

Vuillod, G.
1971   "Exercises sur de courts récit." *Langages* 6, 22:24–38.

Wagner, Norman E.
1976/77   "General system theory, cybernetics, and Old Testament tradition." *SR* 6:597–605.

Walker, H. H., and Lund, N. W.
1934   "The Literary Structure of the Book of Habakkuk." *JBL* 53:355–70.

Walzel, Oskar
1923   *Gehalt und Gestalt*. Berlin-Neubabelsberg: Athenaion.

Waxman, Meyer
1933   *A History of Jewish Literature*, II. New York: Bloch.

Wegener, Philipp
1885   *Untersuchungen ueber die Grundfragen des Sprachlebens*. Halle: Niemeyer.

Weimar, Peter
1974   "Aufbau and Struktur der priesterschriftlichen Jakobs-geschichte." *ZAW* 86:174–203.

Weiser, Artur
1931   *Glaube und Geschichte im Alten Testament*. Stuttgart: Kohlhammer.

Weiss, Meir
1971   Die Methode der 'Total-Interpretation.'" *VTSup*: 88–112.

Weiss, Paul
1958   *Modes of Being*. Carbondale, IL: Southern Illinois University Press.

Weizsäcker, Carl Friedrich von
1971   *Die Einheit der Natur*. Munich: Hanser.
1974   "Evolution und Entropiewachstum." Pp. 200–221 in *Offene Systeme*, I. Ed. Ernst von Weizsäcker. Stuttgart: Klett.

Wellek, René, and Warren, Austin
1956   *Theory of Literature*, 2nd ed. New York: Harcourt.

Welsh, Clement
1974   *Preaching in a New Key*. Philadelphia: United Church.

Wendland, Paul
1900   "Adolf Harnacks Geschichte der Akademie der Wissenschaften." Pp. 229–43 in *Neue Jahrbücher für das klassische Altertum, Geschichte und deutsche Literatur und für Pädagogik*. Leipzig: Teubner.

Westermann, Claus
1960   Ed., *Probleme alttestamentlicher Hermeneutik.* Munich:
              Kaiser.
1964   *Forschung am Alten Testament (Theologische Bücherei,* 24).
              Munich: Kaiser.
1965   *The Praise of God in the Psalms.* Richmond: John Knox.
1977   *Genesis (Biblischer Kommenter,* 1/2). Neukirchen-Vluyn:
              Neukirchener Verlag.

Wharton, James A.
1976   "Redaction Criticism, OT." *IDBSup:*729–32.

Wheelwright, Philip
1959   *Heraclitus.* Princeton: Princeton University Press.
1968   *The Burning Fountain: A Study in the Language of
              Symbolism,* rev. ed. Bloomington: Indiana University Press.

White, Hayden
1973   *Metahistory.* Baltimore: Johns Hopkins Press.

White, Hugh C.
1975   "French Structuralism and O.T. Narrative Analysis: Roland
              Barthes." *Semeia* 3:99–127.

Whitehead, Alfred North
1925   *Science and the Modern World.* New York: Macmillan.
1929   *Process and Reality.* New York: Macmillan.
1933   *Adventures of Ideas.* New York: Macmillan.
1941   *The Philosophy of Alfred North Whitehead.* Ed. P. Schilpp.
              Evanston: Northwestern University Press.

Wieman, Henry Nelson
1975   *Seeking a Faith for a New Age.* Metuchen, NJ: Scarecrow.

Wiener, Norbert
1948   *Cybernetics.* New York: Wiley.

Wilden, Anthony
1968   "Lacan and the Discourse of the Other." Pp. 157–312 in *The
              Language of the Self: The Function of Language in Psycho-
              Analysis.* By Jacques Lacan. Baltimore: Johns Hopkins Press.

Williams, Frederick
1968   *Reasoning With Statistics: Simplified Examples in
              Communication Research.* New York: Holt, Rinehart and
              Winston.

Williams, Raymond
1977   *Marxism and Literature.* Oxford: Oxford University Press.

Willis, John T.
1969   "The Structure of the Book of Micah." *Svensk exegetisk
              årsbok* 34:5–42.

1973   "The Function of Comprehensive Anticipatory Redactional Joints in I Samuel 16–18." *ZAW* 85:294–314.

1974   "A Reapplied Prophetic Hope Oracle." *VTSup* 28:64–76.

Wilson, Robert R.

1977   *Genealogy and History in the Biblical World* (Yale Near Eastern Researches, 7). New Haven: Yale University Press.

Wink, Walter

1973   *The Bible in Human Transformation.* Philadelphia: Fortress.

Wittgenstein, Ludwig

1922   *Tractatus logico-philosophicus.* New York: Harcourt, Brace.

1953   *Philosophical Investigations.* Oxford: Blackwell.

1977   *Bemerkungen über die Farmen, Remarks on Color.* Berkeley: University of California Press.

Wolfe, Rolland E.

1935   "The Editing of the Book of the Twelve." *ZAW* 53: 90–129.

Wolff, Hans Walter

1969   "Zur Thematik der elohistischen Fragmente im Pentateuch." *EvT* 29:59–72. (Engl. trans. in *Int* 26:158–73 [1972].)

Wood, Pearle

1973   *Evolution, Psychology and the Biblical Ideal of Love.* New York: Exposition.

Wright, G. H. von

1974   *Causality and Determinism.* New York: Columbia University Press.

Zimmerli, Walther

1976   *The Old Testament and the World.* Atlanta: John Knox.

Zipf, George K.

1949   *Human Behavior and the Principle of Least Effort.* Cambridge, MA: Addison-Wesley.

Zuckerkandl, Victor

1969   *Sound and Symbol: Music and the External World* (Bollingen Series, XLIV). Princeton: Princeton University Press.

INDEX TO ANCIENT LITERATURE
References to the Hebrew Scriptures Follow the
Hebrew Verse Numbering